o Scott,
Brother I'hopeth
the light.
o life
nthony

SON
— OF THE —
MORNING

ANTHONY KAMINSKI

BALBOA.
PRESS
A DIVISION OF HAY HOUSE

Balboa Press books may be ordered through booksellers or by contacting:

Balboa Press
A Division of Hay House
1663 Liberty Drive
Bloomington, IN 47403
www.balboapress.com
1 (877) 407-4847

Because of the dynamic nature of the Internet, any web addresses or links contained in this book may have changed since publication and may no longer be valid. The views expressed in this work are solely those of the author and do not necessarily reflect the views of the publisher, and the publisher hereby disclaims any responsibility for them.

The author of this book does not dispense medical advice or prescribe the use of any technique as a form of treatment for physical, emotional, or medical problems without the advice of a physician, either directly or indirectly. The intent of the author is only to offer information of a general nature to help you in your quest for emotional and spiritual well-being. In the event you use any of the information in this book for yourself, which is your constitutional right, the author and the publisher assume no responsibility for your actions.

Any people depicted in stock imagery provided by Thinkstock are models, and such images are being used for illustrative purposes only.
Certain stock imagery © Thinkstock.

Print information available on the last page.

ISBN: 978-1-5043-8586-2 (sc)
ISBN: 978-1-5043-8588-6 (hc)
ISBN: 978-1-5043-8587-9 (e)

Library of Congress Control Number: 2017912255

Balboa Press rev. date: 08/15/2017

To God.
If it were not for Him, these words and this work would not exist.

To all the people I have met in the past, all those I
know now, and those I will meet in the future.
It is my desire through this work that the world can
see that there is more to it than meets the eye.

CONTENTS

I.	The Recurrence of Cain	1
II.	Remember Where It All Began	6
III.	The Tradition of the Yellow Footprints	10
IV.	The Recruit	15
V.	The Guide	20
VI.	The Marine	25
VII.	Semper Fidelis	29
VIII.	Phantom Fury	37
IX.	The Art of War	40
X.	Man of Steel	49
XI.	Mein Kampf	54
XII.	The Clairvoyant	59
XIII.	The Mark of the Serpent	63
XIV.	The Fourth Kind	66
XV.	Total Recall	72
XVI.	The Psychic Spy	81
XVII.	The Pharoh	91
XVIII.	Genesis	97
XIX.	The Fall of Atlantis	107
XX.	Jesus Was a Djhedi	113
XXI.	The Cainite Destiny	123
XXII.	The Secret King	131
XXIII.	Parsifal	134
XXIV.	The Messiah Program	143
XXV.	The Knights Templar	150
XXVI.	Morning of the Magician	177
XXVII.	Out of Darkness into Light	201
XXVIII.	The Forbidden Religion	222
XXIX.	The Illuminati	228
XXX.	The Old World Order	231
XXXI.	The New World Order	235
XXXII.	Hereafter	241
XXXIII.	The Divine Revelation	244

And when this cometh to pass, (lo, it will come,) then shall
they know that a prophet hath been among them.
Ezekiel 33:33

I

✠

THE RECURRENCE OF CAIN

In a time far past I began this incarnation not as the men
of the present age did, as the mighty ones of Atlantis lived
and died, but rather from Aeon to Aeon did they renew
their lives in the Halls of Amenti where the river of life
flows eternally onward.

—The Emerald Tablets

I NEVER THOUGHT I came here to start a revolution, but it is all known
to us that God works in mysterious ways. It says he is the maker of the
Bear, Orion, Pleiades, and the constellations of the south. He does wonders
that cannot be fathomed and miracles that cannot be counted.

When I first started this journey, I will admit that I had no idea what
I was doing. All I did know was it had to be done, and the seed that was
planted so long ago has bloomed into this great work, which is irrevocably
a masterpiece. It is nothing but the light of my truth that comes from my
soul.

I was born just as you were on this Earth. I came here in the year 1985
on the nineteenth day of March, born under the great sign of Pisces. Of all
the signs in the zodiac, Pisces are known for their incredible imaginations,
amazing creativity, and strong emotions. And they are known to be the
most psychic.

Before I even came to this Earth, my grandmother had a reading done
on me, and it said I had held the staff of power before and I would hold it

again. Also she said, when I came, I would come fast, but who believes in prophecies anyway, right? My mother was very young when she had me. Because of this, it looked as if I would not come in through her, as the family was unsure about my birth.

Luckily for me, a miracle happened before I was born that helped my passage into this world. One night, my grandfather had a dream that he was on death row, and he attributed it directly to me not being born. So as destiny would have it, I came into this world with a mission. But having drank from the wine of forgetfulness, I came in blind to who I was. I mean, who in this world is really going to remember who he or she is when he or she is given a number at his or her birth? So my mission here would be to remember who I was. And then after, I had reached that point to then be a light in the world.

I have few memories of my father. He wasn't in my life much. I believe that, at such a young age, he wasn't prepared to take on the responsibility of a child. I can understand that, and because of that fact, I have no resentment or anything like that in my heart for him.

When I was three years old, my mother and I moved to Ellensburg, Washington, so we could live with my grandfather and grandmother. My mother was young still, and she obviously needed support. My grandparents are two extraordinary people. My grandfather, an engineer, came from the Kaminski family from Poland. *Kaminski* means "stonemason."

My grandfather had worked on and developed numerous governmental contracts. He has patents for work he did on such projects as the SR-71 Blackbird and the Abrams tank target designating laser, and he even worked on the extremely super-secretive Star Wars defense system from the Reagan administration days.

My grandmother, a gifted natural healer, had many years of experience working as a nurse. Her name is Armstrong. When she was the mother of six children, her bathroom was basically like a hospital with her kids constantly coming in to get patched up. Not only did her own kids need medical attention, the whole neighborhood would come to her house when they needed aid. She is now a naturopathic healer who does very important work that this world is in desperate need of.

Obviously healing and technology run in our family's lineage, which I would find out later in my life that it was quite important. So if anything they say is true, I obviously inherited some good genetics with their DNA being passed on to my mother to me.

From a very young age, there was clearly something special about me. One time when I was young, one of my aunts was feeling sad. So I walked up to her, put my hand on her forehead, and said, "May the Father within you make you whole." Needless to say, she about fainted. The fact of the matter was that, I was spiritual at a young age, like I had wisdom that had come from another life.

I can recall things quite clearly from those days. They were some of the best in my life. Those days of youthful joy—where the simple pleasures in life could be enjoyed and where one could live moments of pure freedom and happiness—are hard to forget. Those were the days when the world was truly magical as you made known the unknown through discovery with an unlimited mind.

My grandfather would take me to the university where he taught engineering. I loved being there with him and seeing all of the projects his students were working on, for example, propulsion systems, robots, and lasers. So as a child, I developed an interest in technology. My grandfather was like a father to me, so with his influence, I was encouraged to be creative so I would create my own projects and inventions. The things I was coming up with had to be coming from a mind of a child prodigy. I would often create the most intricate things, like a very in-depth board game called Journey to the Center of the Universe. And I even was serious about building an airplane. That was when I was seven or eight years old. I was obviously talented at a young age. I was the boy who cried wolf in the school play. I wore a white sports coat and a pink carnation in front of an audience of people when I was in third grade, and I achieved the Presidential Physical Fitness Award before I was in middle school.

When I was seven, my mother met a man whom she would marry, and he would become my father through adoption. When I was ten years old, it was decided that we would move to his hometown in Bellingham, Washington. So for me, that was the first major change I remember in my life. I recall crying on the car ride up to Bellingham, thinking about all of the friends I would not see again. I had so many good memories in Ellensburg. As a young child, losing the comfort of the life I knew and leaving it behind is a traumatic event.

Moving into the unknown is always hard, no matter who you are. When we moved there, we lived with his parents in their white house on the corner of the street. I started my new life in elementary school in fifth grade. It didn't take me too long to make friends. I've always had a charismatic personality, and my personal talent allowed me to fit in with my new surroundings. I started really competing in sports in seventh grade when I started to wrestle. I caught on very quickly, and that was when I recognized my talent. I was dominant by the eighth grade, when I defeated everybody in my county and won the district championship.

During my freshman year, I made the varsity team and wrestled at 103 pounds. That was when I started to get a real taste of competition. At my very first match, I wrestled a senior who had wrestled in the state tournament the year before. He was much bigger than I was, and his hair was bleached, which symbolized that you were a badass in the wrestling world. It was truly a match of a man versus a boy, no doubt the resemblance of David and Goliath. The stands were full of his fans, as we were wrestling away from home. They all had signs and were chanting his name.

Everybody undoubtedly expected that I would be defeated, but I rose to the occasion and came out triumphant. Not only that, I decimated him. The whole time he stood no chance. I proved myself to my team that year as we traveled across the state, competing in tournament after tournament. By the end of the year, I had compiled a record of nineteen wins and nine losses, which was very good for an incoming freshman. I was going to go to state that year with the team, but I ended up injuring my knee and could not compete. They went on to win the state title, which I should have been a part of.

I would get another chance to prove myself my sophomore year. That year, I moved up to 119 pounds, and that was when I started to grow more into my body. I won the district championships, and then I went on to win the regional championship. I finally made it to the state tournament. The Washington State Mat Classics takes place in the Tacoma Dome. For two days, over eight hundred wrestlers battle it out to achieve their dreams of winning a state championship. There is no doubt that it is a spectacle to behold with twenty-four mats spread over a football field with over twenty thousand people in attendance.

Every school from across the state would be represented in a two-day event. If you made it to the second day, you had become a state placer. That year, I made it to the quarterfinals and then lost, so I had to win the next match in order to move on the next day and become a state placer. I ended up winning a close victory and moved on to the second day, where I battled through the consolation bracket and made it to the match that would determine the third and fourth place. I wrestled the same guy who had beat me the day before, and he got my number again. But I ended up being the only sophomore to place in my bracket, and I finished that year with a record of thirty-one and nine.

After that year, I knew I could win a state title so I set my sights on being a champion. I went through that year winning tournament after tournament. I won the district and regional titles again and once again earned a trip to the state tournament. I defeated each opponent with ease on my way to the finals and ended up being matched with a wrestler I had wrestled earlier that year. It was a close match, but I came out on top when we wrestled the first time. For our state finals match, it was close until the end. I was down three to one with five seconds left, and I had to get a takedown to send it into overtime. I went for the takedown and finished it, but unfortunately time had ran out before I was awarded the points. So I lost in the state finals that year and finished with a record of thirty-three and two.

During my senior year, I was on a mission. There was only one thing on my mind, to be a state champion. No one came close to competing with me that year. I won every tournament we went to. I received Wrestler of the Year award for our conference. I won my third consecutive district and regional titles that year and finished the year as an undefeated state champion. My record was thirty-nine and zero, and I finished with a career record of 122 wins and 18 losses.

For me, wrestling was my first passion. The hard work that our team put in day in and day out can only be measured by the blood that had flowed from our wounds, the sweat that poured from our bodies, and the tears we cried when we thought we had nothing left to give. That sport molded me into everything I would become, and it was the basis on which my life would be built upon.

11

✠

REMEMBER WHERE IT ALL BEGAN

> A hundred times ten have I descended the dark way that
> led into light and as many times have I descended my
> strength and power renewed.
>
> —The Emerald Tablets

I WILL NEVER FORGET my high school days. They were times of the utmost joy and also those of the most sorrow. As far as my life was away from home, I got to enjoy many pleasures. I had several friends, and we did many things together. Some things I'm happy I did and others maybe not so proud of. But really the only thing that matters is that you learn from your experiences, and I can most certainly say that I have learned from mine.

Away from home, everything was enjoyable. I even had the chance of falling in love. That memory of summer love is something that will always remain in my heart. The things we will do for love are incredible—whether it be sneaking through a cornfield in the middle of the night to sneak through your lover's window or carrying someone for miles because she can't walk. It is clear that we will do anything for love.

At home, it was a different story. I first realized that there were problems in my mother's marriage when I was around ten years old. With what I know of astrology now, an Aries and a Sagittarius, two fixed fire signs, do not make a compatible match. But astrology aside, it was what it was, and I believe that no one is to blame more than anybody for anything that would happen in the days to come.

To make a long story short, one fateful night everything in our family's lives would change drastically forever. That night I received a call from my younger sister. She was very disturbed, and all she told me was that I needed to come home. On my way home, I noticed as I got closer and closer to our house that the sky was lit up with what were obvious lights from fire trucks, ambulances, and police cars.

When I arrived at our house, emergency vehicles were everywhere, and as I got out of the car, my stepfather came up to me with an intense look in his eye and told me that my mother was dead. At that point, I was in shock from what I heard, and I started to wander around the scene. I had found out that my mom had been walking on the road after she and my stepfather had gotten in an argument. When she was walking down the road, a truck didn't see her and hit her. The driver, one of my wrestling teammates, was going fifty-five miles an hour.

I went into the ambulance he was in. He was crying so I went up to him, hugged him, and told him it was not his fault. He cried on my shoulder. I then went to be with my sister and brother for the remainder of the night and found out that my mom had actually survived the accident. It was a miracle that she had not died, but she was in a coma and in critical condition.

At that time, I had graduated high school and signed up to go into the United States Marine Corps. My ship-out day was coming up, and there was no way that I could leave with my mom being in the condition she was. She ended up coming out of the coma, but when she did, she couldn't talk or move. She only could just lie there with a tube coming out of her mouth that was breathing for her.

It was very hard to see her like that, but over time, she started making a recovery. And after a while, she was able to move and talk. With her gaining strength, I started to think about going into the marines again, so I decided I would ship out on my intended date. I knew it was what she would want me to do. So I packed my bag, said good-bye, and shipped off to Marine Corps Recruit Depot (MCRD) San Diego.

When I arrived in San Diego, all of the recruits were given orders to report to the airport's USO. They were very courteous to us in there. There were sandwiches, cookies, and pop. They had TVs with Xbox machines hooked up to them, and there were lounge chairs that recruits would sit in while they chatted on their phones to their girlfriends.

My mind though was not on cookies and video games. I was precognitively thinking about the times that were ahead as I prepared myself for three months of boot camp so I could be inducted into the finest fighting force in the world. As everybody enjoyed his last moments of freedom, I noticed the door that led out into the parking lot suddenly come open. And for the first time in my life, I would lay my eyes upon the dreaded Marine Corps drill instructor.

Immediately my heart started racing and felt like it was going to come out of my chest because I knew it was about to get extremely real. At the top of his lungs, he shouted an order for us to get our bags and to get on the bus that was waiting for us outside. When we got on the bus, he told us to look down as they turned off the lights. It was silent and dark on the way to MCRD. About sixty of us were crammed into the bus. I was prepared for what was in store though as I had always been up to challenges for all of my life.

When we arrived, a drill instructor came onto the bus. His campaign cover cast a dark shadow over his eyes, and he looked like he was a gladiator. He had flaming skull tattoos on his forearms, and his biceps looked like they were going to bust through the cuffs of his Charlie uniform.

"You have arrived at United States Marine Corps Recruit Depot San Diego. The first and last words out of your mouth are going to be 'sir'! Do you understand that?" he shouted.

"Sir! Yes, sir!" we responded.

"What you're gonna do now when I tell you is you're going to get your bags and get in formation on my yellow footprints! Do you understand that?"

"Sir! Yes, sir!" we responded again.

"Good. Well then, get on my yellow footprints right now!"

And with that command, we all stood up and unloaded off the bus, only to be greeted by more drill instructors who were running around and screaming at the top of their lungs. Recruits were smashing into each other in confusion. Some even were knocked off their feet. Some recruits were wearing their Marine Corps recruitment shirts, which had the motto "Pain is weakness leaving the body." They got their ass chewed out by the drill instructors, accusing the recruits of thinking they were already marines and letting them know that they had no idea what that statement even meant.

After the dust settled and we finally got into formation, we had finally begun our induction into the United States Marine Corps, whose motto is "Semper Fidelis," which means "always faithful."

III

THE TRADITION OF THE YELLOW FOOTPRINTS

Great where my people were my people in the ancient days, Great beyond the conception of the little people now around me knowing the wisdom of old seeking far within the heart of infinity knowledge that belonged to Earth's youth.

—The Emerald Tablets

E VERY MAN OR woman who has ever become a marine has stood on the legendary yellow footprints. As we stood there at the position of attention, we received a brief on how, once we passed through the double doors, our transformation from civilian to marine would begin. For two days, we would be going through the phase that they refer to as receiving. During this time, we filled out paperwork, which took hours and hours on end. Recruits would often doze off, only to get awoken by a drill instructor screaming in their ear. It's actually funny thinking about it now.

But at the time, I knew my life was going to be little different than I had been used to. We walked together in unison from building to building, often having to wait outside for hours before we even got a chance to go in. We received our haircuts, which was more of like a shearing of our head. They made sure they warned us that, if we had any moles or anything like that, to make sure the barber knew. If they didn't, that shit was definitely coming off. We received all of our shots, which they definitely weren't very nice about giving. They issued us our camouflage uniforms, and all of the T-shirts, socks, and boots that we would need.

In the beginning, you don't even get to wear your top. Instead you get to wear a sweatshirt turned inside out to show you are just a receiving recruit at the beginning of his training. During those two days, they taught us all the basic things we would need to know before we were picked up into our training platoons. We learned how to make our racks and all of the military jargon, like how a bulkhead is a wall and a drinking fountain is called a scuttlebutt.

Since we did not know how to march yet at chow time, we would walk in formation over to the chow hall. I will admit that the other platoons that were marching around intimidated me a little bit. On the way over, if we were in another platoon's way, we had to get out of the way, and then they would march through us.

They would all yell in unison, "Out of the way!"

At chow time, every platoon comes marching in while shouting cadences. It is motivating to hear fifteen platoons of sixty marines shouting in unison with each one trying to outshout every other platoon there. When you first get subjected to that, I don't care who you are. You will be shocked.

After the initial receiving phase was complete, it was time for us to be picked up into our training battalion. My battalion was Mike Company, or Mighty Mike. Our platoon number was 3149, and in the company, there were six platoons. The next phase we would go through would be what was known was Black Friday, when we get introduced to our drill instructors.

Everyone knows very well about Black Friday. Black Friday is the worst day of a Marine Corps recruit's life. On that day, we were taken to where all of the platoons train. Once again, I was in awe as I watched platoons on the parade deck, practicing for their final drill. It was hard to imagine that someday that would be us, but that day would not come for quite some time.

When we got to our squad bay, the platoon was seated in formation in the front of what we refer to as the house. We were introduced to our drill instructors one by one as they swore to train us. Our platoon had four drill instructors: Sergeant Escobar, Staff Sergeant Taylor, Staff Sergeant Rodriquez, and Senior Drill Instructor Staff Sergeant Martinez.

If you ask any marine one thing, he will remember his drill instructors. For three months, the equivalent to sixty-three training days, we would be under the instruction of these men who swore they would train us. The company commander made an appearance and gave a motivational speech. He reminded us to keep going, to never quit, and to always remember the reason why we had come. After delivering those words, we stood up to salute him as he left the hatch.

As he left, he turned around and gave the command that would literally turn our world upside down, "Drill instructors, take charge and carry out the plan of the day!"

At that point, the drill instructors erupted into a homicidal rage. They commanded us to pick up our sea bags and to immediately go outside to start running up and down the stairs with them. Once again, recruits were slamming into each other in confusion as the drill instructors swarmed around us like a swarm of bees.

At the same time, the other platoons were getting the same initiation so it was an all-out fiasco of total chaos. The drill instructors were screaming so loud that they have to be specially trained to be able to project as they do. Sometimes they wouldn't even say anything. They would just be running around screaming. Of course the reason for this is to simulate all the confusion and chaos of the battlefield.

After we did that for a while, they had us line up by our racks in the squad bay and hold our bags out in front of us. Our sea bags were completely full of gear so they weighed about fifty pounds. Every time a recruit would drop his bag, he would earn a trip to the quarter deck to receive a period of instruction known as incentive training, or IT. When a recruit is IT'd, he is made to do various calisthenics in front of a drill instructor, who is in his face the whole time, taunting him and telling him to go faster. The rest of us would continue holding out our bags as recruits were dropping like flies.

The drill instructors then made us take our bags and dump them out on the floor. After we dumped them out, they went up and down the aisle, throwing and kicking our gear all over the squad bay. They then would do what is known as a countdown, and when they reached the end of it, we had to be done with stuffing our gear back in our bags. At the beginning, we were running around, looking around for our own stuff. And we were never fast enough, so we had to do it over and over again.

After a while, we learned to just grab whatever we could so the stuff we had in our bags was not our own. After a while, we learned to give up trying to find our stuff amongst a sea of other people's gear. That took too much time, and we knew, if we did not get the task done, we were going to do it until we did.

Some of the recruits would have more gear than the others did, so on some attempts, recruits couldn't shut their bags. So we learned to communicate after some time, and we started to work together. After we completed that little game, the drill instructors had many more surprises in store. They then started to go up and down the aisles, tearing apart our racks and throwing them all over the squad bay. We were then counted down and given the task to reassemble the racks. By that time, we had learned to communicate so we finished that task much faster, but it was still not easy.

We then got introduced to field day, a complete, immaculate cleanup of the squad bay from top to bottom. Every corner and crevice must be so clean that they could take a white glove and there would be no dirt on it. And if you think I'm joking about that, I'm not. While we cleaned, there were recruits still getting IT'd on the quarter deck.

Throughout the night, other drill instructors from other platoons would stop in to have a little fun with us. Sometimes there were at least eight of them in our squad bay at a time, spreading hate and discontent. We cleaned for hours as our instructors continued to play with us. One of the things they made us do was take what we called a scudge brush, which we used to clean the floor. But their twist on it was that we had to run around in a bear crawl position with it. After a while of that, it was clear that recruits were becoming tired when their arms gave out and they were doing face-plants into the floor.

We cleaned and endured that punishment until sunrise when the only reason why they had to stop was because we were required to get morning chow. Reveille was at five thirty every morning. At that time, "Taps" would sound, and everybody would jump out of his rack to get in line to count off. This was to ensure that each member of the platoon was ready and accounted for.

During first phase, they made us do everything by the numbers. First we had to put on our left sock and then right sock. Then the pants, next the shirt, and so on and so forth until we were fully dressed. If we didn't do it by the time the drill instructor was done counting us down, we would have to do it again until we did. Then after that night of chaos, we lined up outside, and we stepped off to morning chow.

IV

✠

THE RECRUIT

Chosen was I from the Sons of men, taught by the dweller
so that his purposes might be fulfilled, purposes yet
unborn in the womb of time.

—The Emerald Tablets

THE PLATOON WAS broken up into four squads, and each squad had a squad leader. There were thirteen recruits in each squad, so the platoon had around fifty of us in it. The top leadership position represented what was known as the guide, or what would be a platoon commander in the fleet.

From the very start of training, I stood out amongst the other recruits. So they made me the guide of our platoon. A typical training day would consist of a morning physical training (PT) session where the whole regiment would run out to a field where a red platform was set up. Then our regimental gunnery sergeant would lead us in various stretches and calisthenics. Then we would each break off into our separate platoons and go on a morning run. After that, we would return to the house to receive periods of instruction.

Our first period of instruction was over the M-16 rifle, the standard issue rifle for the marines. The M-16 is a 5.56mm semiautomatic rifle. It is an air-cooled, gas-operated, magazine-fed assault rifle. We had to learn everything about our rifles from the rate of fire, which is 12–15 rounds per minute sustained, 45–60 semiautomatic, and 750–950 cyclic. The maximum effective range is six hundred meters on a point target and eight hundred meters on an area target. A detachable magazine of thirty rounds feeds the rifle, and it comes equipped with iron sights that can be adjusted for the daytime and the night. We learned how to disassemble and reassemble it until we could do it with our eyes closed, and we had to memorize the rifleman's creed. The rifleman'creed is recited as follows, This is my rifle. There are many like it, but this one is mine.

My rifle is my best friend. It is my life. I must master it as I must master my life.

Without me, my rifle is useless. Without my rifle, I am useless. I must fire my rifle true. I must shoot straighter than my enemy who is trying to kill me. I must shoot him before he shoots me. I will...

My rifle and I know that what counts in war is not the rounds we fire, the noise of our burst, nor the smoke we make. We know that it is the hits that count. We will hit...

My rifle is human, even as I, because it is my life. Thus, I will learn it as a brother. I will learn its weaknesses, its strength, its parts, its accessories, its sights and its barrel. I will keep my rifle clean and ready, even as I am clean and ready. We will become part of each other. We will...

Before God, I swear this creed. My rifle and I are the defenders of my country. We are the masters of our enemy. We are the saviors of my life.

So be it, until victory is America's and there is no enemy, but peace!

After our morning periods of instruction, which were three hours in length, we would march to the chow hall again for afternoon chow. Each time we went to chow, it was my responsibility as the guide to go into the chow hall and request permission for the platoon to enter. Approaching a table full of drill instructors is always a little intimidating at first because you never know how much shit they are going to give you. I mean, after all you are interrupting their meals.

So after a while, I learned I had to go up there with confidence; otherwise they would literally eat me for lunch. After I requested permission, I had to return to the platoon back outside and stand in front of them to inform them where the platoon would be seated.

So at the top of my lungs, I would get the platoons attention and yell, "Ears forty-nine!"

And they would reply, "Open, guide!"

I would then again yell, "Ears forty-nine!"

And they would again reply, "Open, guide!"

Then I would yell, "The platoon will be seated in this section. Does the platoon understand?"

They would then reply, "Yes, guide!"

I would then say again, "Does the platoon understand?"

They would then reply again, "Yes, guide!"

Then I would yell, "Attack!"

And they would reply, "Kill!"

Then I would yell again, "Aattaacckk!"

And they would yell back, "Kill!"

Then I would finally at the top of my lungs yell, "Aaaaaaattttttaaaaaccccckkkkkk!"

And they would belt out, "Kill kill kill them all."

I never had any time to eat because I was always the last one to sit down, and by the time I would get my food, the first recruit was already done eating. But as time went on, things slowed down, and we got a little more time.

After afternoon chow, the platoon would then go out to the parade deck, where we would spend countless hours learning how to march and drill. Needless to say, at the beginning, we looked like we were like a newborn baby deer trying to walk, but in a few months when we had reached third phase, it was going to be a different story.

As the guide, it was my responsibility to carry our company's guidon, the company's battle flag. It goes everywhere the platoon goes, and it was an honor to be the one to carry it. As the guide, I was taught how to glide when I moved as opposed to marching. The guide had to be the example for everyone to follow, and throughout training, I constantly stood out to retain my position. Throughout boot camp, many guides from other platoons who were selected were getting iced, and if the platoon were really in trouble, they would make us carry our guidon upside down to disgrace us. I lost my position for a day, but it wasn't because of something I did wrong. It was more of a punishment for our platoon. That day, they put the least motivated recruit in the position. That recruit was not able to handle it for too long, so it wasn't long before they put me back as guide again.

After hours on the parade deck, we would march over to evening chow and finish off the day cleaning ourselves and the squad bay. Then we would have about an hour to organize our things and write letters before we hit the rack for our guaranteed eight hours of sleep. While the platoon was sleeping, one recruit would stay awake to stand fire watch, or what is also known as interior guard. It was this recruit's duty to stand guard over the platoon and challenge anyone who came within our platoon's squad bay. Going to sleep was undoubtedly the best part of the day, but waking up to reveille the next morning was certainly a dread. It takes some time before it really sinks in that your life is not going to be the same. Those days of being a civilian were definitely over for me now, and the only cornfields I would be sneaking through would be probably be in some distant country instead of my girlfriend's backyard.

As each training day went on, we would learn something that every basic marine should know. We received periods of instruction on first aid, where they taught us how to apply tourniquets and use QuikClot, a gel you can put over a wound that it will seal it closed. They also taught us CPR, and we learned the Heimlich maneuver. For combat, the Marine Corps has a martial arts system that they developed, McMap. By the end of boot camp, every recruit would learn up to a tan belt, the first belt out of five. The others are gray, green, brown, and black.

For me, martial arts came easy. With my wrestling background, the throws came quite naturally, and the drill instructors were definitely impressed with my amplitude. That was when they found out I was a state champion in wrestling, and they let me know that they thought I was a badass.

Following that, we learned about Marine Corps history, for example, the origins and famous battles the Marines were involved in. We also were told about such heroes as Dan Daley and John Basilone. The Marines take heritage very seriously. For 273 years, they have spilled their blood to protect this country and will continue until the end.

At the end of our first week, we took an initial physical fitness test (PFT), which consisted of a three-mile run, sit-ups, and pull-ups. To get a perfect PFT, a recruit would have to do a hundred sit-ups in under two minutes, complete twenty pull-ups, and finally run a three-mile run in eighteen minutes. The sit-ups were easy to complete. The pull-ups were harder for recruits to get the maximum amount. One of the things the drill instructors would do is not count pull-ups they didn't like, and sometimes they didn't like any of them. I ended up getting twenty-eight so all I needed to do now was finish the run in eighteen minutes.

At the start of the run, everyone always starts out sprinting, but as the run goes on, it's clear to see who really has what it takes to push himself. At the midway point, about ten of us were battling for the top spot. Then there were five and then three. And finally I pulled away in front of everybody because, in the end, there can only be one.

It was extremely motivating when my drill instructors joined me at the end of the run. They were encouraging me to run faster as I neared the finish line. When I finished, I ran it in a time of seventeen minutes and forty-five seconds so I received a perfect PFT. I was the only one in my platoon to get a perfect score. One other recruit in the company received a perfect score, but I ended up doing more pull-ups than he did, so for the time being, I had the company high PFT.

On Sundays, they allowed us to attend religious services, which allowed us to get away from the drill instructors. It wasn't uncommon to see recruits in there who had never been to church a day in their life. Then they would give us about three hours to write letters and work on our uniforms. Sometimes we even got a chance to read the newspaper, only to catch a glimpse and dream about what was going on outside of the walls. So that concluded week one, and now there were only twelve more weeks to go.

V

THE GUIDE

Far to the Stars I journeyed until space and time became
as naught then having drunk deep of the cup of wisdom,
I looked into the hearts of men and was glad. For only in
the search for truth could my soul be stilled and the flame
within be quenched.

—The Emerald Tablets

O N THE SECOND week of boot camp, our platoon moved on to pugil
stick fighting. The first stage took place in a sand pit. We had to fight
through three stages, each simulating a different environment. During the
second stage, we fought on a bridge, and for the final stage, we rumbled
in what they called the thunder dome, a octagonal-shaped arena that was
covered in camouflage netting.

In this final stage, two recruits would run into the dome from opposite
sides while warrior crying. The drill instructors would watch from above,
like nobles in Rome in the time of gladiators. I got a surprise when it was
my turn to go into the dome. The recruit they paired me against was the
biggest recruit by far. I was much faster though and ended up finishing
him with a horizontal slash. The drill instructors yelled out in satisfaction
from above.

The next physical challenge was the obstacle course, which is made up
of various tests that assess a recruit's balance, dexterity, and strength. The
confidence course is the next step up. It is similar to the obstacle course,

except everything is much higher and more difficult. Probably the most famous of the obstacles is the stairway to heaven, a forty-foot-high ladder that must be conquered before any recruit can move on. It is no wonder why they call it the confidence course. It instills exactly what it says it does.

Throughout phase one, we learned various types of Marine Corps knowledge. Each recruit would be tested on how well he knew this knowledge when the platoon had its senior drill instructor inspection. During the inspection, our drill instructors would check our uniforms for any discrepancies. If there were one thread sticking out, we would fail the inspection. Some recruits would buckle under the pressure, stuttering when they didn't know an answer to a question. If a recruit didn't know something, he failed, and when there was failure, there was sure to be punishment that followed. And there was.

The next week, the platoon moved on to swim qualification, which had four phases that a recruit could progress through with one being the most advanced. For stage four, we had to swim with full pack and gear on. For stage three, we had to demonstrate how to use our uniforms for flotation devices. And for stage two, we had to demonstrate different methods of strokes for swimming. I made it through all the stages, and I was one of the few selected to move on to stage one, that is, rescuing someone else, a Marine Corps drill instructor. We were given the task to swim out and properly demonstrate a successful rescue.

When I was given my chance, I swam out to retrieve the victim, and once I got to him, he rose up out of the water and took me under. My first reaction was to kick him off me because he caught me by surprise. So I put my boot in his stomach and kicked him off me. When we returned to the surface, he was pissed off. He told me to get the hell out of the pool and said I failed. So unfortunately I didn't pass the phase one swim qualification.

At the end of phase one, the platoon conducted our initial drill. We were graded on all the drill movements we had been practicing all those hours for weeks. At the end of boot camp, we would receive a final drill, the most prestigious event during Marine Corps boot camp.

By that point, we had reached the end of phase one, and it was time to move up north to Camp Pendleton for phase two, combat training. For a month, we would move from the warm, sunny skies of MCRD San

Diego to the cold, dark hills of Camp Pendleton, California, to undergo marksmanship training and combat instruction.

At the end of phase two, the platoon's final test would be a fifty-hour challenge known as the Crucible. So with phase one being complete, our platoon packed our sea bags, got on a bus, and left MCRD for Camp Pendleton.

On the outside of the MCRD's walls, I felt a sense of freedom once again. It was like I was a kid in awe, looking around at everything like it had been the first time I had seen it. Just to observe people walking on the streets was a sight to see. Of course though, it would be a sight to see for anyone who had been locked away for four weeks. The California coast is beautiful. I have always loved beaches for as long as I could remember. Just the thought of one reminds me of paradise.

On the way to Edson Range, my mind was given a moment to escape my current reality. It was silent, and I'm sure that everyone was thinking of one thing, home. It was dark and gloomy when we arrived at Edson Range. The wind was blowing from the ocean, which was kicking up dirt all over the place. Since we had moved locations and now we were going to be in a new squad bay, the drill instructors decided to reenact Black Friday again, but this time with a few new surprises.

While the platoon was going through Black Friday 2, one of my drill instructors took me aside and asked if I wanted to go on his "little island tour." Of course I gave him a "Yes, sir," so he told me to grab my tube of sunscreen and took me to the first destination, one of the other platoon's squad bays. My drill instructor told me to put on the sunscreen and to start doing mountain climbers. Since we were in another platoon's squad bay, all three of their drill instructors proceeded to yell IT commands at me as I did mountain climbers, push-ups, and jumping jacks while they screamed at me, circling around me like vultures.

After we were done there, he took me to the next platoon's squad bay, and the same thing happened again. Then after that, it was on to the next one and the next one after that. I ended up getting IT'd on all five of the other platoon's quarter decks, and even then, we were not done yet. Our final destination was literally a mound of sand with a palm tree sticking out. By the time we got there, the sunscreen I had put on had melted away from my face from all the sweat that spilled from me. My drill instructor, with much concern in his voice, noticed that my sunscreen was gone. So he gave me another tube, which I put on my face, and he then commenced to finishing our little island tour.

The one thing I remember about up north is it was cold. Every morning we would hump out to the rifle range to receive periods of instruction for hours. It was about a two-mile hump to the range where we would receive our training. For the whole morning, we huddled together to keep warm while we were taught the ropes about the range. Before we even got to step on the range, we did hours and hours of "snapping in," that is, when there are no rounds chambered in the rifle but you fire it as if there were.

After we spent a few days doing that, we were ready to step on the range to begin live-firing our weapons. The way they had it set up is we were all put into pairs. One recruit would work pulling targets in the pits while the other would shoot from the firing line. I had never heard what it sounds like to have a bullet pass by me until I experienced the pits. You can definitely hear the crack as it passes over you. Sometimes they even ricochet off the metal of the targets.

On the firing line, we were to shoot from the distances of 150, 300, and 500 meters. Of all the services, the marines are the only ones who shoot from five hundred meters out. There is no doubt they take pride in marksmanship. We fired from various positions. There was the standing, kneeling, cross-legged, and prone. Three awards could be earned depending on how a recruit performed on qualification day. The marksman badge was given to recruits who finished with the lower scores. The sharpshooter badge was given to those who finished in the middle, and the expert badge was given to those who finished the highest.

On prequalification, I shot an expert, but the next day I shot a marksman. The drill instructors from the other platoons made sure they gave me a hard time because I shot like shit. Because everything was a competition, how you performed on the rifle range was huge, and with me being a guide, that was going to hurt when it came down to selection for company honor man.

After our two weeks of marksmanship training, the next stage was field week, when we would learn all of the basic combat skills our platoon would need to be able to finish the Crucible. Now that we knew how to fire our weapons, the next step was to learn how to patrol.

A squad is made up of twelve to thirteen marines. That squad is then broken down into three fire teams of four marines. In a fire team, there are three different roles: the rifleman, automatic rifleman, and team leader (grenadier.) Marines use different variations while patrolling for various purposes, but the most common one used is the staggered column.

After we learned how to patrol, we learned how to move in the movement course. We performed the movement course during the daytime in the light, with speed being the main objective. And then we performed it again at night, with stealth being the emphasis. When we completed those tasks, we worked on being able to work as a team, moving ammo crates through all sorts of obstacles. This was all while they had simulation artillery and machine gun rounds going off.

Then after that fun was over, it was on to the gas chamber. If you ask any marine one thing he or she hated about boot camp, most would say it was the gas chamber, where the platoon lined up along the walls of a room that had a canister of gas in the middle of it. We stood shoulder to shoulder while the chamber filled up full of gas.

At one point, I couldn't see more than a foot in front of my eyes. They made us take our gas masks off, and we could feel the burn of the gas on our face. Some recruits couldn't hold their breath for very long, so they got a lung full of gas, which made them violently erupt into a choking, coughing state. We were then allowed to put our masks back on to get air.

We stayed in there for about three minutes, and then they let us out. Once we came out, everyone was choking and coughing with drool and snot coming from his nose. So that was definitely an experience I would not like to ever have to go through again in my life.

VI

※

THE MARINE

> Down through the ages I lived seeing those around me
> taste of the cup of death and return again to the light of
> life. Gradually from the Kingdom of Atlantis passed waves
> of consciousness that had been one with me one with me
> only to be replaced by the spawn of a lower Star.
>
> —The Emerald Tablets

AFTER WE HAD acquired all the necessary basic skills, we were then ready to take on the Crucible. For two days, we would march fifty-two miles around the hills of Camp Pendleton, working together to complete various challenges. We were given two MREs to eat during the forty-eight-hour journey. Sleep and food deprivation would be felt to simulate battle fatigue. At the end of the Crucible, the platoon would finish a six-mile hike, ending with a motivational finish up a mountain called "The Reaper." The focus and key of the Crucible was teamwork.

Communication was essential in completing the various challenges.

For one challenge, our four-man team had to simulate a case evac. One recruit pretended as if he were hit while the rest of us transported him on a gurney to a pickup location. When we were lifting him up, someone in my team busted his eye socket on the muzzle of another recruit's M-16. So ironically, we ended up needing to actually do a real case evac for him.

After we finished each challenge, we would march on to conquer the next one that awaited. Then when we finished all of them, we gathered together for the final hump up The Reaper. And when I look back on my life, that was probably one of the most motivational times in all my years.

The company commander joined in, and our platoon was leading the company. When we reached the top, we could see as far as the eye could see in all directions— the ocean to the west and, to the east, the hills with the sun rising over them. We could feel the breeze from the ocean on our faces that were covered in dirt and smeared-on camouflage paint. That was a majestic moment that I will remember forever.

After the company commander gave us a motivating speech, the company humped back to the squad bay to clean up for the warrior's breakfast. That day, we got to eat like kings that had just returned from battle. I had never seen so much food in my life, and they had everything we could think of. And the best thing about it is we got to go back for as much as we wanted. It was safe to say, at that point, we were done with the hardest part of boot camp. Now it was time to return to MCRD for phase three back in warm and sunny San Diego.

Phase three was the final four weeks out of thirteen that were to be completed if a recruit wanted to earn the title of "Marine." For that final month, we would receive the final touches on all we needed to know when we returned to MCRD. The first thing they let us do was give us the honors of wearing our boots bloused and unbuttoning the top button of our uniforms. Now we looked like marines. We received the high and tight haircut that marines are known for. Because of that haircut, marines are known as "Jarheads."

Phase three was a lot more relaxed, you could say. Now that we weren't nasty recruits, they treated us with more respect, and we were given more freedom. For the first week, which was known as team week, our platoon was split up into various teams to do work around the base. We were now allowed to march around the base without a drill instructor accompanying us. The drill instructors were now acting more like sergeants than drill instructors. They didn't have to get involved with us so much now because now we were trained.

During that time, I was selected to go on a trip over to mainside to a lunch where teachers from my state were attending. Mainside is totally separated from the MCRD. When we went over there, I had to keep my bearing because I was not used to being around so many civilians.

Families were walking around. Kids were laughing and playing, and I had just gotten done with the Crucible. Needless to say, it took me a while to adapt to these surroundings, but luckily for me, every marine knows about adapting and overcoming.

When the teachers came, one was actually from an area that was close to where I lived back home. She actually knew who I was because she was a fan of her school's wrestling team. I felt like I was living the high life, eating in an elegant dining hall, but that would soon come to an end when lunch was over and I had to return to the squad bay.

Throughout boot camp, I was given a book of Marine Corps knowledge to study that all the guides would be tested on to determine who would be company honor man, the person who received the honor of graduating the highest-ranking marine in the company. If selected, I would be graduating a lance corporal, the number-one recruit in the company.

In the company, there were two series. The first series was platoons 3147, 3148, and my platoon, 3149. Out of the guides of those platoons, I was selected to be the series honor man so I was to square off with the other guide, who was selected to be his series honor man.

For the selection, we had to stand in front of a panel of all the company's top-ranking marines. They asked us to answer various different Marine Corps knowledge, along with other questions, to determine our intentions in being a marine. To select the company honor man, all of our performance throughout boot camp would be assessed and graded. Then whoever they decided would receive the honor of being company honor man.

We continued to practice day after day to get ready for final drill. It was every platoon's goal to be the best. When we drilled, we were encouraged to hit our weapons so hard that they would fall apart. Every time a handguard from our rifle would fall off, the drill instructors would go crazy. Just as much as it was a competition between the platoons, it was a rivalry among drill instructors as well. We also had our company commander platoon inspection, where we wore our Alpha dress uniforms as opposed to our camouflage. This time around, every recruit was locked on, as opposed to when we had the senior drill instruction (SDI) inspection during third phase. It was clear that we were now ready to be marines.

As graduation day neared, we learned how to conduct ourselves as marines in a garrison environment. We received our nametapes on our cammies, along with the US Marine tape as well, and we prepared for the ceremony where we would finally earn the title "Marine."

As the guide, I earned the honor of getting to graduate in my dress blues. So I had finally made that childhood dream come true that I had imagined so long ago. We ran another PFT, which I ended up receiving a perfect score again.

On visitors' day, the platoon was released to spend the day with his family. I had everyone from my side of the family show up, and amongst them was my mother. She had made a miraculous recovery while I was in boot camp, and when I saw her, it brought tears to my eyes.

The next day for our graduation, the company lined up on the parade deck to begin the graduation ceremony. Before graduation day, the company had decided who was going to be company honor man. Unfortunately I was not chosen, but they decided to allow me to graduate as a lance corporal as well. If you ask any marine, he will tell you that it is not often that two lance corporal graduate from out of his company, so my case was definitely a special occasion. Our company marched across the parade deck now as highly trained recruits.

The difference between when we first stepped on those yellow footprints and now was astounding. As the ceremony commenced, the guides were brought out to receive their awards. I graduated as the series honor man. Then it was time for the reason why we came, the reason why we had just spent thirteen long weeks training day in and day out. Our drill instructors awarded us with our eagle globe and anchor and gave us the title "Marine." From that point, our drill instructors were given instructions to release us for ten days of liberty, so with that command, they gave us the order to take charge and carry out the plan of the day.

So we all took one step back, did an about-face, and yelled, "Aye aye, sir. Ooorah!"

VII

✠

SEMPER FIDELIS

Downward into darkness turned the thoughts of the
Atlanteans until at last in his wrath arose from his agwanti
the dweller speaking the word calling the power.
            —The Emerald Tablets

W HEN I RETURNED home for my liberty, I had the best time in my
life. I partied like it was 1999 for every one of those ten days. I had
never felt that much emotion before in my life. I had literally moved into
a new life where it was work hard and play even harder. Needless to say, I
made the best of the time I was given, but all good things must come to
an end. And after those ten days were up, it was back to Camp Pendleton,
California, for infantry training.

The Marine Corps School of Infantry (SOI) is eight weeks long. When
I reported in for duty, I was one of the lucky ones and got picked for guard
duty. That meant all of the marines I graduated with would go on without
me to start training in their platoons. For guard duty, a platoon of marines
was tasked out to guard all of the armories around the base. There were six
armories around the base, and it was our duty to stand eight hours post.
The rotation for us was eight hours and eight hours off continuously for
two weeks. Standing in a box for eight hours is extremely boring. One of
the post we had to guard literally had a four-foot by four-foot box that we
could not step outside for the whole time we were there. It's amazing what

kind of things the mind can dream up when it is not given any other choice but to go to another place.

Night after night, my mind wandered as I stood in my box all alone for hours and hours on end. When we got our time off, we were allowed to watch TV, play video games, and listen to music. I was only supposed to be on guard duty for two weeks, but once again, lucky for me, my time was extended to a month, and that was because there was a gap between companies being picked up from MCRD. I made it through that month without losing my mind, and I finally was picked up into an incoming training platoon.

When marines graduate boot camp, they are sent to one of two schools. All the marines who have noninfantry military occupational specialties (MOSs) would go to a five-week long Marine Combat Training course, which went over basic combat skills. Those who had an infantry MOS would attend the School of Infantry. Infantry Training Battalion (ITB) is a fifty-nine-day course. The mission is to train, mentor, and evaluate infantry marines in specific entry-level tasks under the leadership of combat instructors. Marines are instructed in marksmanship, patrolling, grenade usage, the identification and countering of improvised explosive devices (IEDs), and land navigation, among other various infantry skills.

With this training, the ITB provides the Corps with Marines who are fully prepared for service in the operating forces of the fleet. The infantry is the core component of marine ground forces. Infantrymen are trained to locate, close with, and destroy the enemy by fire and maneuver or repel the enemy's assault by fire and close combat. Riflemen serve as the primary scouts, assault troops, and close combat forces within each infantry unit.

The primary role of the SOI is to ensure, first and foremost, that "every marine is a rifleman." All Marine Corps assets exist to support the rifleman on the ground, and every marine is prepared to do whatever it takes to ensure the safety of the marines to his left and right.

Despite the intense training that was ahead of us, SOI was a lot more relaxed than boot camp. The instructors' focus was more on teaching rather than discipline. After we were done training for the week, we were given weekend liberty. For forty-eight hours, we could go out within a hundred miles of the base, which extended out to the cities of San Diego and Los Angeles. Wherever we went, everyone knew we were marines due to our high and tights and our demeanor. Needless to say, there were times when people didn't like us. But we never cared, and oftentimes that would lead to fights. I never personally partook in any though. But I remember a few times where there would be an altercation and then all the sudden there would be people knocked out all over the place.

One of the weekends, another marine and I joined a couple girls to cross the border to go to Tijuana, which we were not supposed to do. I have done many things that were risky in my life, but that was surely one of the biggest risks I have ever taken. If I would have been caught at that time, I would have been in big trouble. I did have an amazing time that night. It was like Mardi Gras in New Orleans with people packed in the streets. Inside, people filled the clubs. Waitresses were running around, pouring shots in people's mouths. Girls were dancing in cages hanging from the ceilings, and everyone was going absolutely wild. It was definitely a time I will remember, and lucky for us, we made it back without waking up in a bathtub in a hotel with our kidneys missing.

Wherever we went, we certainly had a good time, whether it was on Mission Beach, Long Beach, or Redondo Beach. We drank, and we partied. And then we got our asses back to the base to continue with our training. The Monday following the weekend was always a sight to see. It was always obvious who had too much fun that weekend. Some marines could hardly stand while others would literally collapse from being hungover in formation. Those who didn't make it back when others actually did got dishonorable discharges and were kicked out. Also those who had done drugs and got caught received dishonorable discharges.

After the first month, we took tests to determine what specialty we would be within the infantry squad. The MOSs are 0311, which are infantry. 0331 are machine gunners. 0341 are the mortarmen, and the 0351s are assault men. I chose to be an assault man, so for the next month I would be trained in the 0351 MOS. The assault man has several different purposes. Mainly we are used for breaching.

We were trained in various types of explosives. We learned how to make door charges, cratering charges, and junk charges, which were ammo cans that we filled with C4 and shell casings. We were also trained to take out vehicles and tanks with the Mk153 SMAW, a shoulder-fired rocket used for buildings and small vehicles.

We were also trained on the Javelin, a much more sophisticated system, a fire-and-forget missile that locks on to heat signatures. It was also capable of targeting helicopters. One missile cost around $80,000, so we never live-fired one in training. We only trained on simulators.

Every day we would have classes on all of the different types of tanks from around the world. We had to learn all the weak spots on each so we knew where to hit them. Throughout our training, we did humps of various lengths, the final one being a twelve-mile hump. On the hump, we had to carry all of our weapons systems along with us. The machine gunners had to carry their 50-calibers. The mortarman had to carry his 80mm mortar tubes, and the assault man had to carry his SMAWs and Javelins. Along with the seventy-five to eighty pounds we were carrying, adding a Javelin missile to that definitely puts you over a hundred. On one of the field exercises, I had to be case evac'd because a brown recluse type of spider bit me. They took me to the base where the medical staff took a pair of tweezers and removed all the puss after they sliced it open. That happened to me twice during my time in the marines. Maybe that is the reason why I have never been too fond of spiders.

After our fifty-nine days of training were complete, we were now ready to be tasked out to our battalions. We had a graduation ceremony, but it was nothing like the one we had in boot camp. We received our orders to what battalions we would report to, effective immediately. There was no liberty for us after we graduated. It was just hop on the bus, and off you go.

Some marines were sent to Camp Lejeune in North Carolina. Others were sent to Hawaii, and the luckiest ones were sent to 29 Palms, California, or otherwise known as "the stumps." Once again, I was one of the lucky ones, so it was off to the stumps for me to report in to my duty station, where I would be joining 3rd Battalion, 4th Marines, or otherwise known as Thundering Third Battalion.

* * *

The Marine Corps Air Ground Training center is located in 29 Palms, California, smack dab in the middle of the Mojave Desert. It is the perfect simulation of Iraq and Afghanistan combined due to its mountain ranges and heat. When we arrived there, our battalion was still deployed in Iraq. They were going to be over there for another month before they would return to base, so for the first month there, we did nothing but work parties around the base, and we stood a lot of late-night duty.

When it was time for the battalion to return home, we were tasked to unload all of their bags off the bus so they could go to their families. When they returned, a crowd of their loved ones was there to greet them. I had never seen or felt so much emotion in my life. For a marine, there is nothing like returning home after war. When you really get down to it, making it back is the only thing that really matters.

I was tasked to India Company, where I was put into weapons platoon. Four platoons make up a company. Three of those platoons are infantry, and the squads of the weapons specialists make up the other one. When we were introduced to our squad, a variety of reactions greeted us. Some the guys invited us to drink with them telling us about what happened over there. They told us about the march into Baghdad and when they toppled the statue of Saddam. One of the marines even showed me his belt, which he used for a tourniquet when a round hit him in the leg when he was sitting in the back of a Humvee. The others made us do stupid things as part of a rite of passage into their ranks. Either way I was finally a part of the fleet, and I would be going to war with these marines.

Six teams of two marines made up the assault squad of weapons platoon. One of the marines was designated the gunner, and the other was the assistant gunner. In our case, the junior marines were the gunners, and the senior marines were the assistants. That way, they could give their guidance to us when it came time to fire our big stuff.

A typical day for us would consist of waking up for reveille at five thirty. We would then have morning formation to do our PT, which consisted of a run, obstacle course, or some sort of other physical combat training. After we were finished with morning PT, we would have about an hour to have morning chow. One thing about the military is that they most certainly make sure you are fed. The most incredible smorgasbords around fill chow halls on bases. They have everything you can think of for all of the meals of the day.

After chow, our squad would gather together to go over book knowledge, or we would do some sort of specialized training. After that, we would have lunch, and then we usually just sat around after that and played video games or whatever we wanted in our rooms. There was always the chance that there would be working parties to do during the day. In that case, we would have to do those since we were the junior marines. The average time they would let us off at would be around four o'clock, and after that, we were free to do what we wanted to with the rest of the day.

It didn't take long for me to be accepted in the platoon, although in the beginning they all gave me shit about being a lance corporal. After I proved myself time and time again, it was clear that I was a hot-shit marine, and I actually befriended some of the noncommissioned officers (NCOs). I believe I earned my rite of acceptance when our platoon ran the first company PFT.

Halfway through that PFT, I lost my shoe, but I did not stop to put it back on. And I ran the rest of it with only one shoe on. Needless to say, they all thought that was impressive. And it's kind of hard to treat someone like he's an idiot when he's outperforming you.

The Marine Corps deployment rotation is eight months out and eight months back. During the eight months back at base, we would train in numerous different activities to prepare our company for the next deployment. One of the first company training exercises we did was a simulated company assault on a base. Our objective was to use the four platoons in our company to set up an assault on a base that was dug into a mountain range. Since it was an assault, it was our section's job to initiate the assault with a breach on a concertina wire obstacle that kept the platoon from advancing. Beforehand they had prepared a Bangalore torpedo before the assault to breach the obstacle. A Bangalore torpedo is a pipe that is packed with about thirty pounds of C4, and that makes one hell of a bang.

As the platoon advanced up the dried-out riverbed, two of the senior marines from the assault section ran up to the obstacle and placed the Bangalore torpedo in it. They popped smoke on the torpedo and ran back to the platoon as we waited for the explosion. When it went off, not only did it clear the obstacle, it ended up blowing up all of the rocks that were around it. It was raining baseball-sized boulders on us, but as soon as the dust cleared, we commenced the attack. The weapons section split off to take their overwatch positions while the infantry set up to attack the base. It was my and my gunner's task to set up on top of a hill and fire a SMAW round into one of the bunkers. The machine gunners were to set up in another position while the mortar team did the same thing. On the company commander's command, weapons section was to initiate the attack with a multitude of mortar rounds, a barrage of bullets, and an array of rockets. At the same moment, the infantry squads would bump and bound up to the target while another squad flanked and cleared through the base after it was suppressed. The assault section was tasked with hitting a pile of Humvee tires that simulated a machine gun nest. When I hit my target, the stack of tires flew up into the air, and fire engulfed everything. I could hear all the marines yelling from below me as they commenced their attack. They bumped and bounded up to the target while machine guns suppressed and motors dropped, and finally the squad swept through the base to finish off the enemy with close quarters combat.

Another range was set up to resemble a city so we could get practice in an urban environment. We conducted the range as if we were deployed in Iraq. That is, the platoon would set up a forward operating base (FOB) while squads conducted patrols and marines stood post to watch over the base. We learned many different essential skills that we would need while we were over there. During our patrols, we practiced clearing houses and then capturing and detaining people, and we also worked on patrolling with tanks. At the end of training, we had a mini war game simulation where we would have to eliminate any op-4 (opposition force) that was throughout the mock city. The instructors would dress up like the enemy and run around throughout the city, causing mayhem. So we engaged them in our first real taste of what it was going to be like in urban combat. We used the skills we were taught to locate, close with, and destroy the enemy, but it did not come without casualties. We found out just how hard it is to clear a house with combatants bunkered in. If someone got hit, he would have to pretend he was dead.

At one point, we had to enter a house through a window, but everybody who was getting in was getting shot. It took us a while before we found out that one of the op-4 was hiding behind a mouse hole located right outside of the room, and he was just waiting for people to pop up in the window. Once we established that situation, one of the marines decided he would throw in a grenade to suppress him while as many marines got in as they could.

Once we got in, we piled up against the door. We prepared to go throughout the rest of the house. I was the first man to go, and right when I entered into the other room, I got shot by one of the instructors who was laying in the prone position in the middle of the floor. After that one thing I learned about clearing rooms is that it's always wise to use a grenade and to always look down first instead of straight ahead. After we completed that scenario, we had to do it at night, which was even more challenging.

At night, we had to utilize our night vision goggles (NVGs) and PEQ-2s, a laser targeting system and infrared flood light that attaches to the end of an M-16. Both the laser and the flood light can only be seen with NVGs, so when we entered a room, to us, it would be lit up. But to them, they would see nothing, that is, of course, unless they had their own pair of NVGs.

As the deployment neared, our training intensified bit by bit. On the humps, we traveled further. On the ranges, we stayed out longer, and the military knowledge got much more intricate. We conducted convoy ops where we would drive around the base, practicing getting ambushed. We learned Arabic and how to conduct ourselves in a foreign country, and we learned how to observe the population to identify any potential signs of enemy threats.

When December came around, our battalion received the call to deploy early with the reason being that they had just conducted Operation Phantom Fury, the second invasion of Fallujah. In that operation, our forces lost more marines in a single battle than in any battle of the war. So we received our orders to deploy a month early to replace them because of the heavy casualties that they sustained. We were given ten days to go home for Christmas, and then we returned to get prepared to go war.

VIII

✠

PHANTOM FURY

Over the world then broke the great waters drowning and
sinking changing Earth's balance until only the temple of
light was left standing on the great mountain on Undal
still rising out of the water, some there were who were
living saved from the rush of the fountains.

—The Emerald Tablets

THE SECOND BATTLE of Fallujah was code-named Operation Al-fajr,
which means "the dawn" in Arabic. For the marines, it was code-
named Operation Phantom Fury, and it took place in the months of
November and December 2004. It was a joint American, British, and Iraqi
offensive, which was considered the highest point of conflict in Fallujah
during the war. The marines led the invasion against the Iraqi insurgency
in the heaviest combat that marines had seen since the battle of Hue
City during Vietnam in 1968. The first battle of Fallujah, code-named
Operation Vigilant Resolve, took place in 2004 when coalition forces
received the order to enter into the city and capture or kill the insurgent
elements responsible for the deaths of the Blackwater security team.

In Iraq, Fallujah is one of the most religious and cultural traditional
areas. It is known as the city of mosques for there being over two hundred
mosques throughout the area. It has a population of 350,000 people and
is located forty-three miles west of Baghdad. Following the collapse of
the Ba'ath infrastructure in early 2003, local residents had elected a town

council who kept the city from falling into the control of looters and common criminals. The town council was both considered to be pro-American, and their election originally meant that the United States had decided that the city was unlikely to become a zone of activity. Public opposition was not noticed until seven hundred members of the 82nd Airborne Division first entered the city on April 23, 2003. On April 28, a crowd of approximately two hundred people gathered outside a school past curfew, demanding the Americans vacate the building and allow it to reopen as a school. The protesters became increasingly heated, and the deployment of smoke gas canisters failed in their attempt to disperse the crowd. The protest escalated as gunmen reportedly fired upon US forces from the protesting crowd, and the US Army returned fire, killing seventeen people and wounding more than seventy of the protesters.

After that, Iraqi insurgents in Fallujah ambushed a convoy containing four American private military contractors from Blackwater. Machine gun fire and a grenade thrown through a window of their SUVs killed them. They then set their bodies on fire, and their corpses were dragged through the streets before being hung over a bridge crossing on the Euphrates River. So the first Fallujah campaign was launched on the night of April 4, 2004. With two thousand troops, the marines encircled the city and commenced an assault that lasted for a month. There were estimated to be 3,600 insurgents in the city, so they did have more numbers. But with the help of aerial strikes, the odds are always evened out. At the end of it, all 228 of their combatants were killed with 27 of our marines dying, as well as 581 civilians.

In May, the marines withdrew from the city and turned over control to the Fallujah brigade. The United States armed them to be able to maintain control of the city, but as soon as the marines left, it wasn't long until the weapons were underneath the control of insurgents by September. This then led to the second invasion of Fallujah, which was to be a much bigger conflict that would cost a lot more people their lives.

Before beginning their attack, US and Iraqi forces had established checkpoints around the city to prevent anyone from entering the city and to intercept insurgents attempting to flee. US, Iraqi, and British forces totaled about 13,500. The United States had gathered some 6,500 marines and 1,500 army soldiers that would take part in the assault with about

2,500 navy personnel in support roles. [US troops and about 2,000 Iraqi troops assisted with the assault.] All of the ground element was supported by aircraft and US Marine and Army artillery battalions.

In April, about five hundred hard-core and two thousand-plus part-time insurgents defended Fallujah. By November, it was estimated that the numbers had doubled to equal three thousand. The Iraqi insurgents and foreign Mujahideen present in the city prepared fortified defenses in advance of the anticipated attack. They dug tunnels and trenches, prepared spider holes, and built and hid a wide variety of IEDs. In some locations, they filled the interiors of darkened homes with large numbers of propane bottles, large drums of gasoline, and ordnance, all wired to a remote trigger that an insurgent could set off when troops entered the building. They booby-trapped buildings and vehicles, including wiring doors and windows to grenades and other ordnance. Anticipating US tactics to seize the roof of high buildings, they bricked up stairwells to the roofs of many buildings, creating paths into prepared fields of fire, which they hoped the troops would enter.

Fallujah suffered extensive damage to residences, mosques, city services, and businesses. The city, once referred to as the "City of Mosques," had over two hundred pre-battle mosques, of which sixty or so were destroyed in the fighting. Islamist forces had used many of these mosques as arms caches and weapon strongpoints. Of the roughly fifty thousand buildings in Fallujah, between seven and ten thousand were estimated to have been destroyed in the offensive, and from half to two-thirds of the remaining buildings had notable damage. The 1st Marine Division fired a total of 5,685 high-explosive 155mm artillery rounds during the battle. The 3rd Marine Air Wing (aviation assets only) expended 318 precision bombs, 391 rockets and missiles, and 93,000 machine gun and cannon rounds. The battle proved to be the bloodiest of the war and the bloodiest battle involving American troops since the Vietnam War. Coalition forces suffered a total of 107 killed and 613 wounded during Operation Phantom Fury. Estimates of insurgent casualties place the number of insurgents killed at around 1,500 with some estimates as high as over 2,000 killed. Coalition forces also captured approximately 1,500 insurgents during the operation. The Red Cross estimated directly following the battle that some eight hundred civilians had been killed during the offensive.

I X

✠

THE ART OF WAR

> Gathered I then my people and entered the great ship of
> the master, upward we rose on the wings of the morning
> dark beneath us lay the temple. suddenly over it rose the
> waters, vanished from earth until the time appointed was
> the great temple.
>
> —The Emerald Tablets

F ROM LOS ANGELES, we departed on our eighteen-hour journey across
the world to Iraq. We flew on a commercial jetliner to JFK in New
York, and then we crossed the Atlantic to Ireland. Flying over Ireland was
breathtaking. I've never seen such a green land my whole life. I've always
wanted to go to Ireland. I will admit I've always had a thing for redheaded
girls, and now I had finally set foot in the land of them. We only touched
down for a little while though, so I did not have the time to explore the
land of my dreams.

From Ireland, we departed to Kuwait, where we would wait for a
day for the C-130s to return from Tikrit, an airbase in Iraq. Kuwait was
not a warzone, and we stayed at an army base called Camp Victory. The
next morning we boarded our C-130s to depart to Tikrit, Iraq. When we
arrived in Tikrit, we received a brief from our battalion commander. Our
battalion was to board a convoy and travel ten hours to get to the city of
Fallujah.

It was in December so the ride was very cold and dark. As we drew nearer to the city, it definitely became more apparent that a war was taking place. When I started to see all the burnt-up cars that lined the road on the way into the city, I knew it was getting serious.

Our battalion's area of operation was located on the northeast part of the city. We were replacing 2/7, who had just been through the heaviest fighting of the war. When we arrived in Fallujah, the entire city was evacuated before the fighting took place. A lot of the city had been destroyed. There was rubble everywhere from people's houses, and many of the mosques had been taken down. The city was a ghost town, and our rules of engagement were clear. If we saw anyone, he or she were to be considered an enemy combatant, and we had orders to engage on sight.

Our company's area of operation was located in the northern part of the city. The city was split up into four quadrants, which were assigned to each company in our battalion. Our AO was made up of half-industry and half-rural environment. The platoon's base had been set up in a compound that 2/7 had taken over during the assault. We called it the "soap factory" because, before we took it over, it was used to make soap. Our squad stayed in one of the buildings that were located in the compound, and we slept six to a room. As soon as we got set up, it was right to work, and we started operations from our FOB.

For patrols, the team that was assigned to go out would meet before to go over the pre-patrol briefing. During this time, we would go over the patrol route and do all of our safety and gear checks. When everything was ready to go, the squad would then step across the line out of the base in a staggered column to conduct the patrol. For four hours, we would scout out the city to assure there was no activity going on.

When we first arrived in Fallujah, there was no one there, and it was a complete ghost town. Before the second invasion, the city had been evacuated before the heavy fighting ensued. The people fled to surrounding cities such as Baghdad, Ramadi, and Nassarea. Since no one was supposed to be in the city, we had orders to engage anyone we saw. For the first month and a half, we didn't see anyone, so there was no action going on. After our patrols, we would then rotate to stand guard at positions that were set up around the base. Some of the post was set up with machine guns, and others were set up on rooftops overlooking the surrounding area. The post was four hours long, but there were a lot of times where we had to do eight hours. Sitting for eight hours either in the hot sun of the day or the cold chill of the night is boring and uncomfortable, and it is challenging to stay awake at times. But it's amazing what you can do when there is no other choice.

After post, the next job in the rotation was Quick Reactionary Force (QRF), whose job was to be ready on standby to respond with a squad of marines in Humvees with machine guns mounted. Since there was no one in the city for the first month and a half, QRF never needed to be called out so we used the react time to sleep. That was nice while it lasted, but that would definitely change when we were going to have to start letting people back into the city. The city was destroyed, and now they had to come back to their homes being in rubble. Although we did not know what to expect, any person would conclude something was going to happen.

When the day came to let people back in the city, the cars were lined up for miles. At first we had only set up one entry control point (ECP) in to the city, and once we shut it down, everybody who didn't get in would be turned away until we opened it up again in the morning. The ECP was set up on the main road into the city, which was called "route fran." To get through the checkpoint, cars would have to weave in and out through various obstacles before they would reach a marine who would check their IDs to let them through the checkpoint, which was watched over by a 50-caliber machine gun. Then the car and the people in it would be searched for any weapons or bombs. Since it was not customary for us to interact with the women, we had female marines convoyed in from Camp Fallujah to search the women. After they had passed the necessary inspection, they were allowed to return into the city to start picking up and rebuilding their homes.

Throughout the city, we had various observation posts set up. For a couple days at a time, a team of two marines would be sent out to man observation posts that were around the city. Two marines would man each post, along with two Iraqi soldiers. During that time, I literally watched people clean up their houses from off the streets. When the sun rose in the morning and after morning prayer, the people of Fallujah would go to work to rebuild what had been destroyed. As more people came into the city, it didn't take long to realize that it was not going to be the same as it had been for the first part of the deployment. Things were surely going to get more complicated as angry citizens returned to their obliterated homes, and it didn't take long before gunshots could be heard in the air. There would be nights where I would be sitting on post hearing a firefight going on in the distance, hearing the commentary over the radio of how the situation was unfolding. Another time, I was actually shot at when I was on an observation post. Someone had fired at our post, and I heard the loud cracks go right past my head. Needless to say, I took cover, and my teammate called into the combat operations center (COC) and reported that we were taking fire. Since the post had been compromised, we left it and went back down to where the rest of the team was. QRF came to pick us up, and as a squad of marines swept the area, they never found anyone.

Urban combat is a lot like hide-and-seek. You can go anywhere to escape, and then you could be anyone. A lot of the times, the combatants knew what they could get away with, and they would fire pop shots at us, only to fade away into the night, never to be found.

One time, our squad was out on a mounted patrol, and out of nowhere, an explosion happened about fifteen meters back. My heart jumped, and my adrenaline pumped as we turned the Humvees around to move to contact. We figured it had been an RPG or an IED, so we searched and swept around the area for a trigger man, but once again we didn't find anyone. We returned to the site where the explosion happened, and we found something that was peculiar. It appears that what had been shot at us was a Chinese rocket, which is not your typical RPG. The casing was half-exploded and lodged into the ground.

That event was the first time I ever thought I was going to be shooting at someone. When your life is threatened and the only thing you can do to protect yourself is return fire, it's not hard when it really comes down to it. You or them. Kill or be killed. But we never found who fired the rocket at us. So we never got a chance to get our revenge.

As more people entered the city, there would be more disputes between the marines and the people. There was no electricity or water, food was scarce for them, and people were obviously not happy about that. We organized humanitarian missions to help disperse water and MREs to some of the city's people. One time I saw a couple kids fighting over a MRE. They were definitely hitting and attacking each other for possession of the food we were giving out.

After everybody had entered back into the city, our battalion was tasked with going through and searching every house. That is a city of 350,000 people to be searched by 800 marines. All day and all night, we searched through every house in the city. Some of the houses we knocked on the door, and they let us in. And others we didn't knock and had to blow open because they had been locked. And there were some houses we had to clear that were expected to be Mujahideen hideouts.

We also conducted raids where we would get intel on a house of someone who knew information. A squad would roll up to the target house, and we would clear it definitely without knocking. We would then commence to separate the women who would be screaming from the men, and then we would identify whomever we were supposed to take. When we found them, we zip-tied them, put a bag over their head, put them in the back of the Humvee, and took them to get interrogated.

During the day when we ran patrols through the city, the people of Fallujah would just be going about their daily lives. As time went on, businesses started to open up again, which led to people filling the streets. We would patrol amongst them during the day, and kids were always playing around outside. When our patrols would pass by, they would always run up begging for chocolate. Some of those kids were even little swindlers who were always trying to sell us all kinds of things.

Our platoon was also given an interpreter to take on patrols with us. He was a fat Kurdish guy who wasn't too fond of the people of Fallujah. Most of the interpreters wore something to cover their face, but our interpreter obviously didn't care. He was actually a pretty funny guy. So that made it easier to trust him.

One night out on an observation post, he went and got a lamb and some rice. And I'm not talking about from the grocery store. We killed it, cooked it up, and had one of the best meals I can remember in my life. After eating MREs for five months, a real meal is like going to heaven. A hot meal is the best thing in the world.

Occasionally we would be given a chance to travel to Camp Fallujah, which was located ten miles outside of the city. For the day we were given a day of rest and relaxation. At Camp Fallujah, they had a chow hall that was just like the one back in the States. That was always the first place we went to. It was apparent that we had come from the battlefield, as we were covered in dirt and our cammies were worn to pieces. Everybody else in the chow hall looked as clean-cut as being on base back home. We didn't care though because there were burgers, fries, cake, and ice cream. There was also a chance to take warm showers, which felt like heaven as well. Up until that point, we dumped water over our heads, so taking a shower was like being born again. We were also allowed to make phone calls back home, which with the eleven-hour time difference it was always the opposite time of the day back home. They also had a PX that sold all kinds of stuff, from pop to cookies to movies and Playstations. So at least we got a chance to spend some of the money we were making over there. After a day of rest and relaxation, it's hard to have to go back into the city again, but regardless we headed back into the night, right back to the city.

After the city was starting to get back up on its feet again, a new government was going to be installed, so elections were going to be held throughout the city. Throughout the city, there were going to be voting booths that would be opened so the people of Fallujah could safely vote. Our mission was to provide security from an observation post that overlooked one of the voting booths. We were expecting something to happen that day as we stood overwatch on a roof all day on high alert, but the elections went through without any attacks.

As time went on, our rapport with the people grew. Since we were patrolling their streets every day, we would see the same people every day, and after a while, there was enough trust built between us where we opened ourselves up to their hospitality and joined them in their houses when they asked us in for tea. The kids who were around started to become helpful by letting us know where unexploded ordnance was located. In that case, we would have to call in EOD (Explosive Ordinance Disposal) to come to take care of it. The procedure for taking care of unexploded ordnance is to cordon off the explosive and then wait for EOD to come. Sometimes that would take up to four hours, but if there is one thing a Marine can do, it's wait.

One time we found a car that had been hooked up to be a VBIED (Vehicle Born Improvised Explosive device). There were ten 155mm shells in the trunk that EOD removed. Ten 155 mm shells is more than enough to take out a city block. So it is a good thing that thing never had a chance of being used. After EOD removed the artillery shells, we had to tow the car back to the base. Another marine and I sat in the car while the rest of the squad towed us back to the soap factory in a Humvee.

During the ride back, the car alarm started to go off, and my friend and I did not waste any time getting our asses out of the vehicle. Even though EOD had cleared the car of explosives, it was just our reaction to get out of the car as quickly as we could. It didn't end up blowing up, but it was a very intense moment because you never know when that time could come.

That wasn't the only time we had car trouble. One night on a mounted patrol, I was driving one of the Humvees with NVGs on. The field of vision for the NVGs is very limited. With those things on, it's not the easiest thing in the world to navigate through the middle of the city streets with no light. I ended up running over some rebar that was sticking out of the ground, which ended up jamming into the engine block and causing the engine to catch on fire. Once again we all had to bail out of the Humvee. That one wasn't so funny at the time, but we all laughed about it the next day.

There were periods during the deployment where complacency crept among us. After doing the same thing every day, it's easy to fall into a hypnotic state. With the heat of the sun draining the energy out of the body during the day and the long hours of post we stood at night, the fatigue was undeniable, especially after being in a combat zone for seven months. It's always when a group is in its most complacent state that an event happens that rocks them back into reality. For us, it was on a day where six marines would lose their lives.

It was a dusty evening in the middle of May. Our squad was on a mounted patrol in our AO (Area of Operation) when we heard and felt something that shook our world. An explosion happened about five blocks away from us. We responded immediately to the area, and when we arrived, we saw that a VBIED had hit a seven-ton transport truck. The truck was on fire, and it was charred black. Six bodies were pulled off to the side. Sniper fire was holding down the seven-ton, and one of the marines got hit. Our job was to dismount and create a cordon around the scene while a medical unit responded from Camp Fallujah.

There was absolutely no visibility that evening because a dust storm was passing through. I could not see more than seven feet in front of my face, so identifying any trigger men or snipers was going to be difficult. Once the medical unit arrived, we were given permission to leave the scene after we had been there for hours. When we arrived back at the COC, we received a full debriefing of the situation. What happened was a convoy of women marines were exiting the city to return to Camp Fallujah. A VBIED then slammed into the side of one of the seven-tons in the convoy that had thirteen women marines in it. Five were killed, and seven were wounded. Then a sniper hit the driver of the vehicle.

Up to that point, that had been one of the most catastrophic events in the war. That many women marines dying is a tragedy, and shaking off a disaster like that isn't the easiest thing to do. I went through a lot of emotions after that happened, but I knew I had no choice but to keep it together.

After that, our deployment ended up getting extended for another month longer so we ended up being in country for eight and a half months. The last month was the hottest time of the year. It was August, and temperatures were reaching up to 120 degrees. At the time that we occupied the city, there were definitely no air-conditioners in the buildings we occupied. So we were very uncomfortable for the last part of the deployment. It was funny because sometimes we would joke about the army having air-conditioning in their Humvees along with refrigerators with ice-cold Cokes. They didn't have the refrigerators, but ironically we found out later that they actually did have air-conditioning. Our Humvees were pieces of crap compared to theirs. They had much more advanced versions with way more armor. For our armor, we zip-tied metal plates to the sides and put sandbags on the floor. Needless to say, that wasn't going to do much if we ever got hit.

Finally the day came where we received the order that we were going to be relieved, and when I heard that news, I can honestly say I had never heard anything that had made me so happy in my life. The only thing we ever did over there was count down the days we had left until it was time to go home. Eight and a half months is a long time in a combat zone, and I remember being over there, never thinking that day would come when we would finally get the order to leave. But it finally came, and our battalion packed up and left the city of Fallujah.

As we left the city, I looked back and remembered when we had first rolled in on that cold night when I saw the burned-up cars on the side of the road. The war I experienced in Fallujah is something I will remember for the rest of my life. Being part of it has made me into who I am today, and I am proud of who I am.

We departed for some C-130s to come take us out of the country to Camp Freedom in Kuwait. We stayed in Kuwait for a couple days of rest and relaxation. After being in a combat zone, it was amazing to be around safety again. We were at an army base so there were some soldiers out having BBQs, playing volleyball, and having a good time listening to music. We got to enjoy some things like a couple of fast-food restaurants, and they allowed us to call home again to tell all our loved ones that we were on our way back.

From Kuwait, we departed on some commercial jetliners to fly to Germany. When we reached Germany, we were allowed to get off the plane for a little while. The USO had a stand set up, and a couple of cute German girls were handing out cookies. Needless to say, everyone went over there to get some cookies. I hadn't seen a Western girl for a long time, and when I did, my heart about came out of my chest.

From Germany, we left to JFK in New York. We got to get off for a while there as well. For those of who were old enough, they let them have some drinks at the bar. I was only twenty at the time so I did not get to partake in that.

Finally from JFK, we made the trip back to Los Angeles, where we boarded some buses at the airport and departed back to Marine Corps Air Ground Combat Center (MCAGCC) 29 Palms, California, where crowds of people were lining the streets in celebration of our arrival.

X

MAN OF STEEL

Emissary on Earth am I of the Dweller fulfilling his
commands so many might be lifted. Now I return to
the Halls of Amenti leaving behind some of my wisdom.
Preserve ye and keep ye the command of the dweller lift
ever upwards your eyes to the light surely by right you
are one with the master, surely by right you are one with
the all.

—The Emerald Tablets

I DO BELIEVE THAT there is no greater feeling that I've ever felt than that of
returning home from a war. The overwhelming emotion is indescribable
and can only be felt and not heard in words. When we stepped off the plane
at the air force base, I saw a row of fire trucks that had their lights on and
were spraying their water cannons. They were saluting us for our return
back home, and I had never felt so honored in my life. As we returned to
29 Palms, there were people lining the streets, shouting, holding signs, and
welcoming us back home. I remember when I first arrived at 29 Palms,
when I was the marine getting the bags off the bus for the guys who had
returned. Now I was the one who was stepping off the bus, returning home
from a deployment.

My family was not there to greet me, but I was not disappointed. I
knew I would be seeing everyone I knew shortly for a celebration of a
lifetime when our command released us for our thirty days of leave.

When I arrived back home, I did not hesitate to party like it was goddamn 1999. All those months I had been imagining being back home, having the best time of my life with my friends, was finally upon me. And once I got home, I did not hesitate from making all of those dreams come true. So for thirty days, I enjoyed myself like I never had before.

When my leave had expired, I returned to base to return to my battalion and to start the next training cycle. Each cycle the battalion switches up the command so the battalion has a fresh set of officers for the next deployment. To my luck, our new commanding officer was a wrestler who wrestled for the navy. He noticed I had a little cauliflower ear, and from there, we bonded as one wrestler to another. I had always wanted to try out for the All-Marine Wrestling Team ever since I had seen the team at the state championship my senior year in high school. I had asked earlier before, but the command needed me to go to Iraq. Now that we were back in the States again and my commanding officer was the avid wrestler he was, I was given the opportunity to try out for the All-Marine Wrestling Team in Quantico.

The All-Marine Wrestling Team tryouts took place for a month. When I arrived at Camp Lejeune, I realized I was going to like this job a lot more than being in infantry. The base was located on breathtaking scenery, especially after being stationed in the stumps of the Mojave Desert. Quantico is located on the Potomac River. It's densely populated by lush forests that brought that old colonial feel to the base. The barracks I stayed in were an officers' barracks so the rooms were much more comfortable than the jail cells we had in 29 Palms. Everything was nicely furnished, and there was even a nice leather reclining chair.

My roommate was a heavyweight from Wisconsin. He had been temporarily assigned to the wrestling team from 8th and I, the ceremony marines who are stationed in Washington, DC. 8th and I was made of the silent drill team and the body bearers. He was a body bearer, and their whole platoon was his size. All the body bearers were required to do was lift weights all day. When the marines bury someone, they only use four men to carry the casket, as opposed to the six that the other services use. So it's no wonder they were all six-foot-three and 250 pounds.

I realized real quick that being on the wrestling team was way more relaxed than being in the fleet. The first thing I noticed is that we never had formations. In the morning, all we were required to do was meet up and go for a little jog or lift weights. Then later in the day, we had afternoon practice. After that, we had the rest of the day off. It was more like being a civilian again. We didn't even have to wear our camouflage.

The All-Marine Wrestling Team was made of fourteen marines with ranks from private to major. The fraternization rule was out the window as everybody treated everybody equally and called each other by first names and last names only. This was quite different from the strict rules in infantry where everybody was called by his rank.

All together, about thirty marines tried out, and eight guys were trying out in my weight class. For a month, we practiced the international styles of Greco-Roman and freestyle, which were different than the style we wrestled in high school. For Greco-Roman wrestling, wrestlers can only use their upper body and are not allowed to touch the legs. In freestyle, it's legal to touch the legs. In high school, if someone slammed someone else, he would be penalized. In international rules, competitors are encouraged to throw their opponents higher and harder.

At the end of the trials, each of the weight classes wrestled off with each other to determine who would earn the honors of making the team. The top two wrestlers in each weight class were awarded with positions on the team.

At the end of the finals, I had made it, and I was going to be wrestling against a sergeant who had been on the team for a few years. He ended up defeating me, but regardless I earned a spot. Being on the All-Marine Wrestling Team was nothing like being in infantry. Some marines would call it a glamour job, and that was a job where you never really had to work.

Quantico is located around a sparsely populated area and is nothing like 29 Palms. There was a lot more to explore and do around there. Washington, DC was only a half hour away. So I had a chance to see our nation's capital, along with other places of interest such as the CIA headquarters in Langley.

Our first competition we prepared for was the Armed Forces Championship (AFC) at Camp Lejeune, North Carolina. For the AFC, the branches of the army, navy, marines, and air force would compete against each other to see who was the best among all the services. The team decided that I would wrestle freestyle while my teammate wrestled Greco-Roman.

Our first match was against the navy, where I ended up defeating my opponent, and our team ended up winning the match. Our second match was against the air force, where I ended up coming out victorious, and our team won as well. For our final match, we faced off with the army, who had won the championship the previous three years. The army had a very good team full of NCAA champions and Olympians, so we were definitely the underdogs going in. The army's wrestling team also had the privilege of being stationed at the Olympic training center where they would train with the Olympic team every day.

I ended up losing my match against my opponent, but he was definitely pretty good. He ended up qualifying second at the Olympic team trials that year. Our team got beat as well, but it was clear that they were just more experienced than we were. So once again, the army ended up winning the AFC, but it was still an experience I will always remember.

I ended up wrestling in three more competitions that year. The first was the University National Championship in Chicago. The second was the National Championships in Las Vegas. And my final competition was in Waterloo, Iowa, for the Olympic trials qualifier.

At the Olympic trials qualifier, I was heavier than usual so I wrestled up a weight class. For my first match, I was paired with a Turkish national champion who wrestled for the army. During our match, he ended up locking me up for a belly-to-back suplex, and he launched me for a five-point high amplitude throw. I ended up landing on my arm and snapped it in half. At first I didn't realize that it was broken until we went back to the center to shake hands, and I realized my arm wasn't raising when I went to shake his hand. That was when I looked down and saw that my arm was broken, and then the pain came.

I collapsed to the ground in agony as medics came to my aid. They sent me to the hospital to get x-rays, and when they came back, they showed that I snapped my humerus in half, right above the elbow. I then was transferred to Bethesda Hospital in Maryland, where they put arm in a cast and told me it was going to be seven weeks before the cast would come off. I had never broken a bone before, so being completely immobilized was new to me. I couldn't do anything I could before, and when I tried to, there was nothing but pain. And now that I couldn't wrestle, the team needed to replace me, so that was when my wrestling career came to an end. I was sent back to my battalion in 29 Palms.

My arm was in a cast when I arrived there, so I stayed on the light duty list while the rest of the battalion prepared to go on deployment back to Iraq again. By the time the deployment date came, my arm wasn't healed up enough to go with them so I stayed back with the Remain Behind Element, a team made up of marines who were either getting kicked out or about to be discharged. So I spent the final months of my Marine Corps career in the Remain Behind Element, waiting for my discharge to come.

When my discharge date came, I had a feeling of joy come upon me that cannot be described in words. When I first arrived in 29 Palms, I noticed there were boots hanging from wires on telephone poles around the base. I wondered what that was all about, and a marine told me that, when marines get out, they tie their boots together and throw them up on the wires to signify they had been discharged. I never thought the day would come where I would be throwing mine up there.

But that day did come, and before I left the base, I made sure to take part in that ritual. So I tied a pair of my boots together, threw them up around the wire, and left the base with a honorable discharge from active duty.

XI

✠

MEIN KAMPF

Far in the past lost in the space time the children of light
looked down on the world. Seeing the Children of men in
their bondage bound by the force that came from beyond.
Knew they that only by freedom from bondage could man
ever rise from the Earth to the sun.

—The Emerald Tablets

I HONESTLY NEVER THOUGHT the day would come where I looked back
on MCAGCC, knowing it would be the last time I would see it. Don't
get me wrong. Now that I look back, I miss those glory days of old. But
at the time, I made sure to stick my whole body out the window and give
the base the bird and the loudest "fuck you" I've ever yelled in my life.

When I first got home, it was just like all the other times I was on leave
at first. I partied and had a lot of fun. It was truly a celebration in my life,
but that only lasted for a little while before I realized that things were not
going to be like that forever. Now that I wasn't in the Marine Corps, I had
to find something else to do with my life so I decided to use my GI bill that
I earned to start college. I attended a community college for a semester, but
after that, I decided I was done with that. The classroom environment on
a civilian campus was just not the place for me at the time.

After that, I worked a couple jobs, but those didn't last very long
either. They were only small temporary jobs such as Abercrombie & Fitch
and Kirby Vacuums. After I realized that there wasn't much meaning for

me in those jobs, I just left them without even giving two weeks' notice or anything. It was hard for me to take jobs like that seriously after I had been to Iraq.

So not having any real source of income, I moved from couch to couch and apartment to apartment, searching for my place in life. I ended up getting a DUI one fateful night, so that experience even brought me down further.

After a while, I reached rock bottom, or otherwise known as the "dark night of the soul." And once that happened, little did I know then that I was about to begin a spiritual quest that would take me to a definite understanding and knowing of God.

At the time of my happening of the dark night, I was staying on a friend's couch while I tried to find my place in life. My friend's grandfather was a Christian pastor who had written a series of books that caught my attention. I was hearing the words, and they were calling me. I read them all and realized I wanted to know more so I started reading the Bible and going to church. I became a devout Christian.

When I was born, I was baptized Catholic, but now that I was a born-again Christian, I took it upon myself to baptize myself and accept Jesus Christ as my Lord and Savior. So from that point on, I considered myself to be a true Christian.

Since I did not have a job, I basically became a monk and started reading and writing scriptures all day. I was reading from all the religious holy books: the Bible, the Koran, and the Bhagavad Gita. During this time, I was getting close to God as I was getting the very most out of life despite not having anything materially. Also then, I realized my creativity and started practicing martial arts. I was becoming very devoted to my martial arts. I was getting very into it. I built weapons and shrines, and I studied different moves as I started to progress each day. I then took those skills I learned and used them to become a professional martial artist. I began to fight in mixed martial arts competition. There was no doubt that I had tapped into something, and it seemed as if the only thing I yearned for was to quench my thirst for knowledge.

It didn't take long for me to go further into my quest for spiritual knowledge and explore the esoteric or occult side of the spectrum. It was destiny for me to go down that path, as my zodiac sign is associated with secrets, mysteries, and illusions. Most do not dare to learn about the occult.

The word *occult* is a very misunderstood word in our society today. To put it quite simply, all *occult* means is "that which is hidden." So I broadened my perspective on the universe, and I started learning how to read the tarot, which took me into a whole new world. I crossed the threshold from the outer world and entered into the inner world of life.

For most Christians, I am sure the emotion of fear comes up when the tarot is mentioned. After all, the Bible says to beware of psychics. That warning did not stop me though from expanding the box I lived in and making it a little bigger by allowing for something new to come in. From what I have learned in life, we will never get anywhere by being parochial, and the only way to understand something is to learn about it.

I started off with the Thoth tarot deck, a set of seventy-two cards that represents archetypes in human consciousness. They are nothing more than symbolic representations of one's states of mind that are linked with certain thoughts, feelings, and emotions. Every soul is on a mission to get home, and the tarot is a map of how to get there.

It didn't take long for my Christian friend to notice my dabbling into the occult. I noticed that he had some documentaries on Atlantis and UFOs. I watched them, and a spark of curiosity was ignited in me. One night he made sure to show me that passage in the Bible about not trusting witches, psychics, and astrologers. I acknowledged it, but it did not stop me from continuing my practice. He was a very intelligent guy, but it's clear that people fear what they don't understand.

Where he gave up, I went further. What he couldn't find out, I wanted to know. So needless to say, he didn't want me there anymore, so I departed from that place of residence and went to the only place I had to go, back home.

I started to study magic and alchemy, and I was guided to an alchemical text known as the *Emerald Tablets* written by an Atlantean priest king named Thoth. Thoth founded a colony in ancient Egypt after the sinking of Atlantis. He was the builder of the Great Pyramid of Giza, and he incorporated his knowledge of ancient wisdom and also secreted records and instruments of ancient Atlantis.

The history of the *Emerald Tablets* is beyond the belief of modern scientists, simply meaning that, unless one is initiated, it will be hard to believe. I have found in life that the hardest thing to do is believe in something that is impossible to believe. But until one truly wants to broaden his or her understanding and step out of the box, the unknown will always stay unknown.

From 50,000 BC to 36,000 BC, Thoth ruled the ancient race in Egypt. At the time, the Egyptians were a barbarous race, which he then rose to a high degree of civilization. Thoth was an immortal, meaning he conquered death, passing only when he willed and, even then, not through death. His vast knowledge of wisdom made ruler over numerous Atlantean colonies in Central and South America.

When his time came to leave Egypt, he built the Great Pyramid of Giza over the entrance of the great Halls of Amenti, where he placed his records and appointed guards from among the highest of his people to keep his secrets. As time passed, the descendants of these guards became the pyramid priests, who entitled Thoth as the god of wisdom during the age of darkness after he left. The Halls of Amenti is the psychic underworld that resides in another dimension, where the soul passes after death for judgment. It is also known to be the place in which luminaries reside, teach, and facilitate planetary evolution.

The tablets were left in custody of the pyramid priests for safekeeping. In 1300 BC, Egypt, or otherwise known as Khem, was in chaos, and many priests were sent to other parts of the world. As they traveled, they carried with them the Emerald Tablets as talisman to exercise authority over less advanced priesthoods. The tablets are known in legend to give the bearer authority from Thoth. One of the groups of priests journeyed to South America, where they made contacts with the Mayans, a flourishing race. The priest settled among these people, enlightened the Mayans to the ancient wisdom, and placed the tablets underneath the Temple of the Sun God.

Twelve tablets are emerald green, and they were formed from a substance created through alchemical transmutation. The tablets cannot be destroyed. They violate the law of material ionization. Their atomic and cellular structure is fixed, so no change ever takes place. The tablets are inscribed with characters from the ancient Atlantean language that respond to attuned thought waves that release an associated mental vibration in the reader's mind. Golden hoops and a rod bind them together. The wisdom found in them is the foundation of the ancient mysteries, and for one who reads them, his of her wisdom can be increased infinitely.

The Great Pyramid of Giza, one of the Seven Wonders of the World, has been and still is a temple of initiation into the ancient mysteries. Abraham, Enoch, Moses, Solomon, Jesus, Mary, and Apollonius of Tyana were all initiated in there, among others.

XII

✠

THE CLAIRVOYANT

Down they descended and created bodies taking the semblance of men as thier own. The masters of everything said after their forming. We are they who were formed from the space dust partaking of life from the infinite all, living in the world as Children of men like and unlike the children of men.

—The Emerald Tablets

I REMEMBER THE DAY when I first began the path of the Illuminati. I was sitting on a dock on a beautiful lake, deep in a meditation, when, all of a sudden through the darkness of my mind, I saw the all-seeing eye appear in a flash of light. I focused in more on it, and it started blinking. From that point, the eye disappeared, and then I was flying above what I made out to be the desert. I could make out rocks and sand, and then I started to see palm trees.

As I was floating over the desert, I looked ahead and saw a large structure. I identified that structure as a pyramid. After putting two and two together, I realized that, at that point, I had bilocated to the Great Pyramid of Giza. Bilocation is described as the supposed phenomenon of being in two places simultaneously so from that point on, my destiny took a different path.

The tarot is a book of wisdom and a map, a consciousness. In its study, historians have attempted to understand the word "tarot" to attempt to solve its origins. Some have said that the tarot comes from the Egyptian word *tarosh*, which means "the royal way." Others have asserted that it is an anagram of the Latin word *rota*, meaning "wheel." The cards symbolize the circle of life from birth to death. Some have seen the word "Thoth" as a corruption of the word we all know as the Egyptian god of magic and wisdom. This theory reaffirms the legend that the cards were created in the initiation temples of Egypt.

The word "Gnostic" is derived from Greek and implies much the same as the Anglo-Saxon word "wizard" or "witch," or someone who knows, a wise one, or initiate. Gnosticism mixes together Indian, Caldean, Persian, and Egyptian magical doctrines and seasons them with Greek philosophy and Hebrew Cabalistic beliefs. During the ancient times, these unorthodox Christian sects were known as the Cathars and the Knights Templar.

The tarot is a visual map of consciousness and a symbolic system that offers insight to professional contribution, personal motives, and spiritual development of each individual. The tarot operates primarily through the symbolic nonrational aspects of consciousness, which is the same state from which dreams communicate. No one knows the origin of the tarot cards. Teachers often refer to the ancient Egyptian and the Hermetic school as the originators, and the earliest decks were either Egyptian or European.

The tarot deck consists of the Minor Arcana, which has four suits each with fourteen cards, an ace through ten, a knight, queen, and a prince and princess of each suit. And there's the Major Arcana with twenty-two cards that bear the zero and Roman numerals I through XXII. The Major Arcana reveals life principles, universal laws or collective experiences that all humankind has.

Tarot is symbolic behavior or vision consciously performed. Those who participate sense they are doing an act that has symbolic meaning, and they consciously seek to transform that act into a dynamic symbol that is represented in the tarot symbol and reflected back to them. The meaning thus attributed reflects the movement that has the power of making a symbol in motion carry or bridge an inner world into a visible and physical form.

Ancient and primitive cultures have always understood instinctively that ritual and symbol had a true function in their psychic lives. They understood that the performance of rituals brought them into immediate contact with the gods. Symbols allow us to reclaim the language that enables us to approach the soul, which is reflected to us in our dreams and contemplative states.

Just like psychological and spiritual information is revealed to us in our dreams or contemplative states, the tarot functions as an outer mirror of external experiences and internal psychological states as well. The use of the tarot as a psychological and mythical portraiture of oneself is validated by the ancient saying of Novalis, "The seat of the soul is where the outer and inner worlds meet."

When an individual selects a tarot card, the card itself represents an outer mirror of an internal process, and in that moment, one could say that seat of the soul or human psyche is revealed in the connection between the outer portraiture of the tarot and its synchronistic appearance reflecting internal processes.

The use of the tarot as an outer mirror for internal processes align the basic functions of mythology or the essential services that mythology provides for human growth and development as a resource for self-reevaluation and self-reclamation process. Major Arcana means major teachings or universal principle laws that we will experience in different aspects of our life at various times of our life. Jung called the principles as major archetypes, or those universal experiences that are collectively experienced regardless of cultural or family imprinting. An example of a reading of the twenty-two cards of the Major Arcana would sound like this:

> In our lives, there will be times where we will experience the state of no fear (the fool). Daily we are practicing the art of communication (the magician), which includes our self-trust and insight (the high priestess) as we extend love with wisdom (the empress) and incorporate our own power and leadership for the purposes of empowering others (the emperor). Through our life's lessons and challenges, we learn and teach others that reveals to us our sense of faith and deep spirituality (the hierophant), which allows us to explore the different types of relationships (the lovers). In all aspects of transformation, we are faced with the effects of what we cause (the chariot) and are required to make creative changes that simplify, clarify, and balance the human experience in fair,

just ways (justice). Through introspection and contemplation and trusting our experience (the hermit), we are able to turn our lives in more fortunate positive directions (fortune), which places us in our canes where we can experience our strength and luster (lust) and allows us to break patterns that bind, limit, and restrict us (the hanged man). Breaking old patterns requires us to let go and move forward (the death card) and experience the state of detachment. Following the process of letting go, we are required to integrate our experience (temperance/art). It is that integration or the temperance process that we are able to retain and regain our sense of humor (the devil) and look at our bedevilments from places of sure-footedness and stability. Through sustaining our humor and sense of balance, we are capable to renovate and restore our authenticity (the tower) and to dismantle that which is artificially and false to fact. When we have awakened to our inherent nature (the tower), we radiate our self-esteem and confidence (the star) as we make choices about leaving old known worlds and go through the gates to explore new worlds (the moon). Making choices that honor our authenticity rather than our dutifulness, we are able then to be natural generators, motivators, and stimulators (the sun) in teamwork, partnership, and collaborative endeavors through utilizing good judgment and looking at history and the whole of relationships and creative endeavors. Thus we are able to transform the judge to fair witness (aeon/adjustment). Once we have moved through self-critical patterns and our objective about our professional contribution and personal relationship, we are able to build new worlds within and without (the universe) and have a sense of our own individuality and wholeness.

So as it can be seen the tarot is nothing more than a tool for transformation. It's time for the darkness, any mystery that surrounds the hidden secret, to come to light. It's time for the truth to be known. It's time to remember that, if you so choose, you can attain the Holy Grail. But one must be willing to take on the greatest opponent that he or she could ever face in order to achieve it. And that great villain that awaits at the end of the quest is none other than you.

XIII

✠

THE MARK OF THE SERPENT

He who by progress has grown from the darkness lifted
himself from the night into light. Free is he made of the
Halls of Amenti free from the flower of light and of life.
Guided he then by wisdom and knowledge passes from
men to the master of life. There he may dwell as one
with the masters Free from the bondage of the darkness
of night.

—The Emerald Tablets

THE FIRST TIME I experienced the Kundalini was at a time when I was
going through a spiritual shift in my life right after I had become a
Christian and started searching for answers. One day my friend and I were
sitting down and watching TV, and out of nowhere very spontaneously, I
felt something from inside of me coming from the base of my spine. I shot
up out of my chair in shock as I did not know what was going on. My
friend looked at me like I was out of my mind, so I then went to find a spot
where I could be alone. When I got there, the feeling happened again, and
I jumped up into the air again, startled because it had caught me off guard.

For a moment I was scared because I did not know what was going on.
It felt like the fear of God had been struck into me. At that time, I had just
began my spiritual journey so my knowledge about what was happening to
me was nonexistent. After that spiritual experience, I felt led to get some

answers about what was transpiring from within me. So I searched and was brought upon the knowledge of the Kundalini and the chakric system.

The Kundalini is the life force of a person that descends from the higher seals to the base of the spine. It is a large packet of energy reserved for human evolution. It is commonly pictured as a coiled serpent that sits at the base of the spine. It is often described as the sleeping serpent or sleeping dragon. The journey of the Kundalini energy to the crown of the head is called the "journey of enlightenment." This journey takes place when the serpent wakes up and starts to split and dance around the spine, ionizing the spinal fluid and changing its molecular structure. This action causes the opening of the psychic midbrain and opens the door to the subconscious mind.

This process is known as the "Great Work," the practical application of the knowledge of the ancient schools of wisdom. It refers to the disciplines by which the human being becomes enlightened and is transmuted into an immortal divine being. This process is also known as "alchemy," the transmutation of spirit from base material into gold and is known as the "royal art."

In the body, seven chakra points also represent the seven seals. The first four seals are the seals of sexuality, pain and suffering, control, and power. These are the seals commonly at play in all of the complexities of the human drama. The seals are as follows:

- The first seal, or the Muladhara Chakra, is associated with the reproductive organs, sexuality, and survival. This also correlates with the first plane of consciousness, the material or physical plane. It is the plane of image consciousness and the Hertzian light frequency, and it is the slowest and densest form of coagulated consciousness.
- The second seal, or the Swadiswana Chakra, is the energy center of social consciousness and the infrared frequency band. It is associated with pain and suffering and is located in the abdominal area.
- The third seal, or Manipura Chakra, is the energy center of conscious awareness and the visible light frequency band. It is associated with control, tyranny, victimization, and power. It is

located in the region of the solar plexus. It is also known as the light plane and the mental plane.

- The fourth seal, or Anahata Chakra, is associated with unconditional love and the thymus gland, and when this seal is activated, a hormone is released that maintains the body in perfect health and stops the aging process. The fourth plane of existence is the realm of bridge consciousness and ultraviolet frequency. This plane is described as the plane of Shiva, the destroyer of old and the creator of new.

- The fifth seal, or Vishuddha Chakra, is the energy center of our spiritual body that connects us to the fifth plane of consciousness. It is associated with the thyroid gland and with speaking and living the truth without dualism. The fifth plane of existence is the plane of super consciousness and the x-ray frequency. It is also known as the golden plane or paradise.

- The sixth seal, or the Anja Chakra, is the energy center associated with the pineal gland and the gamma ray frequency band. The reticular formation that filters and veils the knowingness of the subconscious mind is opened when this seal is activated. The opening of the brain refers to the opening of this seal and the activation of consciousness and energy. The sixth plane is to the realm of hyperconsciousness and the gamma ray frequency band. In this plane, the awareness of being one with the whole of life is experienced.

- The seventh seal, or Sahasrara Chakra, is associated with the crown of the head, the pituitary gland, and the attainment of enlightenment. Enlightenment is the full realization of the human person, the attainment of immortality and unlimited mind. The raising of the Kundalini energy sitting at the base of the spine into the seventh seal opens dormant parts of the brain.

Needless to say, when this process started to happen to me, I began to experience things that I've never seen, heard, or felt before. Little did I know then that I was in for the spiritual journey of a lifetime.

XIV

THE FOURTH KIND

Seated within the flower of radiance sit seven lords from the space-time above us helping and guiding through infinite wisdom the pathway through time of the children of men. Mighty and strange they veiled with their power, silent all knowing drawing the life force, different and yet one with the Children of Light.

—The Emerald Tablets

As MY JOURNEY to enlightenment progressed, I started to have several paranormal experiences. I became aware of this one night when I was watching TV. As I walked the fine line between the state of being awake and asleep, I started to feel a tingling around my face, and I also felt a loud buzzing and heard a faint ringing. At that moment, I knew there was something in my presence, but I never had an experience like that before so I wasn't sure what to do. I sat there and felt the presence around me, and I thought to myself, "Is this a ghost?"

As soon as I thought that contemplation, synchronistically as if by magic, the TV answered me. The movie was playing in perfect timing with the finishing of my thought, and it replied, "We are not ghosts," which astonished me because it was a definite answer to my question.

After that experience, I took a profound interest in extrasensory perception (ESP). I started to study day and night to learn everything I could to help me understand the phenomena I was experiencing. During my time of intensive study, I decided I would go see a psychiatrist at a local American Legion.

When I went there, we didn't talk about things that most war veterans would discuss. Instead we talked about my spiritual experiences I was having, and he took notice that I was carrying a book about ESP. When he noticed, he mentioned to me that I had a gift. He gave me a couple techniques to relax, like the ol' "putting your worries in a box, putting them on a rocket ship, and sending them to the sun" trick. Then he sent me on my way and told me to come back the following week.

As time went on, I kept having more experiences. One night I was just lying in bed half-asleep and half-awake when, all of a sudden, I felt tingling around me, along with buzzing and ringing. I just laid there with my eyes closed as it continued. It went on for about two minutes, and then all of a sudden, it was like I was being lifted up in a rainbow-colored tube of light, sort of like the tunnel you go down at Space Mountain at Disneyland. The frequency was extremely high, and then I don't remember anything after that. I just woke up in my bed the next morning, thinking it was very peculiar, but of course I had no explanation of what happened.

When the next week came, I went to my appointment with my psychiatrist, and when I arrived, I saw a man who was in his mid-fifties in the waiting room. He was talking to someone else, and I noticed him as I was waiting to see the psychiatrist. He approached me and introduced himself, which was unusual of course. He was very informed.

He told me that he had been a commander in the navy and he had been on different aircraft carriers and submarines. There was a bar there, so he led me there to sit down and talk to him. The things he was discussing were very out of the ordinary. He mentioned things, like how easy it would be to get a nuke into the United States and all someone would have to do is put it in a boat and row it to shore. He also mentioned that, if it were up to him, he would have the president of Iran assassinated. I wasn't sure what that was all about at the time, but he did give me his number and told me to call him for lunch sometime, which made it clear that he wanted to talk to me.

Around this time, strange events kept happening. One time I noticed a car pull up to the house and start to take pictures. Another time when I went to church, the man who talked to me from the American Legion was there. When I entered the building, they were having service, and he was in there, coincidently talking to someone I knew from high school. He knew I was going to be there. After the service was over, he approached me again and offered me a ride home. I rode home with him, and our conversations were, of course, not the usual discussion. It was all about the military, which was easy to talk about.

At the end of the conversation, he made a comment to me nonchalantly about a topic that most people never bring up. He mentioned to me that he had always been interested in aliens. At that time, I had no solid knowledge about extraterrestrials so I could not carry that conversation any further. So we ended the chat there, and I got out of the car to return to my house.

The extraordinary experiences did not stop. One night I was lying on my stomach in my bed, and all of a sudden, I heard a noise, and then I was completely paralyzed. I tried to get up, but I could not. I felt something behind me, and I wanted to turn to face it. Once I was released, I quickly turned around, but nothing was there. That experience did scare me little bit, and I am not afraid to say that I slept with the light on for some days after that.

After that experience, things were really starting to get interesting. I read *The Reconnection* by Dr. Eric Pearl, and his work really intrigued me. Every night I would be having the most elaborate dreams, most of them having to do with UFOs and being out in the middle of the desert.

Not too long after, I got kicked out of my house for being too spiritual, with the combination of the tarot cards and all the spiritual books I was reading. It was obviously a challenge to my father-in-law and his beliefs. One time he even tried to steer me away from continuing my study in the tarot and the occult. He tried to explain to me about who the serpent in the Bible is, who he thought Satan was, and who was evil. But that is only in the Abrahamism side of the tale of serpent. The Gnostic version tells a much different story about who the serpent is, and little did I know then that I was on a quest to find out who the serpent in the Bible really was.

Since I was very young, I have always been able to have conscious awareness in my dreams. I always thought it was normal and everyone experienced what I did. But as I got older, I realized the ability I had to see in my dreams was unique and rare.

I have memories of being a pharaoh during the times of ancient Egypt.

I have seen inside the pyramids where hieroglyphics cover the walls. And there's the memories of waking up in a bed draped with a white cloth that hangs from the ceilings and is blowing in the warm wind coming from the balcony.

When I was young, I had a peculiar fascination with ancient Egypt. It is now clear why that was. That fascination didn't just spawn from nowhere. It came from the remembrance of a past life and the understanding that my lineage was from the pharaohs.

I also had a fascination with stars and the universe when I was younger. My dream was to be an astronaut of course. My knowledge of astronomy was very impressive for being so young, and I clearly had a passion for the heavens at a young age. I even created my own observatory made out of a giant black garbage bag, a fan, and Christmas lights that were poked into the garbage bag in different constellations. This fascination of these topics at an early age, I now know, were carried over from a past life to be used in the one I am living right here and right now.

I had been out of the Marine Corps for five years at the time of my divine intervention. As I gathered more and more information over the years, I started to put together the puzzle pieces to form the big picture on what exactly had happened to me.

I started noticing that something was much different in my life one night when I was lying in bed late at night and a plane started circling the apartment I was living in. At first, it did not catch my attention, but as it kept circling and circling, I knew this was not normal, especially at one o'clock in the morning. It got to the point where I got up and went outside to see what exactly was going on. I started to walk down a pathway, and I noticed that, as I was walking, the plane would fly right over my head every time. I stayed outside for about an hour as it did circles around me, and then finally it changed its light patterns to that that of the FAA regulation.

The "plane" was not that low. Actually it was high enough to not cause any disturbance to anyone else around. But I certainly knew that, whatever it was, it was there for me and that no one else around was even aware of its presence.

My dreams began to get a lot more intricate at the time of these experiences. I was constantly having dreams of UFOs, Star Wars, and military operations. I also had dreams of nuclear bombs being detonated, along with catastrophes like earthquakes, tsunamis, and alien invasions. I know that several people have dreams during the night, but these weren't dreams that I was having. They were experiences, and there is a difference between dreams and visions. They felt real because I was in control of myself in them. It felt like I was being trained for something that would happen in the future.

One night I had a dream where I remember seeing an envelope of money in my hands. At that time, I had been applying for VA disability, and my paperwork was taking a long time to be processed. I was completely broke and had probably survived off about $7,000 for five years. At the time, I never really could even imagine what it felt like to have money, but I kept having dreams of having envelopes of money. That was nice, but I really couldn't quite grasp yet what my subconscious was preparing me for.

As I was barely scraping by each month for five years, my life definitely allowed me to experience poverty and deprivation. But in having these hard times, I also learned independence and self-sufficiency. And in learning that, I was prepared to receive a reward that would allow me to be relieved of all my financial troubles for life.

One day I had called in to my bank to see how much money I had for the month's rent. I only expected to have around $300, and the automated voice said my back account had $44,000 in it. I was in complete shock. My VA disability had been granted to me. I had been awarded $1,330 for every month for the rest of my life, and I was paid for the five years that I didn't receive anything. A week later, I got another surprise. I received another $13,000 dollars, and I realized that, in my life, I would never be in debt again. And that was a very liberating moment.

If you are around me, you will notice that the air traffic is a little out of the ordinary. As a matter of fact, I will go out of the way to say it is extraordinary. After the night I noticed the "plane" circling my house, I started to notice that "planes" were constantly flying around me wherever I went. It doesn't matter if I were in the middle of the city or way out in the forest. All types of planes, from Cessna 152s from 747s, were always flying around me. In the daytime, they would appear to be as they presented themselves. But at night, I could tell that their light patterns were different from any plane I had seen before. So I concluded that these "planes" were not planes. They were UFOs.

As time went on, they got closer, and they started to change into military aircraft. At first it was Blackhawk and Chinook helicopters. Then there came the AH-1 Cobras and the AH-64 Apache, both attack helicopters that are not seen flying over civilian zones in America. Then came the C-130 Hercules and C-17 Globetrotters, and the most spectacular plane that appeared was an F-105 Starfighter that circled around me for quite some time. It did a dive bomb, just barely scraping the deck and then pulling straight up and doing an Immelman as it soared away.

Every day at all times of the day, these craft would constantly be flying around me at very low altitudes, doing combat maneuvers over towns full of people who were totally oblivious. Some of the time, people would look at what was going on because it was certainly out of the ordinary. But then they would just go about their business unaffected. Some people didn't even flinch when three C-17 Globetrotters came screaming in over an area, pulling extreme turns over the parking lot at extremely low altitudes.

If I weren't there in those places at that time, I can guarantee that those aircraft would not have appeared. It took me a while to gather enough information about what was happening to me and why, and for a while, you can only imagine how in the dark and confused I was. But as I searched increasingly deeper, I was finally able to make a connection that would bring me an explanation of this unexplainable phenomena.

X V

TOTAL RECALL

Traveled I through the space time, knowing my soul at last
was free, knowing that now might I pursue wisdom, until
at last I passed to a plane, hidden from knowledge, known
not to wisdom, extension beyond all that we know. Now
O man, when I had this knowing happy my soul grew, for
now I was free. Listen ye space -born, list to my wisdom:
know ye not that ye too will be free. (The Emerald Tablets)

M Y FIRST NOTION that I was involved in something extraordinary
came to me as I searched through the field of ufology for answers.
My search brought me upon a topic that is known to the community
as MILABS, or military (MIL) abductions (ABS). I came across this
information when I found a series of videos from a group of people who
were having the same experiences I was. I was so excited when I found
out that people were having these experiences as well. When I found these
people, my curiosity in the subject had been raised even more, so I opened
up Pandora's box to uncover the very secret world of MILABS.

Our government has a classification system for information that has
thirty-eight levels. The information is based on how sensitive it is, meaning
how damaging it would be to national security if it were to be disclosed.
The first three levels are, of course, confidential, secret, and top secret. Then
once you get above top secret, you get into unacknowledged special access
programs, or USAP. Even the president does not know information that

is classified in the higher levels. Most programs are compartmentalized so that secrecy can remain. Compartmentalization allows for no one to really know what he or she is really working on.

The clearance levels classifications are the following:

1. Orbit, which deals with US accountability for orbiting satellites
2. Triad, the federal government's fast-growing crime and prevention partnership with statewide coordination
3. Cosmos (unknown)
4. Astral, which is US government projects that are beyond dreaming
5. Stellar, which is where the NSA wiretapping and eavesdropping takes place
6. Ultra, the covert CIA mind control that began early in the 1950s
7. Luna, a project to study a mining base on the moon
8. Cosmic, the USAF space test program, which studies propulsion, dark matter, and dark energy
9. Majestic, the USAF's official investigation on aliens and UFOs
10. INWA, the USAF's official investigations of nuclear weapons security
11. D-5, which is above presidential, military, and civilian agencies in protecting the United States Constitution and Declaration of Independence and aiding in preventing wars to avoid nuclear Armageddon

In the UFO abduction and general ufology community, the acronym MILABS, or MILAB, which is short for military abductions, has become known as an experience that a contactee/abductee experiences where a military presence or government agency is involved in extraterrestrial abduction experiences.

Ever since it was first created, researchers and contactees/abductees have used the phrase MILABS to reference many types of possible experiences—from the presence of military uniformed personnel in an otherwise extraterrestrial abduction scenario, to government mind control activities, to a sanctioned secret organization that is involved in monitoring the lives of extraterrestrial abductees, and to an outright military cause for abductions with no ET presence being involved at all. The MILABS phenomena clearly needs to be cleared up, and some light should be shed on this dark corner of our reality. Another way that MILABS can be termed is "covert intelligence and paramilitary reabduction, harassment, and surveillance in extraterrestrial abduction experiences."

In these days, targeting, monitoring, and the reabduction of abductees by covert military and intel agencies may provide the strongest evidence for the reality of UFO abduction experiences that intelligence sources can gather. These covert agencies are involved in a quest for extraterrestrial technology and to back-engineer technologies that operate on paranormal functioning (PSI). And because of the development and control of those technologies, it is also one of the reasons behind the government's suppression of the UFO subject and, along with it, the suppression of our dormant human potential.

The first stage of the program is the abductee will find that he or she made a soul contract and a past-life agreement with ancient aliens. Then the abductee will be identified as a genealogical extraterrestrial and may choose to be involved with the government or military. Then the abductee will have UFO sightings and experience psychic contact. Then the abduction takes place.

After that the MILABS will receive threats or warnings in the form of phone calls and harassment, such as gang stalking and black helicopters. Then the MILABS will report that he or she knows he or she is under constant surveillance. The MILABS may then receive a visit from a government agent and, following that, may witness aliens working with the military. He or she then will experience reabduction scenarios where he or she undergoes psychic development in the form of tests and drills. He or she will then be recruited in the future to operate psychotronic technology and will experience military operations and space travel to serve in the roles of extraterrestrial spies and super soldiers in an extraterrestrial war. Finally he or she is involved in time travel, and then he or she repeats activation.

There is quite a large number of programs and subprograms that fall under the MILABS programs. These are all in support of a program that the elite of our world has created that's sole purpose is to create super soldiers. These individuals are identified either through family lineage (genetics) or standardized testing in elementary schools. Usually people have memories of being taken into military and extraterrestrial facilities between the ages of six and eight years of age. (Sometimes it's as early as four years old.) Some are a part of a familial genetic program while others are usually "star seeds" that meet certain criteria.

The training is designed to condition the children and identify their personality types as well as any undeveloped gifts they may possess, such as esoteric abilities that can be enhanced with proper knowledge and training.

After time, as the children grow up, they are split off into further subgroups to focus on developing their gifts and pushing their boundaries based on their personalities and ethics. Many times the MILABS "wash out" before they have completed their training and are "blank-slated" (undergo memory removal) and will never remember any of their experiences. These individuals have a very difficult life, usually feeling rejected and discarded or useless, but with no obvious reason for feeling this way.

Many times some of the strongest skeptics on this information are these individuals. There are also the catch-and-release MILABS, those who are picked up after a chance otherworldly encounter or happen to be in the wrong place at the wrong time. They are put through experiments, have genetic sample collections, and sometimes are implanted and then blank-slated and released, never to have another encounter for the rest of their lives. Those raised in the MILABS programs go through many different types of chemical, mental, and genetic upgrades, many of which must be maintained to remain fully functional.

The MILABS are used as assets throughout their training, depending on the needs of their controllers. They then reach a certain point or skill level and emotional maturity. (And with all they are put through with the trauma-induced training, physical/mental/sexual abuse, and witnessing of death, they tend to mature early in life.) They are then drafted out to various secret Earth governments and their syndicates (for example, cabal, Illuminati, and other secret societies), to where they then infiltrate the military and corporate world. Also they are drafted into various secret space programs and other black operations on every layer of the onion structure controlled by the elite and their off-world gods.

There is a known group of approximately 5 percent of these people whom the blank-slating (memory wipes) did not work on or only worked for a very short period of time, usually the intuitive empaths. These people are identified and watched very closely their entire lives.

Star seeds are beings that have experienced life elsewhere in the universe on other planets and in nonphysical dimensions other than on Earth. Star seeds may also have had previous lifetimes on Earth. A typical star seed may have lived five to fifty lifetimes on Earth. Some of these were preparation lifetimes, which included periods of acclimatization to being a human being on Earth and the development of the life missions, leading to the climax of these activities in this current lifetime.

Earth represents a place of service more than a place of learning for these star seeds who have already achieved higher consciousness on other planets. As there were fewer lifetimes on Earth compared to the average human being, this leads this group of star seeds to retaining some of their extraterrestrial abilities, such as with healing, telepathy, channeling, and general higher consciousness qualities.

Star seeds often come to Earth at times of rising spiritual awareness, as this is the environment that their gifts can be recognized and when they can truly help others. They have often performed the roles of spiritual teachers, shamans, prophets, light workers, temple guardians, healers, all kinds of leaders such as kings and queens, and high priest and high priestess. These star seeds hold the wisdom and spiritual knowledge of the ancients as it has been used on Earth. This includes the human knowledge of astronomy, astrology, tarot, numerology, certain healing modalities, light work, and spiritual ceremonies. This will be the last lifetime as a human being for many of these star seeds, those who are completing the cycles of lifetimes on earth and all the project and work included in these cycles. These star seeds have often mastered the ability to hold a balance between being grounded and being spiritually aligned. This is why they still resonate with their extraterrestrial origins even though they have lives on Earth for so many lifetimes.

The Indigo race is from Sirius. Star seed is a label to represent many different galactic races such as Pleiadian, Arcturian, Andromedan, and so forth. The Indigos and star seeds on earth are hybrids of angelic human and other galactic races. Agreements are made between earth humans and the Indigo or star seed prior to birth, most often prior to the birth of the parents. The Indigos and star seeds came to earth knowing they would go through the "veil of forgetfulness," just like all other humans on earth. This happened because the Indigo/star seed needed to fully experience life on Planet Earth. And none chose an easy life. This choice was made for multiple reasons, one being that, in order to heal it, you have to feel it. Both Indigos/star seeds and angelic humans have the potential to activate enough DNA to ascend, the ultimate goal of the ascension timeline.

In what seemed to be an endless search for truth, I finally was connected with a source that was a secret agent who worked for an intelligence agency, which we will say is a little higher on the hierarchy than the CIA, NSA, and FBI. There are thirty-eight clearance levels in the government's intelligence classification system, and this agency was above all them and clearly an organization that belongs to what is referred to as the "secret government." This intelligence agency was known as the Alien Contact Intelligence Organization (ACIO), and they had a database of every MILABS that there has ever been.

This agent had answers to all my questions: the why me, the who did it, and the what for. And once I was finally told the truth, I finally knew I had come across the answers I had been searching for and the explanation of everything that had happened to me that was unexplainable in my life.

When I first talked to him, he asked me to tell him what was going on in my life. Obviously I didn't know where to start. So I started with the most concrete thing that I could and told him about the black helicopter phenomena that was constantly happening around me. I also told him of a few dream memories where I appeared to be in some sort of advanced armor and I was doing battle with some entity on a building. In this dream memory, the entity threw me through the building walls onto some cars on the street. After that happened, I was then picked up by the same black helicopter that always flies around me and all times of the day.

One night, one was flying over my house, except it was going really slow. Plus there was no noise. It did have lights on the tips of it, and I made out that it was never a "black helicopter." It was actually a large, black triangle, and it came uncloaked over my house one night. It was as low as it could be without landing, and then it just silently sailed away. Of course I could have told him about so many other experiences that I had, but I wanted to hear what he had to say so I stopped and let him tell me the truth.

He confirmed that I was a MILABS/super soldier. At six years old, I was taken for the first time to a secret base in Texas where the military along with aliens and advanced corporations started to turn me into an enhanced human/cyborg because of my genetic lineage to be a generation four super soldier.

The first time they abducted me, I actually look back now and remember. At six years old, one night I had a dream about a hand coming and taking me out the window. I actually wrote a horror story about it and showed it to my grandfather. I now know that was the first time that I was taken, and when that happens, the story of Peter Pan and him being taken away to Never Never Land takes on a whole new meaning.

At the base, they injected me with what is referred to as "black goo." It is a predatory pathological artificial intelligence (PPAI). I was also implanted with a special implant in my pineal gland in my forehead. During the years of eight to twelve, I was taken four additional times. At those times, now that I look back, I was getting random bloody noses. When I had them, it was obviously out of the ordinary, so now when I look back, I know that those were from abductions as well.

During some of these abductions, they were doing something called a soul extraction, and apparently I am lucky to be alive. When I was twelve years old, my body was not having a good reaction to the things that had been placed in me, and one time I got sick and threw up a blue substance. My parents took me to the doctor, and the doctor didn't know what was going on. So in that instance, there was obviously a breach of something that had to remain covert. So the organization wiped mine, my parents', and the doctor's memories of it because they have the technology to do that and they will do anything to keep the program secret.

When I was sixteen, I signed a contract with the Department of Naval Intelligence to be utilized in an extraterrestrial war. When I signed the contract, I was with a girlfriend I had at the time. A mysterious man approached me and convinced me to get in a car with him, and that was when the contract was presented. After I signed it, I was then gone for a week's time and then returned like no time had gone by.

From that point, I became a part of the black operations corporations. These are obviously the corporations that make up the secret government that are involved with advanced technologies. Four major corporations are tied in with the secret government and breakaway civilizations category: Monarch, Kruger, Shoreline, and Ultimate. They are all independent corporations that all have different agendas, and on top of that, they are tied into alien agendas as well.

Behind the scenes, Monarch is attempting to shift our timeline to something where they don't know exactly what the outcome will be with the secret advanced technology they have developed. To accomplish their agenda, they will use any means necessary. Their main facility is located underneath Toronto and the Great Lakes, where the elite in above black operations employ millions for the cabal, where they are working on such projects as eugenics, cloning, and advanced weapons/systems.

In this secret world, there are many different agendas, as there are a variety of secret societies, corporations, and alien syndicates and alliances. They of course are operating in another reality that the mass consciousness of this world does not know at this time. You could say there is a light and a dark side. There are beings that will murder, rape, and steal to accomplish their aims. But there is also a rebel alliance that is fighting against the oppressors of the cabal, and they do not kill unless it is absolutely necessary. They do not rape, and they also are not thieves.

Kruger is also involved in black operations, but their agenda is to oppose Monarch from accomplishing their goals. I was told that I was a sleeper agent for Kruger. I am a manager of super soldier/runners. I am the one who sends them on their missions. Kruger runners are not violent killers. Their mission is to sabotage Monarch by stealing their parts for their machines that they are using as weapons. A runner is a super soldier that can run at speeds that slow down time. They can only even be seen by special cameras that only the most technological spy agencies have. These cameras run at sixty thousand frames per second. This type of ability can be compared to Quicksilver in *The X-Men*. They use parkour to traverse terrain, mixed with martial arts training primarily in the art of Ninjitsu. Super soldier runners are smart, silent, and tricky. They are primarily used for infiltration and sabotage. To put it into words that can be understood, they can be considered as ninjas.

Many different super soldier types are used in various roles. When I first found out that I was a super soldier, I thought I was an assassin and I had killed in what I had been involved in. I was told I had not killed and I was doing good things for good purposes. In my time with Kruger, I have done over 4,138 missions. And in all those missions, I have done around

1,324 of them to infiltrate into Monarch for Kruger. I was involved in the sabotage of Cern, a device that Monarch uses to open portals, a weapon that aids to keep our world in its current state of consciousness.

Monarch is trying to keep this earth from ascending into the next dimension. They are playing around with time and forces they cannot fully control where they do not know what the outcome is going to be. They can be seen as the Empire from *Star Wars*, and Kruger can be seen as the Rebel Alliance. Monarch is tied in with aliens whose agenda is not in humanity's benefit. Kruger, on the other hand, is tied into another agenda that is in support of humanity.

The missions I have done have been over a multitude of lifetimes. During my service as a runner, I was identified as an FQR, an acronym for "fucking quick runner." Because of this, I have donated my DNA to the program at the expense of my own life to advance super soldiers. As a manager for Kruger runners, I was told that I cooperate with other members from different parts of the programs to plan missions for super soldiers. For example, I was told that I worked with an artist who was from Norway who makes designs of cities so super soldiers can plan their missions and routes, just like in the game *Mirrors Edge: Catalyst*.

He also asked me if I knew who Faith Conners was. She happens to be the girl from *Mirrors Edge: Catalyst*. In that game, they even reveal the corporation Kruger. If you want to know what a Kruger runner is, that is a perfect example.

He asked me if Faith reminded me of anyone. And I was honest with him and told him that she reminded me of me. He laughed. And then I asked him if she were my twin flame. He laughed again and said yes. He also told me that she had been asking about me. I asked him if we would meet again someday, and he laughed again and said yes. Needless to say, I was happy to know that the twin soul/flame reality was real.

XVI

✠

THE PSYCHIC SPY

> Then from his throne came one of the masters taking
> my hand and leading me onward, through the halls of
> the deep hidden land. Led me he through the halls of
> Amenti showing me mysteries that are not known to man,
> through the dark passage downward he lead me into the
> halls where sits the dark death. Vast as space lay the great
> hall before me walled by darkness but filled with light.
>
> —The Emerald Tablets

I REMEMBER THE FIRST time that I realized that I was seeing a UFO. The experience came shortly after I moved to live with my grandmother in Tenino, Washington. At that time I was undergoing a tremendous spiritual awakening, so all of the extraordinary experiences I was having were all very new to me. One night, I was about to go to sleep, and out of the corner of my eye, a dancing light appeared in the sky, and it caught my attention enough where I had to go outside to see it.

My grandmother lives in the most magical, peaceful place that one could imagine. Her house is located on the top of the hill where there is no one around and all you can hear is nature around you. I looked out into the night sky to where I thought I saw it, and lo and behold, it showed itself again, and it started to move freely in the night sky. Then another one appeared, and they started moving around each other as if they were playing. I sat there and watched them for about an hour before I decided to go back inside. I could have stayed out there all night, but I decided that I would try to go back and get some sleep.

That night I remember something strange happening to me. It was as if my consciousness were being brought up out of my body in a spinning vortex, and then I recall the same feeling that night right before I woke up. At that point, it was pretty clear what was happening to me. There was no more denying it. I was having alien abduction experiences, and to my conscious knowledge at that point in time, I had three of them. But the truth I would find out later is that there had been more, and there would be more in the future.

The first questions that go through your mind when something like this happens is first "Why me?" and then "What for?" And then of course after that, "Who was it?" The asking of these questions and the courage to inquire and find the truth leads you into a journey of mystery where Pandora's box opens and one dives down the rabbit hole. Ask and it will be given. Seek and you shall find. Knock and the door shall be opened.

After I started having these experiences, it was obvious that something happened to me. Before in my life, I had read a couple books. I was never really a reader. But when these experiences happened to me, I started reading and finishing multiple books at a time. My knowledge and intelligence grew exponentially in my search to find out who the raiders from above were. As I searched, I once again came upon the topic of ESP and the attainment of information by means other than the five senses.

I had always been interested in the psychic life but never really had a chance to explore it. For me, it was destiny that I would have this gift. Coming to this Earth when it is in the house of Pisces makes you very psychic. Both my sun and moon signs are Pisces, so that only multiplies the ability that is latent within me

My interest grew even more in psychics after I saw *The Men Who Stare at Goats*, a film made about the CIA's program for psychic spying. The program was known as "StarGate" and initially was funded with over $20 million from the American government. The Americans started the program when they found out that the Russians had a program for exploring the use of psychic ability for military application. The Americans had received information that the Russians were using psychics to communicate with each other on submarines with successful results. So the Americans decided to counter the Russians and started exploring the occult.

The Americans then started a program and started taking interest in tarot card readers, crystal ball gazers, and all sorts of spiritual mediums that had been singled out by demonstrating some paranormal ability. Those selected hopefuls were then recruited into a program that was definitely beyond belief.

There are a number of abilities that psychics are known for demonstrating. The one that is most commonly known is telepathy, the purported transmission of information from one person to another without using any of our known sensory channels or physical interactions. Many scientifically documented cases prove that telepathy is real.

Another ability is clairvoyance, a French word that means "clear sight or vision." Clairvoyance is the ability to gain information about an object, person, location, or physical event through means other than the known senses. Clairvoyance's more scientific term is "remote viewing."

Another ability that has been demonstrated is telekinesis, the ability to influence a physical system without physical interaction. Examples of telekinesis include moving an object and levitation. Through my studies I have gathered enough reliable information to come to the conclusion the psychic ability is real, and I have demonstrated it myself on several occasions. So if psychic ability is real, where does it come from, and how do we learn to use it? And even more importantly, for what purposes? What is the significance of psychic ability? What value does it have? What does it imply about nature? Is there something that connects all of us together like an invisible anchor? The existence of psychic ability certainly adds another dimension to our perception of the world.

Throughout the history of humankind, individuals have displayed an uncanny ability to predict events before they begun to unfold. Sometimes these persons would act alone, and other times they would come together in groups. Sometimes society ostracized and ridiculed them, and occasionally they were kept at the sides of royalty.

Events such as the witch hunts during the Middle Ages or the burning of Cathars and Knight Templars show what can happen when public opinion turns against a psychic. But while they remained in people's favor, they might find themselves treated like ancient Greek prophets that received gifts of food and gold in order to curry favor. There were also the ancient Egyptian pharaohs who had to do through rigorous initiations and demonstrate psychic ability as a prophet if they were to rule.

The first lessons that an aspirant is to learn are basic concepts that can be applied in practical ways. One of the first things a student will learn as a neophyte is that he or she is a dual being. In addition to the student's five physical senses, the student also has a psychic sense. The exercises in these introductory lessons are designed to gradually awaken and develop the psychic faculty. The exercise allows the students to discover to himself or herself through direct experience how these principles work.

Topics include mystical sounds, spiritual alchemy, time and space, human and cosmic consciousness, meditation, development of the intuition, introduction to the human aura, telepathy, and metaphysical healing.

FIRST ATRIUM

The first atrium includes composition and structure of matter, power of thought and concentration, visualization, telepathy, metal projection, and law of the triangle.

SECOND ATRIUM

The students understanding of the connection between mind and matter will now be expanded to include the connection between the mind and the physical body. The second atrium explores how the students' thoughts influence their health. The role of proper breathing in psychic development as well as well as health, vitality, and Rosicrucian healing techniques is explored. As students develop their body's psychic centers, the student will gradually awaken psychic faculties such as the ability to perceive the human aura. The student will also experience the mystical effects of sounds.

Topics in this atrium include origin of diseases, influence of thoughts on health, mystical art of breathing, Rosicrucian healing treatments, perception of the aura, awakening psychic consciousness, and mystical sounds.

THIRD ATRIUM

The third atrium moves beyond the physical body and the psychic faculties into the realm of the mystical. As the student becomes more attuned with the inner source of wisdom, he or she will become more receptive to the subtle inner prompting of intuition, inspiration, and illumination. These lessons also explore the nature of the soul and spiritual evolution, reincarnation, and karma and cycles of the soul.

Topics include reincarnation, karma, free will, good and evil, intuition, inspiration, illumination, the great religious movements, the nature of the soul, and purpose of our spiritual evolution.

TEMPLE SECTION

Having completed the lessons of the neophyte section, the students stand at an important milestone in progress along the mystical path. The student is now ready to enter the temple. The studies in the neophyte section establish the foundation for the lessons of the temple degrees. The students have been introduced to various elements of the Rosicrucian system and had the opportunity to practice many of the principles presented, providing additional depth and practical applications of principles.

First Temple Degree (Zelator)

The first temple degree introduces the concept of polarity and its relationship to the subatomic world and its differing rates of vibration. It introduces the full spectrum of physical and nonphysical manifestation. An understanding of these subjects gives the student the appreciation for the system and order of the universe. It's the interconnection of all nature and how natural law governs everything.

Topics in this degree include structure of matter, positive and negative as vibratory polarities, electricity, magnetism, electromagnetism and their Rosicrucian definition, subatomic particles, elements, material, and alchemy.

Second Temple Degree (Theoricus)

The second degree explores the workings of the mind. Students will learn how to use various mental faculties to strengthen will, eliminate bad habits and establish good ones, tap into levels of subconscious, reason more effectively, and integrate principles of psychology and mysticism.

Third Temple Degree (Practicus)

The third temple degree explores the meaning of life on many different levels, including living and nonliving matter. Topics include life on a cellular level, the mystery's death and rebirth, and the eternal nature of the soul.

Topics in this degree include cosmic purpose of life, vital life force and reproduction, cellular life, living and nonliving matter, incarnation of the soul, transition of the soul, and initiatic aspects of death.

Fourth Temple Degree (Philosophus)

The fourth temple degree introduces Rosicrucian ontology, the study of the nature of being. It lays out the cosmological framework for all creation. It explores the meaning, understanding, and use of symbols as the language of the subconscious.

Topics in this degree include noumena and phenomena, artificial symbols, mystical symbols, sacred architecture, vital life force, natural symbols, living soul, cycles of life, and constant state of flux.

Fifth Degree (Adeptus Minor)

A mystic by nature is fundamentally a philosopher. In the fifth temple degree, the student will study excerpts from the works of classic philosophers. The students will explore the ancient roots of Rosicrucian philosophy, which will demonstrate the timelessness of these principles. Thoughts of the following philosophers are presented: Thales, Solon, Pythagoras, Heraclitus, Democritus, Empedocles, Socrates, Plato, and Aristotle.

Sixth Temple Degree (Adeptus Major)

The sixth degree presents the physical, mental, emotional, and spiritual components of healing and disease. You will learn specific Rosicrucian healing techniques. Topics include spiritual dimension of food; breathing and respiratory health; Rosicrucian therapy for self-healing; druids and fices ; personal treatment to restore psychic equilibrium; autonomic nervous system; physical, mental, emotional, and spiritual prevention of diseases, and self-healing.

Seventh Temple Degree (Adeptus Exemptus)

The exercise and experiments of all previous degrees have contributed to gradual development, providing the student with the necessary foundation for the advance techniques of the seventh, eighth, and ninth degrees. In the seventh degree, the student will learn how to accomplish psychic projection (astral projection), how to develop his or her personal aura and perceive other people's auras, and how to further develop psychic centers and perceptions. Students will also receive a thorough explanation of the physiological, psychic, and spiritual influence of specific spiritual sounds.

Topic in this degree include the psychic body, the psychic centers (chakras), nature and symbolism dreams, psychic projection (experiments), out-of-body experience, perception of the aura (experiments)(comparing with clairvoyance), and mystical powers of sounds.

Eighth Temple Degree (Magistericus Templicated)

The eighth temple degree explores in depth the theme of immortality, the mysteries of birth and death, reincarnation and karma, and the evolution of the soul personality. The goal is to learn the constituents of the human soul and how it evolves from incarnation to incarnation.

Topics in this degree include universal and human soul, divine and self-consciousness, spiritual evolution of humans, mastery of karma, reincarnation of the soul, remembrance of past incarnations, reincarnation, the mysteries of birth and death, help to the dying before and after death, the work of an adept, psychic contact with great intelligences, prayer, and psychic development using vocalic sounds (mental vibratory).

Ninth Degree (Magus)

This degree involves learning the principles of spiritual alchemy, deriving benefit from the student of divine nature, acting not only different levels of the human being but also in the visible and invisible world's environment. These practices are regarded as the alchemy of matter, consciousness, and life. The ninth degree is a long and careful ascent that gives the student every opportunity to put into practice what has been learned in the preceding temple degrees.

Topics in this degree include microcosm and macrocosm, the four principles (earth, water, fire, and air), symbolism of the cross, triangle, square, circle, rose-cross, mental alchemy, experiment on telepathy, telekinesis, vibroturgy, radiesthesy, invisibility, attunement with cosmic consciousness, the triangle of lights, the power of will, the circles of protection and harmonization, the three planes of consciousness, the cosmic plane, spirals as gateways to other realms, the invisible masters, the lost word, and the assumption of individuality and cosmic assumption.

ILLUMINATI SECTION

Tenth Degree (Magus Later, Illuminitus Minor)

This degree is to learn to walk on the path of the masters. It includes an introduction to the religious doctrines that the masters gave birth to and understanding beliefs that have been available to us for centuries and how humanity is evolving toward a universal religion. It also includes introduction to Zoroastrianism, the Tibet, and the ancient mystery schools of Atlantis, Egypt and the Essenes. It introduces Master Mori-El, the Rig Veda, the Great White Brotherhood, exercises on materialization, telepathy, psychic projection (advanced), the esoteric concept of sin, reincarnation, the psychic senses, the ritual magic, astrology, the human aura, the pineal gland, the fourth dimension, the nature of elections of spirit, Sufi mysticism, and psychic harmonization.

Eleventh Degree (Illuminatus Major)

In this degree, the students must journey through the great traditions, those that have marked the spiritual history of humanity. This journey began in Atlantis and completed this phase through the Martin St. Movement in France in the nineteenth century. It is also the threshold for admission to ordo *summum bonum* (the order of the highest good).

Topics include the heritage of CRC, the Khhurnah method, the dark night of the soul, the gateway keeper, the regeneration, the invisible fraternity, the Rosicrucian inner circle, the Holy Spirit, the mystical Egypt, the cosmic harmonization, the cosmic consciousness, development of the third eye, the signs of psychic development, mantras, the effects of cosmic consciousness, the cloak of invisibility (advanced), esoteric foundations of religions, esoteric teachings of Jesus, the Christus programming, the next incarnation, esoteric formulae, use of the water, the lost word, contact of the invisible masters, and the Rosicrucian hierarchy.

The Twelfth Degree (Illuminati Later, Illumintus Exemptus)

Those who have attained the esoteric hierarchy become, in fact, intermediaries between the cosmic and the imperator, placed in a position to periodically commune with the cosmic and receive inspiration and illumination that one should pass to the imperator for what they may make of the knowledge of the order.

They are to learn how to contact the sacred esoteric hierarchy to serve the order as described above. Also they are to learn how to develop the body of light to be used to attain high states of divine communion.

Topics include Christian Rosenkruez and the Rosicrucian teachings, contact with the masters (El moria and St. Germain), esoteric and celestial hierarchy, mystical silence, cosmic consciousness, the fundamental note or vibrational tone, cosmic harmonization on techniques, planetary influences (moon, sun, and planetary cycles), the cosmic counterpart, the vibration spectrum, Rosicrucian ethics, alchemy of water, benefits of cosmic harmonization (regeneration), masters' chambers, alchemy of fire, cosmic harmonization techniques, astral projection, principles of cosmic harmonization, psychic currents, assumption technique and its application (distance healing), Rosicrucian manuscripts, esoteric principles, the dark night of the soul, astrology, external influences, procedure to recall past-life experiences, development of the inner voice, the Rosicrucian method, use of cosmic forces, the mythic life force of Hervy Spenser Lewis, the Templars, Cogliostro and the Rose Cross, and development of the body of light.

XVII

✠

THE PHAROH

Before me arose a great throne of Darkness, wielded on it
seated a figure of the night. Darker than Darkness sat the
great figure dark with a darkness not of the night. Before
it then paused the master speaking the word that brings
about life. Saying o master of darkness guide of the way
from life unto life before the I bring a Sun of the morning
touch him not ever with the power of night. Call not his
flame to the darkness of night know him and see him one
of our brothers lifted from Darkness into the light. Release
thou his flame from its bondage, free let it flame through
the Darkness of night.

—The Emerald Tablets

THE ANCIENT EGYPTIANS knew the secret to immortality, and they
knew how to attain the key that opens the doorway to the kingdom
of heaven. They knew how to release the full potential of the most powerful
tool that is known in the universe, none other than the human brain.
The ancient mystery schools of Egypt were based on unlocking the full
potential of the human being by activating dormant parts of the brain that
could only be accessed through rigorous discipline and understanding of
extraordinary knowledge.

If anyone were to examine the elder forms of religious worship, they
would find in most of them that God is worshiped under the symbol of

the sun. Not only is it true in those religions that are known to be pagan but also in the Bible itself, the sun is alluded to as the most perfect and appropriate symbol of the creator.

The sun is undoubtedly the most splendid and glorious object in nature. It is the same yesterday as it is today and will be the same tomorrow. Its shining light is an eternal truth that ensures the continuation of life, and its warmth is a reminder of universal love. It is therefore not strange that men in the ancient past selected the sun as the highest and most perfect symbol of God as well as the sign for truth and illumination. The sun thus personified was made the theme of allegorical history emblematic of its passage through the twelve constellations of the zodiac.

The zodiac is the path of the sun among the stars. The ancients divided it into twelve parts composed as clusters of stars named after living creatures. The spectacular belt of stars was thereafter called the zodiac, the word meaning "living creatures." As the sun pursued his path among these wild creatures, it was said that in allegorical language either to assume the nature of or triumph over the sign he entered.

In Leo, the sun became a lion slayer, an archer in Sagittarius, and the Dagon fish god Vishnu in Pisces. These fables are most often absurd enough if understood as real histories, but the allegorical key was kept secret by the priests and philosophers and was only imparted to those who were initiated into the mysteries.

The profane and unworthy crowd were kept in darkness and believed in and worshiped a real Hercules or Jupiter, whom they thought had actually lived and performed all the transformations of the mythology. By these means, the priests of Egypt ruled the people. The fables that were contained within the mythology exposed great scientific truths to them and them only. These fables served three purposes:

1. They kept secrets of science from all but those that understood the key to them.
2. Being themselves easy to remember, they served on the principle of the art of mnemonics or artificial memory to keep alive the recollection of scientific facts that otherwise might be lost.

3. They were the means of keeping people in ignorance. By their use, the priests were enabled to rule them by the superior power of the working of miracles.

The science of the Egyptian priesthood was extremely advanced. One of the most guarded secrets was that of astronomy and astrology. The people worshiped the sun, moon, and stars as gods, and to have knowledge of their true nature would have at once put an end to the influence of the priests who the ignorant crowds believed to be able to withhold the divine favor with prayers, invocations, and sacrifices.

To deny the divinity of the sun, moon, and stars or to permit science to disclose their true nature to the masses of the people was consequently held by the priesthood of Egypt as the highest of crimes. With a knowledge of astronomy, the priest was able to calculate and predict eclipses of the sun and moon events beheld with superstitious awe and fear, but the multitude saw how certainly these predictions, when thus made, were fulfilled. The priests were credited with the power to foretell the future generally. So with that power, they cast horoscopes and were assumed to be prophets.

A knowledge of astronomy spread among the people would have been pretentious. The facts of astronomy were there for these reasons. Most were carefully hidden from the common people, and the priesthood only communicated them to each other, wielded in allegorical fables. The key to which was disclosed to those who had taken the highest degrees of the mysteries and given the most convincing proof of his fidelity and zeal.

The names under which the sun was personified were many, but the one great feature most prolific of fables was his great decline in light and heat during the winter and his renewal in glory and power at the vernal equinox or summer solstice, which gave rise to all class of legends, which represents the sun god as dying and being restored back to life again.

So we are told in the ancient Egyptian legend that Osiris, which represented the sun, was slain by Typhoon, a gigantic monster that represented darkness and the evil powers of nature. The ritual mysteries took place in Egypt and India. And Greece was founded upon this legend, which displayed some form of the death and resurrection of the sun god.

The mystery of Osiris and Isis was in the form of a mystic drama representing the death by violence of Osiris, the search for his body by

Isis the moon, and its finding and being raised to life and power again. Celebrating these mysteries, the neophyte was made to perform all the mysterious wanderings of the goddess through the most fear-invoking scenes. But while being guided by one of the initiated, that spawned a mask representing a dog's head, who represented Anubis, the god of the underworld. The dog's head also refers to the bright star Sirius, or the Dog Star, so-called because the rising of the star each year above the horizon just before day gave warning of the approaching immadation of the Nile.

The candidate was, by this guide, conducted through a dark, mysterious labyrinth. With much pain, he struggled through involved paths, over horrid chasms in darkness and in terror. At length he arrived at a stream of water, which he was directed to pass. Suddenly however, three men, disguised in grotesque forms, assaulted and arrested him. After taking a cup of water from the stream, they forced the terrified candidate to first drink of it. This was the water of forgetfulness. By drinking which, all his former crimes were to be forgotten, and his mind was prepared for new instructions of virtue and truth.

The attack of Typhoon, or the spirit of darkness, typical of the evil powers of nature, upon Osiris, who was slain, was also enacted as the initiation progressed amidst the most terrible scenes, during which the judgment of the dead was also represented and the punishments of the wicked exhibited as realities to the candidate.

The search for the body of Osiris, which was concealed in the mysterious chest or ark, followed. The mutilated remains were at last found and deposited amidst loud cries of sorrow and despair. The initiation closed with the return of Osiris to life and power. The candidate now beheld, amidst effulgent beams of light, the joyful mansions of the blessed and the resplendent plains of paradise.

At this stage of the initiation, all was life, light, and joy. The candidate was himself figuratively considered to have risen to a new and more perfect life. The past was dead, with all its crimes and unhappiness. Henceforth the candidate was under the special protection of Isis, to whose service he dedicated his new life.

The sublime mysteries of religion and the profoundest teachings of science were now revealed to him and satisfied his thirst for knowledge, while the possession of power as one of the hierarchy gratified his ambition to strive forward to make known the unknown.

Egypt is not only a culture that existed in a certain time and place, with certain history, geography, and economics. Egypt is also a state of being that exists eternally in archetypal realms. The historical Egypt was about a backdrop for the essential Egypt, the Egypt of the eternal return. In this view, Egypt did not have but rather a quality of intelligence.

How did it happen that, in a two to five hundred-year period somewhere between 3100 and 2600 BCE, aboriginal people on the swampy delta recovered the land and invented a blank that has lasted over five thousand years? What leaps of imagination caused them to discover the fine points of astronomy, architecture, medicine, mathematics, and literature? What infusion of wisdom, intuition, or intelligence conceived the enormity of the pyramids and their eternal presence and also created the delicate balance of Maat, a system of governance based on principles of cosmic truth?

What priest and kings divined in their hearts a consummate theology and symbology and an enormously artful and enduring culture and written language based on hieroglyphics? How could it be that, in so short a time, the Egyptians' bodies, minds, and souls are entered into a congregant that quickened a surge of creativity that, as far as we know, has not been rivaled yet and what is perhaps one of the finest explanations of nature and practice of creative imagination?

The New and Old Testaments and the myth of Ptah refer to the creation of the material world through the mental plane. Thought finds its form on Earth. John 1:1 declares, "In the beginning was the word and the word was with God and the word was God." The story of Genesis 1:2–3 recalls the same event by saying, "And the spirit of God was hovering over the face of the waters. The God said, Let there be light and there was light."

In Memphis, the Egyptian god Ptah opened his mouth, and light sprang from his lips. The Shekaba stone suggests that Atum made the world, but prior to that, Ptah spoke the magical words of truth (Heka and Maat) across the waters of nothingness. According to the legend, the light from Ptah's lips allowed Atum to see himself for the first time. In that way, he saw he was a god, and only after Ptah created the light was he visible even to himself.

In other words, the solar god Atum made the world, but first Ptah had to make Atum visible. Ptah proceeded Atum. Thought proceeded action. As the world's first architect, Ptah was the god of Egyptian stonemasons, craftsmen, scribes, and priests. They were seen as metaphysicians who crafted, invoked, and operated the sacred energies within the temple. The generation of ideas, the enunciation of truth, and the energy to create order from chaos were the gifts of Ptah. The emblems of the Freemasons, the craftsmen's square and compass, were the hieroglyphs of Ptah's name. The all-seeing eye that appears above the pyramid on the back of the American dollar is another Masonic idea. If one can envision a better world, if one sees it and acts upon it, that world already exists.

Ptah stands upon a solid foundation, the plinath of truth. He wears a gleaming sky blue crown that represents his supreme power, the power of the universal mind to create. The energies of the chakras (the sacred centers of the body) are indicated on the scepter he holds. This staff of life aligns heart and the solar plexus chakra, signifying unifying desire and will. The mind of God manifests through the use of Maat, a feminine principle of unified desire and action. Maat is called the heart and tongue of Ptah.

The priest of Ptah surely knew about name vibration and numerology. Knowing a secret name and the sacred breath of its vowel heightened its vibration. If man knew a man's or even a god's secret name, one acquired a kind of power over him. The shamans of Ptah possessed that kind of power and guarded it. Ptah the creator was also a magician, much like Thoth, god of wisdom. His priests and those of Sekhmet, Ptah's consort, were viewed as shamans. They seemed able to manifest things out of thin air through mind and willpower. Their healings appeared to be spontaneous. Some priests had the power to raise the dead.

XVIII

✠

GENESIS

Forward He led me through many great spaces filled with the mysteries of the children of light. mysteries man may never yet know of until he too is a Son of the light. Spoke he then with words of great power saying thou has been made free of the Halls of Amenti choose thou thy work among the children of men. Then Spoke I O great master let me be a teacher of men leading them onward and upward until they to are light among men freed from the veil of the night that surrounds them flaming with light that shall shine above men.

—The Emerald Tablets

T HE TRUE HISTORY of the world is not written for those to see in plain sight. This secret history, of course, will not be found in history books because these tomes of human civilization go back six thousand years, and if we really want to get a grasp on the big picture, we need to go back about 450,000 years to begin to uncover our origins

First you must realize something about written history. Somebody has to hold the pen and write it down, so written history is always the viewpoint of the person or people who wrote it. Written history began only in the last six thousand years, but would that history be the same if different people had written it? Consider that, in most case, the winners of the wars wrote the history books. If Hitler had won World War II, our history books would be completely different. If JFK were never shot, we would be living in another world today. This hints to the importance of key events in our history's timeline.

The Sumerian records are the oldest written records on the planet, 5,800 years old, but they describe things that happened billions of years ago, specifically detailing things that happened 450,000 years ago. We've been here for slightly more than two hundred thousand years, but there were civilizations on the Earth long before our creators were far more advanced than them. The ancient Sumerians told of a story so outrageous that scientists are having a very difficult time accepting it, even though they know it must be true.

The oldest known culture in the world, the Sumerians, extending back to around 3800 BC, knew exactly what it looked like to approach our solar system from outer space. They knew about all the outer planets and counted them from outer to inner, as though coming in from outside the solar system. The Sumerians also had knowledge of the precession of the equinoxes from the very beginning of their existence as a culture. They knew the Earth was tilted on its axis at twenty-three degrees to its orbital plane around the sun and it rotated in a circle that took approximately 25,920 years to complete. How did they know this? Where did it come from?

Even deeper than these astounding bits of information they knew is the actual story of the writings of the beginnings of the human race before Adam and Eve. This story begins several billion years ago when Earth was very young. It was then a large planet called Tiamat, and it rotated around the Sun between Mars and Jupiter. Ancient Earth had a larger moon than we have in our time. Their records say it was destined to become a planet itself someday in the future.

According to the records, there was one more planet in our solar system that we are only vaguely aware of in these modern times. The Babylonians called this planet Marduk, but the Sumerian name for it was Nibiru. It was a huge planet that spun retrograde compared to the other planets. The other planets are in an essentially flat plane moving in one direction, but Nibiru moves in the other direction, and when it comes close to the other planets, it passes through the orbit of Mars and Jupiter. They said it passes through our solar system every 3,600 years, and when it came, it was usually a big event in our solar system. Then it would go way out past the other planets and disappear out of sight.

On one orbital pass, Nibiru came in so close that one of its moons struck Tiamat (Earth) and tore about half of it off. According to the Sumerian records, this big chunk of Tiamat, along with her major moon, got knocked off course, went into orbit between Venus and Mars, and became Earth as we know it. The other chunk broke into a million pieces and became what the Sumerian records call the hammered bracelet, what we call the asteroid belt between Mars and Jupiter. Nibiru was inhabited by conscious beings called the Annunaki, or otherwise known as the Nefilim from the Bible. The Nefilim were very tall, about ten to sixteen feet tall. They were not immortal, but their lifetime was about 360,000 Earth years.

According to the Sumerian record, approximately 450,000 years ago, the Annunaki started having a problem with their planet. It was an atmospheric problem very much like the ozone problem we are having right now. Nibiru's orbit takes it so far away from the Sun that they needed to hold in the heat, so they decided to put gold particles into their higher atmosphere, which would reflect the light and temperature back like a mirror. They planned to get large quantities of gold, turn it into dust, and suspend it in space above their planet.

The Annunaki had the capability of space travel, yet they weren't at that time much further advanced than we are in the present day. The Sumerian records show them in their spaceships with flames coming out the back. So this is the beginning of space travel. They had to wait until Nibiru got near enough to Earth before they could even make the trip between the two planets. It can be said that, since their space travel was limited and they could not leave the solar system, they searched throughout all the planets that were here and found that Earth had the largest quantities of gold. So they sent a team here over four hundred thousand years ago for one purpose only, to mine gold.

Twelve members headed the Annunaki who came to Earth. They headed about six hundred workers who were to actually dig the gold from the mines, and about three hundred stayed in orbit in their mother ship. They first went into the area of present-day Iraq and began to establish themselves and build their cities. For the gold, they went to Africa. One of the twelve, whose name was Enlil, was the leader of the miners. They went deep into the Earth and dug large quantities of gold. Then every 3,600 years when Nibiru came around, they would shuttle the gold to their home planet. According to the Sumerian records, they dug for 150,000 years, and then the Annunaki rebellion took place around 250,000 years ago.

The workers rebelled against their bosses. They did not want to keep digging in the mines. The rebellion presented a problem for the bosses, so the twelve leaders came together to decide what to do. They decided to take a certain life-form that already existed on this planet, which was one of the primates, like a tiny foot. Then they would take the blood of the primates, mix it with clay, then take the sperm of one of the young Anunnaki males, and mix these elements together. Their plan was to use the DNA of the primates and their own DNA to create a more advanced race than Earth had at that time so the Annunaki could control this new race for the sole purpose of mining gold. So as it can be seen, the mysterious missing link is our creators, who are the Annuanki.

In numerous records, it has been recorded that there were giants here on Earth. When our race was created, these giants became our mother. He said that seven of them came together, dropped their bodies by consciously dying, and formed a pattern of seven interlocking spheres of consciousness. This merging created a white-blue flame, which the ancients called the "flower of life." And they placed this flame into the womb of the Earth, which is known to the Egyptians as the Halls of Amenti, a fourth-dimensional space that's located three-dimensionally about a thousand miles under the surface of the Earth and is connected to the Great Pyramid through a fourth-dimensional passageway.

In this passageway, the glowing force of Vril energy from ancient Atlantis lines the passageway. All initiates of the mysteries walked this passageway at the end of their initiations. One of the primary uses of the Halls of Amenti is for the creation of new races or species. Inside is a room based on Fibonacci proportions, made from what appears to be stone. In the middle of the room sits a cube, and on top of the cube is the flame the Annunaki created. This flame, which is five feet tall and about three feet in diameter, illuminates a whitish blue light. This light is pure prana, pure consciousness, the planetary ovum created for us to begin this new evolutionary path that we call human.

If there is a mother of our race, there's got to be a father. And the nature of the father, the father's sperm, must come from outside the system of body. So when the Nephilim were setting up their flasks and preparing for this new race to develop, another race of beings from a far-distant star from the third planet out from Sirius were coming to Earth. There were thirty-two members of this race, sixteen males and sixteen females. They were also giants like the Annunaki. Though the Annunaki were primarily third-dimensional beings, the Sirians were fourth-dimensional.

The Sirians came here and entered the Halls of Amenti, right into the pyramid and before the flame. These beings understood that all things were light. They understood the connection between thought and feeling. So they simply created thirty-two rose quartz slabs that were about thirty inches high, three or four feet wide, and roughly twenty feet long. They created them out of nothing and placed them around the flame. Then they laid down on these slabs, alternating male and female facing upward with their head toward the center around this flame. The Sirians conceived or merged with the flame, or the ovum of the Annunaki.

On the third dimensional, the Neflim scientists placed the laboratory-created human eggs in the wombs of seven Annunaki women from which the first human being was eventually born. Conception in human terms happens in less than twenty-four hours. But conception on a planetary level is very different. According to Thoth, they stay there without moving for approximately two thousand years, conceiving with the Earth this new race. Finally after two thousand years, the first human beings were born.

Seven of us were birthed at once, not just one Adam and Eve, according to the original stories, and we were sterile. We could not produce. The Annunaki continued procreating little humans, making a legion of beings, and they put them on the island of Gondwanaland, which at the time was off the coast of Africa. So our race's mother is Annunaki, and our father is Sirian. Seven of us were birthed at once, not just one Adam and Eve, like according to the original stories, and we were sterile. We could not produce. It is clear that science doesn't understand how we got here. We seem to come out of nowhere. They do know that we are somewhere between 150 and 250,000 years old, but they have no idea where we came from or how we developed.

Another interesting part of the Sumerian record was that, after they mined gold for a while in Africa, the cities in the north near modern-day

Iraq became quite elaborate and extremely beautiful. They were in rain forests and hade huge gardens around them. It was finally decided, according to the Sumerian records, to bring some of the slaves from the mines to the cities to have them work in the gardens.

One day, Enlil's younger brother Enki went to Eve and told her that the reason his brother didn't want the humans to eat of that tree in the center of the garden is because it would make them like the Annunaki. So Enki convinced Eve to eat of the apple tree, the Tree of Knowledge of Good and Evil, which, according to the records, included more than just a dualistic view. It gave the power to procreate, to give birth. So Eve found Adam, and they ate of this tree and had children.

Now if you think about the Adam and Eve story, it says God walks through the garden. So he's walking, he's in a body, and he's in flesh, which is suggested in Genesis. He's walking through the garden, calling for Adam and Eve. He doesn't know where they are, which is odd. He's God, but he doesn't know where Adam and Eve are. He calls for them, and they come. He doesn't know they at the tree until he sees them trying to hide themselves because they're ashamed. Then he realizes what they've done.

Another thing they use for God is Elohim in the original Bible. In fact, in all the Bibles, he was not singular, but plural. Was the god who created humanity a race of beings? Does that mean that God is actually in fact the gods? When Enlil found out that Adam and Eve had done this, he was furious. He especially did not want them to eat from the Tree of Life because, not only would they be able procreate, they would become immortal. The Tree of Life is also known as the "divine knowledge of the twelve secret sciences."

Therefore, at that point, Enlil removed Adam and Eve from his garden. He put them somewhere and monitored them. He had to have monitored them because he wrote down the names of all the sons and daughters. He knew everything that was going on in the whole family. It was written down over two thousand years before the Bible was ever written.

From the time of Adam and Eve, our race developed in two strains. Ones that could procreate were free (though monitored). And the other that could not have children were slaves. According to scientists, this latter strain continued to mine gold until at least twenty thousand years ago. The bones of this second strain that were found in the mines were identical to ours; the only difference is they couldn't have children. This strain was completely destroyed at the time of the great flood, roughly 12,500 years ago.

After Adam and Eve, there was a major pole shift of the axis, which submerged Gondwanland. Thoth says that, when Gondwanaland went down, another landmass came up in the Pacific Ocean, which we call Lumeria. And the descendants of Adam and Eve were taken from their homeland and brought to Lumeria. The new civilization was growing quite well. But most of Lumeria sank. They knew Lumeria was going to sink a long time beforehand. They knew with absolute certainty. It wasn't even a matter of discussion. The Lumerians were very psychic because of their female right-brained mentality.

The sinking of Lumeria and the rising of Atlantis occurred at the same time, during another shift of the axis. Lumeria went down, and what would be called Atlantis rose. The immortal beings of Lumeria flew from their homeland to a little island north of the newly risen continent of Atlantis. They waited for a long time on an island they named Udal. Then they began to recreate their spiritual science.

When the time was right, the Naacals from Lumeria created a spiritual representation of a human brain on the surface of their Atlantean island. Their purpose was to birth a new consciousness based on what they had learned during Lumeria. The next step was to project onto the surface of Atlantis the form of the Tree of Life. Even though it extended hundreds of miles on the surface of this land, they projected it to the accuracy of a single atom. There is an indication that ten spheres of the Tree of Life were used to designate the size and shape of the cities of Atlantis.

Plato says in his book *Critas* that the main city of Atlantis was made of three rings of land separated by water. He also said that the city was constructed of red, black, and white stones. The last statement will make sense as soon as we talk about the Great Pyramid.

In a single day, those of the Naacal Mystery School breathed life into the Tree of Life on the surface of Atlantis. This created vortexes of energy rotating out of each of the circles on the Tree of Life. Once the vortexes were established, then the brain of Atlantis psychically called forth the children of Lumeria. Millions of millions of Lumerians who had then settled along the west coast of North and South America and in other places began to be pulled to Atlantis. A great migration began, and the ordinary people of the sunken Lumeria started moving toward Atlantis. However, the Lumerian body of consciousness had only reached the age of twelve as a planetary consciousness, and some of its centers weren't functioning yet. They had worked with the energies but only mastered eight of the ten. So each migrating Lumerian was attracted to one of these eight centers on Atlantis, depending on the nature of the individual. There they settled and began to build cities.

That left two vortexes with nobody using them, not a single person. Though Lumerians settled into eight of the vortex areas, Mayan records state clearly that there were ten cities when it fell. These records can be seen in what is known as the Torano document, estimated to be at least 3,500 years old. It describes in detail the sinking of Atlantis. It's Mayan, and it contains an authentic account of the cataclysm.

In the year 6 Kan on the eleventh Muluc in the month Zak, there occurred terrible earthquakes that continued without interruption until the thirteenth Chin. The country of the hills of Muf, the land of Mu, was sacrificed, being twice upheaved. It suddenly disappeared during one night, the basin being continually shaken by volcanic forces. Being confined, these caused the land to sink and rise several times in various places. At last, the surface gave way, and ten countries were torn asunder and scattered, unable to stand the forces of the convulsions. They sank with their 64 million inhabitants.

The ten countries mentioned were referring to the ten points on the Tree of Life. When you see this document, it shows an extremely sophisticated city with volcanoes going off inside and all around it. Pyramids and everything else are being destroyed, and people are getting in boats and trying to escape.

To fill those two empty vortexes, two extraterrestrial races stepped in. The first race was the Hebrews, coming from our future. They hadn't graduated to the next level of evolution, so they had to come back and repeat the grade. They knew a lot of things that we didn't know yet. They had legal permission from the galactic command to step into our evolutionary path at the same time. They brought with them many concepts and ideas that we had no idea about because we hadn't entered into those levels of awareness. This interaction actually benefited our evolution. There was no problem with their coming to Earth and settling. There probably would have been no problem at all if it were just them who came.

The other race that stepped in at that time caused big problems. These beings came from the nearby planet Mars. It has become evident because of the situation that has developed in the world that this same race is still causing major problems. The secret government and the trillionaires of the world are of Mars extraction or have mostly Martian genes and little or no emotional/feeling body.

Mars looked much like Earth a little less than a million years ago. It was beautiful. It had oceans, water, and trees. It was just beautiful. But then something happened to them. It had to do with a past Lucifer rebellion.

From the very beginning of this experiment, we are in all of God's creation, an experiment. Experiments similar to the Lucifer rebellion have been attempted four times. In other words, three other beings besides Lucifer attempted to do the same thing, and each time it resulted in utter chaos throughout the universe.

More than a million years ago, the Martians had joined the third rebellion, the third time that life decided to try this experiment. And the experiment failed dramatically. Planets everywhere were destroyed, and Mars was one of them. Life attempted to create a separate reality from God, which is the same thing that's going on right now.

When someone tries to separate from God, he or she severs his or her love connection with reality. So when the Martians created a separate reality, they cut the love bond. They disconnected the emotional body, and in so doing, they became pure male, with little or no female within them. They were purely logical beings with no emotions. What happened in Mars was that they ended up fighting all the time because there was no compassion, no love. Mars became a battleground that just kept going on and on and on until it became clear that Mars was not going to survive. Eventually they blew away their atmosphere and destroyed the surface of their planet.

Before Mars was destroyed, they built tetrahedral pyramids. Then they built three-sided, four-sided, and five-sided pyramids, eventually building a complex that was able to create a synthetic merkaba. You can have a space-time vehicle that looks like a spaceship, or you can have certain other structures that do the same thing. They built a structure from which they were able to look ahead and behind in time and space to tremendous distances and time periods.

A small group of Martians tried to get away from Mars before it was destroyed, so they translated themselves into the future and found a perfect place to resettle before Mars was destroyed. That place was Earth, but it was about sixty-five thousand years in our past. They saw that little vortex sitting there on Atlantis with nobody in it. They didn't ask permission. They stepped right into the vortex, and in doing so, they joined our evolutionary path.

The very first thing they did when they arrived here on Earth was try to take control of Atlantis. They wanted to declare war and take over. However they were vulnerable because of their small numbers and perhaps other reasons, so they couldn't do it. The Atlanteans/Lumerians finally subdued them.

Once the initial conflict was over, it was agreed that the Martians would try to understand the female right-brained aspect they lacked, this emotional feeling, of which they had none at all. Things essentially settled down for a while. But then the Martians started implementing their left brain technology, which the Lumerians knew nothing about.

The Martians kept putting out these left brain inventions, one after another after another until finally they changed the polarity of our evolutionary path because we began to see through the left brain, and we changed from female to male. We changed the nature of who we were. The Martians gained control bit by bit, until eventually they controlled everything without a battle. They had all the money and power. The animosity between the Martians and the Lumerians never subsided, not even to the very end of Atlantis. They hated each other. The Lumerians, the feminine aspect, were basically shoved down and treated like inferiors. It was not a very loving situation. It was a marriage that the female component did not love, but the Martians did not care. It remained this way for a very long time, until approximately twenty-six thousand years ago.

XIX

✠

THE FALL OF ATLANTIS

Light there was in ancient Atlantis. Yes darkness too was hidden in all. Fell from the light into the darkness, some who had risen to hieghts amoung men. Proud they became because of their knowledge, proud were they of their place amoung men. Deep delved they into the forbidden, opened the gateway that led to below. Sought they to gain ever more knowledge but seeking to bring it from down below.

I T WAS ABOUT twenty-six thousand years ago when we had another pole shift and a small change in consciousness. This pole shift took place at the same point on the polar wobble called the precession of the equinoxes that we have now returned to. At the time of the pole shift, a piece of Atlantis sank into the ocean. That caused a tremendous amount of fear in Atlantis because the thought they were going to lose the whole continent, like what happened in Lumeria. By this time, they had they had lost most of their ability to see into the future.

After they lost some of the continent, things were going along nicely for a while, but out of the blue, approximately thirteen to sixteen thousand years ago, a comet approached Earth. When this comet was in deep space, the Atlanteans knew about it because they were more technologically advanced than we are now. They witnessed the approach. A great conflict began to occur in Atlantis. The Martians, who were in the minority even though they were in control, wanted to blow it out of the sky with their laser technology. But there was a huge movement amongst the Lumerian population against them using the left brain technology. The feminine aspect said this comet is in divine order and we should allow this to take place naturally.

After lots of arguing, the Martians finally and reluctantly agreed to allow the comet to hit the Earth. When it arrived, it came screaming into the atmosphere, plunging into the Atlantic Ocean just off the western shore of Atlantis, near where South Carolina is. The remnants of that comet are now scattered over four states. One of the largest pieces actually struck the main body of Atlantis. This catastrophe left two huge holes in the floor of the Atlantic Ocean and could have been the true cause of the sinking of Atlantis. The actual sinking did not happen at that time but took place at least several years later.

The comet hit near one of the Martian cities and killed a large portion of their population. By allowing the comet to come in, the Martians got hurt the worst, and that humiliated them. This is where Earth began its great fall in consciousness. What took place next was the planting of a seed for a bitter tree, the same tree we live in today. The Martians said, "It's all over. We are divorcing you. We are going to do whatever we want from now on."

So the Martians decided to take over the Earth. Control, the Martians' primary interface with the reality, rose to meet their anger. They began to create a building complex like the one they had constructed on Mars that destroyed the planet. So they built the buildings and began the experiment. That experiment is directly tied to a chain of merkabas that began with the Mars experiments a million years before. One was later done here on Earth in 1913. Another one was in 1943 (the Philadelphia Experiment). And another in 1983 was called the Montauk Experiment.

If the Martians had succeeded in setting up a synthetic, harmonic merkaba, they would have had absolute control of the planet. If they succeeded, they would have been able to make anybody on the planet do whatever they wanted. No higher order of beings would place this kind of control on another if they truly understood the true nature of reality.

The Martians built the buildings in Atlantis and set up the whole experiment. Then they switched to begin the energy flow. Almost immediately they lost control of the experiment, like falling through space and time. The degree of destruction was catastrophic. What the experiment did was begin to rip open the lower dimensional levels of the Earth.

The Martians did something that almost killed the Earth. The environmental disaster we are experiencing today is nothing in comparison, though the problems we are having today are a direct result of what we did long ago. With the right understanding and enough love, the environment could be repaired in a single day. But had this Martian experiment continued, it would have destroyed the Earth forever. We would never be able to use the Earth as a seed base again.

The Martians made a very serious mistake. This out-of-control merkaba field first of all released a huge number of lower dimensional spirits into the Earth's higher dimensional planes. These spirits were forced into a world they did not understand or know, and they were in total fear. They had to live. They had to have bodies so they went right into the people of Atlantis. Finally almost every person in the world was totally possessed by these beings from another dimension. These spirits were earthlings but very different, not coming from this dimensional level. It was a total catastrophe, the biggest one the Earth has ever known.

The Martians' attempt to control the world took place near one of the Atlantean islands in the area we now call the Bermuda Triangle. An actual building is sitting on the ocean floor down there that contains three rotating star tetrahedral electromagnetic fields superimposed on each other, creating a huge synthetic merkaba that stretches out over the ocean and into deep space. This merkaba is completely out of control. It's called the Bermuda Triangle because the apex of one of the tetrahedrons, the stationary one, is sticking up out of the water there. The other two fields are counterrotating, and the faster-rotating field sometimes moves clockwise, which is a very dangerous situation. When the faster field rotates counterclockwise, everything's okay, but when the faster one moves clockwise, that's when time and space distortions happen. Many of the airplanes and ships that have disappeared in the Bermuda Triangle have literally gone into other dimensional levels because of the out-of-control field there.

A primary cause of much of the distortion in the world, the distortion among humans such as wars, material problems, and emotional disturbances, is that imbalanced field. Not only is that field causing distortions on Earth, it's causing distortions way out in the remote areas of space because of the way reality is constructed. That's one of the reasons why this race of beings called the Grays and other extraterrestrial beings are trying to correct what happened here long ago. This is a big problem that extends way beyond Earth. What they did back in Atlantis was against all galactic law. It was illegal. It will be solved, but not until the end of the Mayan calendar, the beginning of the New Golden Age where our planet will have completed a 104,000-year great cycle. And humanity will ascend once again to reclaim its long-lost divinity.

At the time of the synthetic merkaba failure, about 1,600 ascended masters lived on Earth. And they did everything they could to try to heal the situation. The situation at that time began to deteriorate extremely rapidly. All the systems on Atlantis (financial and social) and all the concepts of how life ought to be lived collapsed. The continent of Atlantis and all its people became sick. The situation grew continually worse. For a long period of time, it was hell on Earth. If the ascended masters had not slowed it down, it would truly have been the end of the world.

They were looking for a solution that would heal the Earth, both the dark and the light. They knew that the only way they could do it was to get us back into Christ consciousness, a level of beingness where we can see the unity, and they knew we would proceed from there with love and compassion. They knew that, if we were going to get back on track, we would have to be in Christ consciousness as a planet by the end of the thirteen thousand-year cycle, which is now.

It was finally decided to try a kind of standard operating procedure that usually works in these situations. In other words, it was an experiment. Earth's people were about to be subjects of a galactic experimental project in the hope of helping us. We would experiment on ourselves. It wasn't done by extraterrestrials or anything like that. They simply showed us how to do it. We were given instruction on how to proceed with this experiment, and we actually carried it out successfully.

The project to rebuild the grid was begun by three men: Thoth, a being named Ra-Ta-abin, and a being named Araragt. These men flew to a place in what is now Egypt, to the area now called the Giza Plateau. At that time, it was not a desert but a tropical rain forest, and it was called the land of Khem, which meant the "land of the hairy barbarians."

Many beings and levels of consciousness have been working together to figure out how to get us back onto the path DNA where we were before. Beings from all over the universe who have been trying to help us with our problem have initiated various experiments on us in an effort to assist, some legally and others without license. One particular experiment is resulting in a scenario that no one anywhere had ever dreamed would become a reality, except for one person in a single culture from a long, distant past.

Thoth of Egypt goes all the way back to the beginning of Atlantis. He figured out fifty-two thousand years ago how to stay conscious in one body continuously without dying. Then he moved into a way of being far beyond our understanding. He lived through most of the period of Atlantis and even became king of Atlantis for a period of sixteen thousand years. During those times, he was called Chiquetet Arlich Vomalites. Chiquetet was a title that meant "the seeker of wisdom" because he really wanted to know what wisdom was. After Atlantis sank, Arlich Vomalites and other advanced beings had to wait for about six thousand years before they could begin to reestablish civilization.

When Egypt began to come to life, he stepped forward and called himself Thoth, keeping that name all through the time of Egypt. When Egypt died, Thoth started the next major culture, which was Greece. Our history books say that Pythagoras was the father of Greece and it was from Greece that our present civilization emerged. Pythagoras says in his own writings that Thoth took him by the hand, led him under the Great Pyramid, and taught him all the geometries and the nature of reality.

Once Greece was born through Pythagoras, Thoth then stepped into that culture in the same body he had during the time of Atlantis and called himself Hermes. So Arlich Vomilites, Thoth, and Hermes were all the same person, hence the name Hermes Trismagustus, thrice great.

They had to wait until the right moment until the precession of the equinoxes passed the low ebb in consciousness before they could act, and the low ebb was still far into the future. After that, they would wait about thirteen years to complete everything by the end of the twentieth century. We couldn't go any longer than this, or we would destroy ourselves and our planet.

First they had to complete the grid on the higher dimensions. Then they had to physically build the temples in this dimension before the new infinity grid would manifest. Once manifested and balanced, they were to help us begin to consciously move into the higher world of being and begin a new out path home to god.

So Thoth went to the very spot where the unity consciousness vortex exited the Earth. This point was about a mile away from where the Great Pyramid sits in the desert today, but then it was out in the middle of nowhere in the middle of a rain forest. Centered tight over the axis of this vortex on Earth, they created a hole extending approximately one mile into the Earth, lining it with bricks. It took only a few minutes because they were sixth-dimensional beings, and whatever they thought happened. It was that simple.

Once the hole aligned with the unity axis was created, they mapped the golden mean spirals that emerged from the hole and located where they moved above the Earth. One of the spirals exited the Earth not far from the present Great Pyramid. Once they found it, they built a little stone building in front of the hole. That building is the key to the entire Giza complex. Then they built the Great Pyramid.

X X

✠

JESUS WAS A DJHEDI

Fast we fled toward the Sun of the morning until beneath us lay the children of Khem. Raging they came with cudgels and spears lifted in anger seeking to slay and utterly destroy the Sons of Atlantis. Then I spoke to them in words calm and peaceful telling them of the might of Atlantis saying we were children of the sun and its messengers.

—The Emerald Tablets

THE ANCIENT EGYPTIANS referred to the pathway for the ascent of the serpent power of the Kundalini as the Djed, and the path of initiation was begun when the aspirant began the task of raising his or her life force up the spine. Not only is the myth of the resurrection of Osiris a myth, it is an alchemical treatise on how to attain the alchemical union of male and female to form the tabernacle. The symbol of the serpent has an affiliation to the masters and adepts of many of the world's spiritual traditions. Traditionally these masters have been connected with the snake, serpent, or dragon and referred to by regional names denoting serpent. In India, they are known as the Nagas, Quetzalcoatl in Mexico, Djedi in Egypt, Adders in Britain, and Lung in China. Collectively they have been called the Serpents of Wisdom and are a worldwide network of spiritual adepts that are also known as the Great White Brotherhood.

The Serpents of Wisdom's story began with their appearance on Earth

Anthony Kaminski

at the beginning of a long cycle that was to be 104,000 years. They initially manifested on Atlantis and Lemuria, two large continents located in the Atlantic and Pacific Oceans. During this time, they began to teach their sacred teachings, which were to help mankind achieve spiritual enlightenment throughout the cycle.

When the deluge happened and the continents sank to the bottom of the seas, the Serpents of Wisdom took their ancient wisdom and migrated to all the corners of the world. The indigenous people welcomed these serpent people as prophets under their guidance. Numerous dragon cultures arose, which were comprised of colossal pyramids, multitudinous serpent motifs that were ruled over by dragon kings and pharaohs. All of these cultures reached the heights of civilization and continued to survive for many thousands of years.

There have been many times in history that certain people have claimed to have realized the purpose and goal of existence. Through many teachings and disciplines, these masters successfully joined the male and female principle within themselves, and they had raised their inner transformative fire serpent from its seat at the base of the spine and awakened the consciousness of love within their hearts. For the ones who had completed these tasks, the evolutionary cycle of spiritual transformation had been completed. These enlightened men and women have reached the goal of all spiritual paths and have become Serpents of Wisdom. They are both male and female, which is spirit and matter united in one body.

As fully conscious spirit that inhabits physical form, they wield powers, including the ability to materialize any object at will. They dwell as ghosts in the machines that can survive for hundreds of years and primarily out of a fourth-dimensional immortal body. Contained within this immortal body are the supernatural senses of clairvoyance, clairaudience, telepathy, omniscience, and omnipresence, which allow immortals to remain in continual communion with the heavenly etheric realms that surround and penetrate the physical plane. When they so please, they can extricate their immortal body and travel within it to distant locations throughout the universe.

At death, the immortals can detach from their material body and relocate to the paradise realms of the immortals. When on Earth, wherever they have manifested, they have been seen as gods and goddesses, and they are respected around the Earth. They have served as prophets, magicians, and healers. They are also known as guides or world teachers who show the way to those who strive to achieve the liberated state of an enlightened mind and become one to transcend themselves past the cycles of time. All of the Serpents of Wisdom are part of a global organization known as the Great White Brotherhood. While they live many lives, their souls work for the spiritual uplifting of the entire human race. They all understand the universal language of love and have the ability to teach profound spiritual truths.

The early stages of the Serpents of Wisdom can be traced to the beginnings of time when all that existed was an infinite ocean of consciousness, which was the spirit of god, which has also been referred to as Shiva among Hindus, Tao among the Chinese, Ra among the Egyptians, and Yod Ae Vahe among the Hebrews. And from out of this spiritual sea emerged the first form of spirit, the first Serpent of Wisdom.

Following the first Serpent of Wisdom came the various celestial order of the angels at the head of this angelic hierarchy, which are the sacred seven, the seven archangels of the seven sons of the solar spirit.

Next in line after the archangels are the seraphim. Then came the cherubim. Through the protective assistance from the cherubs, embodied souls can safely pass into the terrestrial temples of wisdom, and disembodied spirits can make a smooth transition into the heavenly realms of the universe. Under the seraphim and cherubim is a celestial hierarchy of a multitude of angelic orders that oversee different aspects of creation within the universal body of the primal serpent.

Below the angelic serpents of wisdom are the orders of the extraterrestrial Serpents of Wisdom who inhabit planets, star systems, and galaxies. As intergalactic and interstellar ambassadors, they move freely among various planets and star groups via the immortal dragon bodies or very advanced spacecraft.

It is known that sometimes they travel to new evolving galaxies in order to assist certain life-forms through their evolutionary stages of growth and development. For millions of years, extraterrestrials have been coming to our solar system to assist in evolution. When a planet and its inhabitants reach a pivotal stage in their evolution, the extraterrestrial serpents often travel there to help facilitate a paradigm shift.

Many of the extraterrestrials chose to come to Earth and assist the human race at the beginning of 104,000 years. This major cycle was considered particularly important as it was destined to end in a unique evolutionary advancement for both the Earth and her children. This wisdom that was brought to Earth in the beginning of this cycle has been divided into four parts or worlds. Each world has been approximately twenty-six thousand years, the length of the precession of the equinoxes, or the number of years required for the solar system to travel through the twelve signs of the zodiac.

According to many of the pre-Christian traditions, every major cycle of time begins with the birth of the serpent goddess, followed by her division into twin dragon lands. The ubiquitous allegory symbolically refers to the creation of the serpent life force, which is given birth to by the spirit at the start of each new cycle of time before dividing into its male/female component parts (positive and negative, matter and antimatter), thereby ensuring the preservation of the universe.

As a reflection of this archetypal model, the current 104,000-year cycle began with the fresh infusion of life force on Earth and the division of the planet's landmasses into two polar opposites, or twin dragon lands. These lands are known historically as Atlantis and Lemuria, and they existed at opposite ends of the planet in what is now the Atlantic and Pacific. They are remembered in world mythology as gardens of Eden, cradles of civilizations, dragon lands, and motherlands.

Each land displayed a civilization consistent with the nature of the polarity it embodied. Lemuria reflected the positive polarity and spiritual principle and therefore produced a spiritually motivated civilization dedicated to the development of certain divine qualities such as love and acceptance as well as living life in harmony with the Earth. Atlantis embodied a negative polarity and material principle and eventually spawned a materialistic civilization devoted to analytical reasoning, technological research, and the domination of the Earth.

THE LINEAGE OF THE DJEDI

Cain the Immortal

According to the hidden wisdom of the Kabbalah, the serpent wisdom and esoteric traditions of the Hebrews and Jews, after Transcendental YHVH projected his manifest aspect and proceeded to create the universe, the androgynous deity divided into two component parts and became Adam the spiritual male principal and Eve the material female principal. In this regard, YHVH translated name "I am Eve" can be expressed as Adam Eve. Adam and Eve were placed in the garden of Eden to mate or reunite in order to produce Cain, the firstborn son. Cain was thus Adam and Eve reunited as YHVH manifests aspect of the androgynous primal serpent, and for this reason, Helena Blavatsky rightfully asserts the Lord God is Cain esoterically and the tempting serpent as well. In the Kabbalistic mysteries, Cain, birthed as the androgynous fire serpent, was revealed in a mysterious allegory that describes an illicit combination between God and Eve. Cain, whose name means both "smith," a worker with fire and the possessor of fire, thus inherited the nature of the serpent fire from his father.

The myth of Cain's mysterious birth and fiery nature was apparently adopted in the Hebrew traditions from its earlier parent orders. It appears as though he may have been a direct evolution of Vulcan, the Atlantean fire serpent.

Besides denoting the primal fire serpent, the name Cain has further implications. It also referred to a lineage of early adepts who were the possessors of the serpent fire. Cain is apparently a title for the fire lineage of Thoth Hermes from Atlantis and Egypt. The city that which Cain built and named Enoch is most likely the pyramid city built by Thoth Hermes on the Giza Plateau. This seems probable since Enoch means "initiator" and the Egyptian city of initiation was synonymous with the pyramids of Giza. Enoch's sacred number is 365, which has been found repeatedly encoded into the Great Pyramid.

Enoch, the Transmitter of the Holy Fire

The master Enoch is either the third or seventh patriarch of the Hebrews, depending on which generation list is used, Seth or Cain's. As third patriarch, Enoch would have been a teacher and a manifestation of the divine mind of God. Three is the number of communication. As seventh patriarch, Enoch would have been the carrier of the power of death and transformation. (Seven is the number of death.) Since he is associated with the numbers, Enoch appears to have been both a true teacher and transforming master.

Like Cain before him, Enoch was a possessor and transmitter of fire. His name denotes "enlightened seer" and "initiator," one who initiates through the transmissions of the holy fire. And like his predecessor Cain, Enoch also apparently refers to one or more masters in the lineage of Thoth, a truth that becomes nearly irrefutable in the light of their identical legends and the fact that, in the esoteric records of the Arabs, they are both referred to by the same name, Idris. Both Enoch and Thoth were manifestations of the divine mind of God and prophets of that aspect of the spiritual wisdom known as the sacred science, which is science united with spiritual principles. Each was associated with the design and construction of certain sacred edifices, including the Great Pyramid of Giza, and both are mentioned as prediluvian masters who preserve the mystery teachings once the floodwaters had subsided.

The brazen serpent was an ancient motif of spiritual resurrection and everlasting life, which the Jedi priest Moses had taken with him out of Egypt during a time when the reigning pharaoh Ramses issued a decree in which all the firstborn male children of the Hebrews were murdered. In order to save Moses, his mother placed him in a reed basket and then set it afloat on the Nile River. He was found by Pharaoh's sister, who took him into their home and raised him as her own.

While growing up within the Egyptian royal family, Moses accorded all the privileges of an Egyptian prince, including entrance into the ancient mystery schools of Khem. According to both Strabo and Manetho, part of Moses' training occurred at the Academy of Heliopolis, where he received ordination as a Djhedi priest within the king's chamber of the Great Pyramid. As a result of his initiation, Moses acquired the supernatural abilities of an Egyptian magician and carried a staff or rod as the symbol of his power.

Moses' serpent power grew until it exceeded that of most magician priests of Egypt. Examples of his superior power are found throughout the book of Exodus. When Moses had to compete with the pharaoh's chosen magicians, his staff turned into a live snake and easily consumed their rods that had transformed to snakes, thereby symbolizing their superiority of his serpent power over theirs. While using his immense power, Moses proceeded to create the plagues and disasters that finally convinced the pharaoh to free the enslaved Israelites.

When Moses left Egypt for Palestine, he took with him all the ancient wisdom instruments and rites of the ancient Djedhi priesthood, and with this knowledge, he began his tenure as a high Levite priest of the Hebrews by designing a temple modeled after the temples of the Djedhi. His temple is referred to in the Bible as "the tabernacle in the desert." Moses' temple had sixty pillars, the number of the Egyptian cycle, and opened to the east like in an Egyptian secular temple. It also reflected the function of the Egyptian initiation chamber by serving as an alchemical crucible for the union of polarity. Moses hired a representative of the tribe of Dan, whose symbol was the snake (female principle), and one member to the tribe of Judah, whose symbol was the solar lion (male principle) to oversee the temple's construction.

The later Solomon's Temple reflected Moses' tabernacle and similarly united the polarity. Besides possessing columns and cherubs similar to the tabernacle, Solomon's Temple further precipitated the union of polarity by incorporating strategically placed metal rods in its design. The rods united the water channels (representing the female principle), which ran under the temple to golden spires (representing the male principle) on the temple roof, thereby completing the fusion of heaven and Earth.

Because of the spiritual guidance of Moses as well as the arcane legacy of Abraham, a Hebrew order of serpents called the "School of the Prophets" eventually crystallized. The secret wisdom of this school of the Kabbalah or secret mysteries coalesced as a synthesis of the knowledge Moses had acquired in Egypt and on Mount Sinai, along with the wisdom that Abraham had brought out of the Kabbalah.

The School of Prophets is first mentioned in the Bible as a group of itinerant prophets occasionally meeting to prophecy together under the watchful eye of the master, the Levite Samuel. This roaming band of prophets eventually acquired a fixed location for a school upon the summit of Mount Carmel, where they built a compound of buildings. Some of the buildings served as monasteries for the resident prophets while others were used as teaching facilities and initiation temples for prophets in training. Famous prophets that studied at the school were Elijah, Elisha, and Jesus Christ.

From their seat on Mount Carmel, the Hebrew Order of Serpents sent and received communication from branches of Serpents of Wisdom from around the world. According to ancient Rosicrucian records, the prophets would occasionally exchange communiques with the Djhedi priesthood of Heliopolis in Egypt. Supposedly at one time, some very valuable records were transferred from the sun temple at Heliopolis for safekeeping. Later these records were carried to the eastern headquarters of the serpents in Tibet and supposedly continue to exist there in a hidden underground vault.

One important branch of the school of prophets was the Essenes. This branch of the Hebrew Serpents of Wisdom served as a vehicle for bringing the ancient mystery teachings from Mt. Carmel as well as founding communities based upon their spiritual principles. Another very important reason for the Essene order was to act as a vehicle for the birth of a divine son, a Messiah who was destined to be born among the Jews. Since the days of the prophet Isaiah, the imminent birth of a teacher and a savior who would establish God's kingdom on Earth was spoken about and anxiously awaited by the initiates of the school of prophets for the reception of this divine leader on Earth.

From out of the Essene sect of Nazaria, a man and women were eventually chosen to act as vehicles for the prophesied Messiah. The communities of Nazaria or Nazarenes have accordingly existed along the banks of the Jordan River for at least 150 years preceding the birth of Jesus. At the time, she was chosen out of a special group of Nazarene virgins. Mary, mother-to-be, was only twelve years old. Her partner Joseph was a carpenter and a high-ranking member of the Nazarenes.

When the birth of Jesus finally occurred, news of a Messiah and future grandmaster of both Hebrew and worldwide Serpents of Wisdom rapidly spread throughout Asia, Europe, and Africa. Some branches of the Serpents (the Magi) sent representatives laden with gifts for the divine infant.

Jesus's spiritual education began as soon as his parents were safe from fleeing the murderous decrees of King Herod and reached safe haven in Egypt. While sitting along the quiet banks of Lake Moeris and listening to discourses from masters of the Essene community of Therapetus, Jesus embedded his first philosophical doctrines and experienced the first extrasensory revelations. Then when safety to his return to Palestine was assured, Jesus was rushed back home and placed under the care of certain esteemed Essene rabbis who were well-versed in the Torah, Talmud, and other traditional Jewish sects. While under their tutorship, the young Jesus accompanied his Essene masters to the temple and even participated in their scriptural debates.

When Jesus was just thirteen years of age, the age a Jew officially becomes a man, he left Palestine and set off to study other Serpents of Wisdom around the globe. His subsequent adventures are currently mentioned within various records.

In the first leg of Jesus's journey, a two-year passage through the deserts of Asia ended safely in India, in the land of Bharat. Jesus became a faithful student of the ancient Vadata philosophy and learned the path of yoga from numerous Mahanga and Siddhas. Jesus also went on pilgrimages and visited many of India's holiest cities and shrines, including the holy city of serpents Kashia and the famous Jagarath temple in Orissa.

Leaving India at the age of twenty-six, Jesus traveled first to Persepolis, the capital of Persia, where he studied the teachings of Zoroaster under the tutelage of the Magi priests. Continuing west, he journeyed to Athens in order to study with the renowned Greek philosophy, and from there, he passed into Egypt via the port of Alexandria. Once upon the soil of ancient Khem, Jesus was escorted by high-ranking Djhedi initiates to Heliopolis, where he learned the wisdom of Thoth while preparing for his final initiation in the Great Pyramid.

Jesus Christ, grandmaster of the Serpents of Wisdom, had his pivotal Egyptian initiation occur on a prearranged auspicious night while members of both the extraterrestrial and planetary Orders of Serpents watched with great anticipation. Jesus was escorted through the paws of the Sphinx and into the holy of holies, the king's chamber. Here he was directed by presiding Djhedi to lay down in the ancient sarcophagus while the mantras of Thoth were recited over his corpse. The fiery transformational process of the upward Kundalini was then officially consummated.

When Jesus finally arose from his tomb three days later, he did so as a resurrected Djhedi. Surrounding his sarcophagus in a moment of glory were the highest Djhedi masters of Egypt, who proceeded to officiate a coronation ceremony in his honor. Having succeeded in achieving a level of consciousness higher than any other soul on Earth, Jesus was anointed not only as a Djhedi priest but grandmaster over the entire worldwide Order of Serpents. He was no longer simply Jesus, but Priest-King of the Earth. He became a Christ, which, with its hard K sound, became an immortal Serpent of Wisdom.

From the etheric realm, the immortal Kumaras also acknowledged Jesus's newly acquired high spiritual status from their omniscient

Anthony Kaminski

perspective. However, Jesus's enlightenment was not new. He had simply removed the veil of ignorance that separated him from his true soul vibration and identity that of Avatar Sananda Kumara. As an avatar, an eternally illuminated Son of God, Jesus had taken numerous incarnations during the current cycle for the spiritual uplifting of Earth's inhabitants. Apparently the first of his impediments during the 104,000-year cycle was that of the Lemurian Avatar Sanada Kumara, who had arrived with his brothers' other immortal avatar, Jesus Christ. Sanada Kumara's mission would be to complete the work he had begun at the beginning cycle by preparing humankind for the projected end times (end of the cycle), a period when there would be an opportunity for souls to achieve immortality en masse. This he would do by revealing the timeless venisian path of polarity through both yoga and love.

The serpent is a most ancient and primordial symbol in human consciousness. Mythologies throughout the world abound with stories about snakes and their relation with humans. In Genesis, the serpent tempted Eve to taste of the fruit of the Tree of Knowledge, driving her and Adam forever out of paradise.

Interestingly the Gnostic Christians held a different view of the serpent. The Gnostics believed in direct contact with the divine without the need for intercession; thus they were not popular with church of Rome. To the Gnostics, the serpent was a hero, not a villain. By persuading Eve to partake of the fruit of knowledge, the serpent lead humankind to the path of the spiritual sovereignty. This requires man to leave paradise where all his or her needs are met but at the cost of subservience and consciousness. The quest for understanding that the serpent of Eden symbolically represents is attained by leaving the blessed ignorance of unconsciousness for the hard-won fruit of increased awareness.

The Kundalini refers to a kind of magnetic energy coiled up at the base of the spine. The serpent is feminine. According to ancient yogis, this feminine power ascends upward through the Satsuma, a subtle etheric pathway into the brain. As she enters the brain, she moves upward to the crown chakra there to meet Shiva, Lord of the Universe. The merging of electric (Shiva) and magnetic (Shakti) energies rapidly expands the awareness of the yogi. The cosmic merging of male and female energies of an individual is called the sacred marriage and is a potent symbol used in alchemy.

122

XXI

✠

THE CAINITE DESTINY

Deep neath the image lies my secret. Search and find in
the pyrmid I built. Each to the other is the keystone; each
the gateway that leads into life. Follow the Key I leave
behind me. Seek and the doorway to life shall be thine.
Seek thou in my pyrmid, deep in the passage that ends in
a wall. Use thou the Key of the seven, and open to thee
the pathway will fall.

I N THE MI5's headquarters in London, there is a document that is
referred to as the Cainite Destiny that, even to this day, has never
been explained. Shortly after the end of World War II, British soldiers
found a document concealed in a compartment in the heel of one of SS
Frederick Veldt's shoes. When the officers from MI5 questioned him,
he committed suicide by biting down on a cyanide capsule that he had
hidden in a fake tooth.

The document was only partial, and the rest of it has never been
recovered. The entry describes the moment when Hitler seized the Spear of
Destiny. When the page had been translated, it was said that its contents
defied any conventional vision of history on Naziism of which had been
known. It was believed that it was the most significant document on Earth
and the world's future is dependent on it.

This document gives an inexplicable version of the Nazi ideology
that is based on the occult. When a professor analyzed the document, he

concluded that its implications were terrifying, and the document was given the highest possible security clearance available because it was feared that it was a coded reference to a Nazi plot that neo-Nazis might resurrect in the future.

The document is called the Cainite Destiny because it suggests that there is a direct link between the Nazis and the biblical figure Cain. This means there are people out there who are part of an incredible secret history of the world that has been buried deep in time.

The Cainite Destiny is the key to something that is unbelievable and astonishing. It is a reinterpretation of history based on ideas that we have never dared to take seriously in the West. The Nazis were anything but a political party, and the war they waged was unlike anything that had ever gone on before. They were more like religious zealots fighting a crusade. Many of those who helped set up the Nazi party were members of the Thule Gesellschaft, or Thule Society. They believed that a mythical land known as Thule was the home of an Aryan master race who later populated Atlantis. A central part of the Nazi dream was to create Atlantis on a global scale. A member of the Thule Society chose the ancient Aryan symbol as the Nazi emblem. The SS had a specialized division called the Ahnenerbe whose task was to find scientific and anthropological evidence to support the Thule Society. They went on expeditions to Tibet to uncover the legend that the descendants of the original master race of Atlantis had settled there.

The legend described huge underground cities in Tibet where the descendants of the first master race still lived in the high-tech cities in a subterranean paradise. These hidden Aryans were masters of an astonishing power known as Vril. It was one of the tasks of the Ahnenerbe to make contact with the people in these cities and learn the secrets of the Vril. Right up to the end of the Second World War, the Nazis believed a secret weapon would save them. The weapon they had in mind was Vril. When Russian troops entered Berlin in 1945, they made one of the most extraordinary discoveries of the war. They found a thousand Tibetan monks dressed in SS uniforms who all committed suicide. These monks were the Third Reich's last futile attempt to harness Vril as a weapon of mass destruction against the Russians.

The two secret societies that worked together to create the Nazi Party were the Thule Gesellschaft and the Vril Society. For those who want to know anything about how Hitler rose to power, these two societies need heavy consideration by any researchers, be they believe in what these societies adopted as truth or not. They both influenced the political climate in Germany behind the scenes and were the forces that helped to bring Hitler to power.

The Thule Society (*Thule-Gesellschaft*), originally the *Studiengruppe für Germanisches Altertum* (Study Group for Germanic Antiquity), was a German occultist and *völkisch* (group for the people) in Munich, named after a mythical northern country from Greek legend. The society is notable chiefly as the organization that sponsored the Deutsche Arbeiterpartei, which Adolf Hitler later transformed into the Nazi Party.

The primary focus of Thule-Gesellschaft was a claim concerning the origins of the Aryan race. "Thule" was a land located by geographers in the farthest north, said by Nazi mystics to be the capital of ancient Hyperborea. They identified Ultima Thule as a lost ancient landmass in the extreme north, near Greenland or Iceland. These ideas derived from earlier that a lost landmass had once existed in the Atlantic and it was the home of the Aryan race, a theory reference to the distribution of Swastika motifs supported. He identified this with Plato's Atlantis, a theory further developed by Helena Blavatsky. Thule-Gesellschaft maintained close contacts with Theosophists who were the followers of Blavatsky. Just like Freemasonry and many other secret societies, these orders are ancient and have survived throughout history under different names but always had the same mission and agenda.

In our world everyone knows about the Wright Brothers and how they where the pioneers of flight in or day. But what about the Vril sisters? The Vril Society is the inner circle of Thule, and they work with the US government and have done so since the end of World War II when German Thule and Vril members were secretly moved over to the United States in a project called Operation Paperclip. The Vril Society was founded as "The All German Society for Metaphysics" in 1921 to explore the origins of the Aryan race, to seek contact with the hidden masters of Ultima Thule, and to practice meditation and other techniques intended to strengthen individual mastery of the divine Vril force itself. It was formed by a group of female psychic mediums led by the Thule-Gesellschaft medium Maria Orsitsch (Orsic) of Zagreb, who claimed to have received communication from Aryan aliens living on Alpha Tauri in the Aldebaran system. Allegedly these aliens had visited Earth and settled in Sumeria, and the word "Vril" was allegedly formed from the ancient Sumerian word Vri-Il, "like god." Some other sources state that a group of Rosicrucians founded the Vril Society in Berlin before the end of the nineteenth century. The Vril Society was also known as the Luminous Lodge, or the Lodge of Light, though others claim it was originally called the Brothers of the Light and its purpose was the realization of the great work.

Not only did the society allegedly teach concentration exercises designed to awaken the forces of Vril, their main goal was to achieve Raumflug, which is space flight to reach Aldebaran. To achieve this, the Vril Society joined the Thule-Gesellschaft and the alleged DHvSS (*Die Herren vom schwarzen Stein*)(The Masters of the Black Stone) to fund an ambitious program involving an interdimensional flight machine based on psychic revelations from the Aldebaran aliens who are actually the Annunaki.

Obviously hidden masters (the members of the Vril Society and their antagonist, the Jewish World Conspiracy), an escape by Hitler and other Nazis from Berlin to the South Pole, flying saucers, secret Nazi inventions, psychic channeling powers, and aliens from Aldebaran clearly are clearly the elements of a conspiracy theory. But as I said before, there's always more to history than we are told, and that of course is for a reason.

Hitler's right-hand man Heinrich Himmler thought of the SS as an order of knights as modern-day successors of the Knights Templar. He was obsessed with the Spear of Destiny and the Holy Grail, both of which were strongly linked to the Templars.

Years before the outbreak of World War II, Himmler sent an SS officer to the south of France to look for the Holy Grail. The officer, Otto Rhan, was convinced the last owners of the Holy Grail were the heretical sect known as the Cathars, who the Catholic church exterminated in the Middle Ages. They were the first people to face the inquisition, and in fact, it was invented specifically for dealing with them. Rahn thought the Cathars were descendants from Celtic druids, and they were steeped in the legends surrounding King Arthur. The legend of the Holy Grail is indeed actually a recasting of old fertility rituals from ancient Egypt. The main aspects of the Holy Grail stories are similar to the myth concerning the ancient god Osiris.

The Cathars are one of the strangest sects in history. Their name comes from the ancient Greek word meaning "the pure." The pure ones were known for living simple lives. They had few possessions and were peace-loving. During their time, several Catholics saw the Cathars as living much more holier Christ-like lives then the Catholic. Before long, many Catholics started converting to Catharism. It did not take long for the Catholic church to see the danger that the Cathars displayed. So they assembled a war of extermination against the Cathars. Sensing a war was coming, the Cathars knew that, if they did not find a way to pass on their knowledge to future generations, it would be lost forever. They had to come up with something that communicated their beliefs without attracting attention from the Catholic church. The legend of the Holy Grail was their final solution.

On one level, it seemed like an orthodox Catholic story, but it was actually the opposite, which was pure heresy. It's a fact that, before the Holy Grail romances appeared, there had never been a mention of anything called a Holy Grail. The Holy Grail legends actually describe in coded form the initiation ceremonies and religious rights of the Cathars but now transformed into chivalrous stories. Everything was symbolic all the characters in the stories carefully chosen. Many of the Troubadours, the great romantic poets of the Middle Ages, were Cathars, and they brought all there to bear creation of the legends. These were the greatest romances ever devised, inspiring everyone who read them as incredibly powerful heretical ideas.

On June 24, 1209, Pope Innocent III ordered a crusade against the Cathars. This day was significant, as it was the feast day of John the Baptist. The Cathars did not approve of violence, but they fought back against the church. And they drug out the war for decades. In 1231, Pope Gregory IX set up the inquisition to permanently eradicate all heresy. In 1243, the Cathars made what was effectively their last stand at their mountain stronghold of the Montsegur. The Catholic army besieged it for months before it fell in 1244. Those in the garrison who refused to recant their heresy were taken to the bottom of the hill and burnt at the stake.

According to the basic legend, the Holy Grail is in the keeping of a man called the Fisher King who lives in the Grail Castle, surrounded by warrior monks. He has a mysterious wound on his upper thigh that never heals. The symbol of the fish is known to represent divine life. Only one person can offer divine life so the Fisher King is another name for

God. According to the Cathars, those who converted to Catharism and understood the truth would be caught up in the Fisher King's net while the unworthy Catholics would swim right through. It saddened God that so many fish in the sea could not be saved. They were his metaphorical wound that never healed. Only when all humanity returned to him would his wound vanish.

The Fisher King's Grail Castle hidden from the unworthy was heaven, the wasteland outside hell. The wasteland would only disappear when the Fisher King was cured, and that would happen only when the Cathars triumphed.

So how is it that those in the wasteland could find the hidden Grail Castle? Only those who rejected their old false beliefs and started seeking the truth of Catharism would succeed. In the castle, they would be shown a solemn ceremony where the Holy Grail hallows a spear, cup, sword, and dish would be presented to them.

If they understood the meaning of the ceremony, they had been fully initiated into Catharism. The Holy Grail seekers would know to ask the king a particular question because they were still clinging on to the false doctrines of other religions. They'd leave the castle and never find it again.

The Holy Grail hallows separates into two pairs: the spear and the cup and the sword and the dish. The first pair represents Christianity. The spear was the Roman lance thrust into Christ's side at the crucifixion and the cup he used at the Last Supper. The sword was the one used to behead John the Baptist. His head was placed on a dish to be presented to Salome for dancing for King Herod. So the sword and dish stood for John the Baptist. Holy Grail seekers had to choose between the two pairs. If they chose correctly, you were a true believer. Otherwise you were damned. John the Baptist was related to Jesus by blood. Their mothers were cousins. Some people thought John was more important than Jesus was. The Cathars were the descendants from an earlier Gnostic sect called the Johninnites, who considered John the Baptist the true Messiah. Even Jesus openly said, "There is none greater than John; he is more than a prophet."

The Knights Templar were also known to be Johninites. Every grandmaster of the Knights Templar took the name John. The Catholic church accused the Templars of worshiping a severed head called baphomet. This of course was none other than John the Baptist's preserved head. Also at the inquisition, the Templars were accused of trampling and spitting on the Christian cross. Even the Templars' famous red cross was far from conventional. It was a Latin cross not with the unequal type of arms used at Jesus's crucifixion, but a cross with equal arms. This allowed them to masquerade as Christians while actually showing they weren't Christian at all to those who understood the symbolism.

The quest for the Holy Grail was the symbolic representation of the Cathars' search for God. The procession of the Holy Grail hallows was a reconstruction of the Cathars' most sacred ceremony. Many Templars came from Cathar families. The Templars refused to join in with the Catholics persecution of the Cathars, even though, as elite crusaders, they should have been the ones leading the attack. They actually aided the Cathars during the Inquisition.

The Cathars were subjected to a savage crusade and eventually exterminated a few decades later. The Templars were arrested and accused of heresy. They were brought in front of the inquisition and burned. The Johnnites, the followers of John the Baptist, created the Templars and the Cathars. The Cathars were an overt challenge to the Catholic church, while the Templars pretended to be orthodox but were in fact completely heretical.

The secrecy demanded of every member of the Templars was the perfect way to discover the truth about them. New members were warned of the appalling retribution that would be taken against them if they ever revealed any of the order's secrets. They would have their tongues removed, their eyes poked out, and their hearts taken from their chests while they were still beating. This oath of course is similar to the oath that the Freemasons make, and it is no mere coincidence. The Templars founded the Freemasons. They were the next step of the revolt against Catholicism. The papacy forbade Catholics from becoming Freemasons and accused Masons of worshiping a false god. The Freemasons' ceremonies and rites are all connected with Solomon's Temple, and the proper name of the Knights Templar is the Poor Knights of the Temple of Solomon.

Himmler thought of the SS as an order of knights as the modern successors of the Knights Templar and their Germanic counterpart, the Teutonic Knights. He was obsessed with the Spear of Destiny and the Holy Grail, both of which were strongly linked to the Templars. The Cainite

Destiny suggests that the Nazis thought they could trace their lineage back to Cain, and two of the points in Nazi ancestry are the Cathars and the Knights Templar.

On his expedition, Otto Rahn discovered caves where the walls were inscribed with Templar and Cathar symbols side by side. There were also depictions of the Spear of Destiny, the Holy Grail, and the ark of the covenant.

So if one has been astute in this long journey to truth, the big picture comes together, and that links just about every conspiracy theory imaginable: Atlantis, Cathers, druids, Freemasons, Nazis, psychics, UFOs, aliens, the Knights Templar, the ark of the covenant, the Spear of Destiny, and the Holy Grail. Everything is covered, and even more astoundingly, everything is connected.

What if all the conspiracies that the world was familiar with were just fragments of a much bigger conspiracy? A super conspiracy with each minor conspiracy theory gives a tempting glimpse of the super conspiracy.

What would the super conspiracy be about then? Who's doing the conspiring, and who or what are they conspiring against? Every conspiracy is connected with religion. What were the Knights Templar really up to? What did the Cathars really believe in? Why did the Catholic church hate and fear them so much? What was the ultimate Nazi objective? What was the quest for the Holy Grail really about? What power does the Spear of Destiny have? What was the ark of the covenant really used for? And so on.

Every conspiracy theory comes back to just one thing, the identity of the true God. What if you were in in a world where you knew the truth but were forced on pain of death to embrace a lie and openly expressing your opinions would get you killed? So to convey your message, you were forced to create secrets and codes that your enemies wouldn't notice or understand. But your enemies were smart. They cracked your codes, exposed your secrets, and killed you in huge numbers. The survivors had to create even more complex codes and pass on the keys to unlock them. What if the keys were lost? What then? Without the keys, the codes would eventually become incomprehensible, their true meaning lost, unless there was one group that never lost the key, that maintained the secret perfectly intact right from the beginning and through everything thrown at them by their enemies.

XXII

✠

THE SECRET KING

Hark ye O man to the wisdom of magic. Hark to the knowledge of powers forgotten. Long Long ago in the days of the first man, warfare began between darkness and light. Men then as now were filled with both darkness and light and while in some darkness held sway, in others light filled the soul.

RETURNING TO THE story of Adam and Eve, Qabalistic masters maintain it was not the serpent (Enki) who was the deceiver, as we are led to understand. The deceiver in this instance was Enki's half-brother, Enlil, or otherwise known as Jehovah. He told Adam he would die from eating the fruit, and Eve believed this truth. Jehovah had therefore told a falsehood to Adam, who was afterward enlightened by Eve who listened to the serpent. And so Adam was not conclusively deceived.

Its time to learn about the truth: who we are, where we came from, why we are here, where we are going, and why we have forgotten who we were. This world does not know the true story of Cain and Abel. There is another side, which reveals an astonishing truth about our origins and those that created us.

It transpires that Cain and Abel come to be the first and second sons of Eve. They actually have different fathers. While Abel was the straightforward product of a Homo sapien union with Adam, his elder half-brother Cain was an advancement, with Eve's ovum further enriched with Enki's Annunaki blood. This means that Cain emerged as the most advanced product of the royal seed of our creators.

In Genesis, we read that Abel was a keeper of sheep, while Cain was a tiller of the ground. By a better translation, however, the text should read more accurately that Cain acquired domination over the Earth. And he did, in kingship. When we then read that Abel's offerings were acceptable to the Lord but Cain's were not, we get the impression that Cain's offering were in some way inferior. But the original emphasis was on the premise that offerings were acceptable from Abel as a subordinate subject as a slave who was on his knees, whereas for Cain to make offerings was unacceptable because of his kingly status. This actually makes the point that Cain's seniority over Abel was significant.

We then move when it is said that Cain is to have slain Abel in the field. The word was indirectly translated and recorded. "Slew" is "yaqam," and the text should have read that Cain was "elevated, raised, or exalted above" Abel. The terminology that Cain "rose up" against Abel is used in the English translation, but in quite the wrong context. Abel was a man conditioned according to his station, time, and location. His blood was therefore symbolically swallowed into the ground, another way to say that he became so mundane that his life was indistinguishable from his toil. Abel is actually a translation from "hevel" in Hebrew. The meaning of the name Hevel means "puff" or "vapor."

The most important aspect of the story is the mark placed upon Cain because, although it is not defined in the Bible, the mark of Cain is the oldest recorded grant of arms in sovereign history. In the Phoenician traditions, the mark of Cain is defined as being a cross within a circle. It was, in principle, a graphic representation of kingship, which the Hebrews called Malkhut (kingdom from the Akkadian word *mallku*, which means sovereign). This was a legacy of Tiamat, who was the dragon queen and great matriarch of the Holy Grail bloodline

In accordance with the history of the imperial and royal court of the dragon, which was an ancient fraternity with Egyptian origins from about 2170 BC, the outer circle of the mark of Cain was emblematic of a serpent or dragon clutching its own tail, a symbol of wholeness and wisdom known as the Ouroboros. In more recent representations, it is shown precisely in this form. The cross (called the "Rosicrucis," from "rosi" for "dew" or "water" and "crucis" for "cup" or "chalice") is a sign of enlightenment.

And on this account, the sacred Rosicrusis was the original mark of foundation of the kingly bloodline. The cup, itself emblematic of the womb, represents the maternal aspect of kingship, where the blood royal (the waters of enlightenment) flowed.

The mark of Cain is also associated with the all-seeing eye of Enki, who was called Lord of the Sacred Eye. The aiyn is associated with the all-seeing eye. It is more correctly attributed to blackness (or nothingness) by alchemists, who associate its mystery with the cerebellum, the posterior part of the brain. The all-seeing aspect is that which perceives light from out of blackness. The very word "alchemy" comes from the Arabic "al" (the) and the Egyptian "Khame" (blackness). "Al khame" is defined as the science that overcomes the blackness or that which enlightens by intuitive perception

The term "qayin" also means "smith" as in metalsmith or, more precisely, as in blade smith, a required skill (or kenning/knowing) of the early kings. In this regard, his given name is Genesis, like that of Hevel. And like many others in the Bible, it is a descriptive appellation rather than a real personal name. In the alchemical tradition, he was indeed a qayin, an artificer of metals of the highest order, as were his descendants, particularly Tubal-Cain, who is revered in Freemasonry.

Cain's heritage was that of the Sumerian metallurgists. The master craftsmen whom we encountered at the court of El Elyon and the supreme master of the craft was Qayin's father Enki, described as "the manifestation of knowledge and the craftsman par excellence, who drives out evil demons who attack mankind." The alchemical pursuits of this family were of the utmost significance to their history, and the expertise of their craftsmanship held the key to the Bible's mysterious bread of life and hidden manna.

XXIII

✠

PARSIFAL

Adepts have there have been filled with blackness,
struggling always against the light; but others there are
filled with brightness, have ever conquered the darkness of
night. Where ere ye may be in all aages and planes, surely
ye shall know of the battle with the night. Long ages ago,
the Suns of the morning, descending, found the world
filled with the night. There in that past time began the
struggle, the age old battle of darkness and Light.

PARSIFAL IS AN opera written by Wolfram von eschenbach that is about
the knight who found the Holy Grail. It's set in medieval Europe. It
takes place in a mountain castle stronghold called Monsalvat, the Grail
Castle almost certainly modeled on the Cathars' stronghold at Montsegur.
The Grail king is called Amfortas, and Grail knights, men who have vowed
to protect the Holy Grail with their lives, serve him. Their great enemy is
Klingsor, a black magician of the highest degree who once tried to join the
Grail knights but was rejected because of his uncontrollable sexual lust.
Insanely Klingsor castrates himself to try to cure his condition, but the
knights still refuse to allow him to join their order. So Klingsor becomes
their sworn enemy, pledging to do everything to destroy them.

The Grail knights guard the Grail hallows, including the Spear of
Destiny, but Klingsor manages to steal the spear and later uses it to wound

Amfortas in the genitals. It represents a spiritual as well as a physical wound that never heals, no matter how many medicines are applied to it.

From his dark castle, Klingsor, with the power of the spear flowing through him, dominates all the lands around. Meanwhile, Amfortas lies in agony in the Grail Castle, tormented by his incurable wound, powerless to resist Klingsor, and praying for the return of the lost spear.

A prophecy says that an innocent fool will find the spear and cure Amfortas. Parsifal chances upon the Grail Castle and is allowed to witness the Grail keepers' most sacred ceremony. In the great hall of the Grail Castle, Amfortas and the grail knights prepare to commemorate the Last Supper with Parsifal looking on. When Amfortas tries to remove the veil that covers the Holy Grail, the pain of his wound grows worse than ever.

When the chalice is uncovered, it glows. Parsifal watches the strange ceremony but takes no part and doesn't ask Amfortas any questions about his wound. Parsifal is then ordered to leave the castle and told never to return.

Klingsor, aware of the prophecy regarding the innocent knight, guesses Parsifal is the knight in question and lures him to his wondrous castle. In the castle's magic garden, enchanting flower maidens beg to make love to Parsifal, but he turns them all down. Klingsor then uses a beautiful sorceress to try to seduce Parsifal. The sorceress is Kundry, a Jewish witch who was present at Jesus's crucifixion and mocked him as he hung on the cross. Cursed to live forever because of her crime, she's despicable and tragic. It was she, with promises of perverted sex, who entrapped Amfortas, which led to the Grail King's wounding by Klingsor.

When Kundry kisses Parsifal, the young knight recoils, but at the same time, he's overcome by profound insights. He understands why Amfortas was tempted, and he feels the Grail King's longing and suffering. The world, he realizes, is an unending circle of pain and despair. Only through compassion and renunciation of the pleasures of the flesh can the circle be broken. He's full of regret for the lack of pity he showed at the ceremony in the Grail Castle. Why was he so insensitive toward the Grail King? Now he knows what he must do to help Amfortas.

Klingsor, thwarted, flies into an uncontrollable fury and throws the Spear of Destiny at Parsifal, but it miraculously stops in midair. Parsifal reaches up and grasps it. As soon as he does so, Klingsor's castle of enchantment disappears.

For years, Parsifal struggles in vain to find the Grail Castle once more. It seems to have vanished from the real world. After many trials, he's allowed a second chance to enter the sacred castle, which is full of gloom. The knights are sunk in despair because they've been deprived for years of the spiritual sustenance provided by the presence of the spear. As Parsifal brings the spear close to Amfortas, the tip begins to bleed, and he touches the king's wound with it. Instantly the king's wound vanishes. One interpretation is Parsifal is regarded as a symbol of Christianity and Klingsor is a symbol of Paganism, and the story is about how the purity and compassion of Christianity triumphs over the primitive passions of paganism.

Hitler interpreted Parsifal very differently. Hitler believed it was a story about the purity of blood-racial hygiene. Amfortas' incurable sickness was caused by his perverted sex with a Jewess. His blood had mixed with hers and was now eternally tainted. The Grail knights' sacred task was to protect the purity of Aryan blood. Untainted blood was the secret to life, the real Holy Grail.

Klingsor's enchanted castle was the world of temptation, where pure Aryan blood was in danger of being contaminated by non-Aryans. Parsifal was the great hero because his blood was never corrupted by non-Aryans. Parsifal was the great hero because his blood was never corrupted. He was able to resist Klingsor's blandishments and Kndrys' offers of wild sex. The recovery of the spear was the restoration of Aryan purity. Amfortas had sinned by having sexual intercourse with the Jewess. His genitals were the source of his downfall. When the holy spear was to touch his genitals, his blood was miraculously purified again, and he was cured. The Grail Castle was the perfect Aryan world. Klingsor's realm threatened that purity, and it was the task of all good Aryans to take the role of the Grail knights and resist the corruption of their Aryan blood.

A final interpretation says Amfortas symbolized Gnosticism, while Klingsor was Christianity. The Grail Castle was the true God's pure world of light while the Castle of Wonders was the material world of the demiurge. Amfortas' incurable wound was the loss of so many souls from heaven to the evil world of matter. He could only be cured by the return of all souls to heaven. The lesson of Parsifal is that only an innocent fool can achieve that by using the Spear of Destiny. So as it can be seen, the spear is the key to it all, not the Holy Grail.

There is more than just a historical link between the elite members of the Cathars, the Knights Templars, the Freemasons, and the Nazis. There was a physical connection too. They were related by blood, and all bore the mark of Cain.

There are many speculations on what the Holy Grail actually is. The most common in modern-day is that it is the bloodline of Jesus Christ. The truth is that no one really knows what the Holy Grail was. That was deliberate of course. The best way to camouflage something is to give it multiple identities or no identity at all.

There's a special mountain in the northern foothills of the Pyrenees in the Languedoc region of France. It's almost four thousand feet high and commands spectacular views. The mountain is called Montsegur, meaning "Mount Safe," but in the spring of 1243, it was anything but safe. It was the site of the last stand of the Cathars against the Catholic crusaders to completely surround the mountain and cut off supplies to the Cathars. The Cathars had several expert mountaineers in their sheer rock face on one side of the castle, easily evading besiegers.

Three peculiar incidents happened at the end of the siege. When the defenders finally realized their position was hopeless, they negotiated with the crusaders and were offered abnormally good terms. All of the Cathar mercenaries were to be set free, and the Cathars themselves would all be pardoned if they recanted their heresy. Any heretic who refused would suffer the normal penalty of being burned at the stake. The defenders asked for two weeks to consider the terms. It appeared they were trying to buy time to allow them to hold one last special ceremony inside Montsegut, which would take place the night before the official surrender.

There is no record of what happened that night of what the ceremony entailed. What is known is that many of the mercenaries who would have been allowed to go free the following day insisted on converting to Catharism, knowing certain death awaited them.

The following day, March 15, over two hundred men and women who had refused to abandon their Cathar beliefs were led down the mountain to a stockade erected in a field. They were tied to stakes and burned to death en masse. That place is known to us this day as the "field of the cremated."

But the incident that lies at the heart of the mystery of the Cathars' concerns what four members of the garrison did immediately after the end of their sacred ceremony. The four were Cathars' most expert climbers. They had a very special job to do, one that has ensured that the Cathars have been veiled in mystery ever since.

The Cathars supposedly had a great treasure they wished to prevent from falling into the hands of the crusaders at all costs. The treasure, whatever it was, was somehow essential for the vernal equinox ceremony and had to be kept inside the fortress until that date, despite the risk it might fall into enemy hands. With the ceremony over, the elite Cathar mountaineers were able to take away the treasure hours before the official surrender. The crusaders found no trace of the treasure, and none of the garrison divulged a word about it, despite being tortured.

To this day, there are all sorts of bizarre suggestions about what the mysterious treasure was. Some claim it was a miraculous elixir that extended life and had special healing properties, a bit like the philosopher's stone, except this was literal rather than metaphorical. But as a Gnostic sect, the Cathars hated the material world, so they would scarcely be looking for something that prolonged their stay in this hell. By the same token, they wouldn't wish to be cured of any life-threatening illness. Their ambition was to achieve Gnosis and die as soon as possible so they could go straight to paradise. That was why so many of them went willingly to the stake, even though they might easily have lived.

Others claimed that the Cathars had the skeleton of Jesus Christ in their possession, thus proving he didn't die on the cross and was never resurrected. Allegedly the Catholic church was so afraid of this secret being revealed that they went to all the trouble of wiping out the Cathars. This version of events is preposterous on every level. How could anyone in those days hope to prove that a skeleton belonged to Jesus? More to the point, it was one of the central beliefs of the Cathars that Jesus Christ didn't have a physical body. So how could they have his skeleton? You can see how easy it is for the Cathars to be misrepresented.

Many people have said the Cathar treasure was the Holy Grail itself, but why would anti-materialists place any value on a material object? It's ridiculous. Nor would their treasure consist of gold, precious stones, or any other type of material wealth.

What was it that made the mercenaries convert to Catharism? They were given incontestable proof of the truth of Catharism.

The vernal equinox wasn't the date of the Cathars' ceremony. The Catholic church invented it because they hoped to wipe out all trace of the truth of the date most sacred to the Cathars, April 30, the day Hitler allegedly committed suicide, the day of the supposed end of the world. Why do you think Hitler made the defenders of Berlin fight so ferociously for so long against impossible odds? Just like the Cathars at Montsegur, he was trying to buy time to allow a special ceremony to take place.

On April 30, 1945, the Nazis in Nuremberg were able to reenact part of the ceremony performed by the Cathars. The Nazis were Gnostics, and so were the Cathars. The roots of Nazism go as far back as can be imagined. Now back to Cain. The Cainite Destiny could not be accurately interpreted. It defied everyone. The truth is always the most bizarre thing of all.

The Nazis are so far beyond comprehension that to begin to try to conceive of their true nature is unthinkable. The senior Nazis thought Cain was the father of the Aryan race. The Nazi leadership, for obvious reasons, didn't openly divulge that they were Gnostics. Only senior Nazis knew they had inherited the mantle of the Cathars and the Knights Templar. They hated the Jews because the Jews were the self-proclaimed chosen people of Jehovah, or Satan as the Nazis saw him. They were Satan worshippers as far as the Nazis were concerned. They weren't fighting a political war. In fact, it was a Gnostic holy war.

The ultimate mission of the Nazis was to assemble all of the Grail hallows and the ark of the covenant because they believed that, with these, they could somehow correct the mistake made by their alleged ancestors, the people of Atlantis, when they accidentally destroyed their own island. That was why the Nazis carried out excavations at sites of religious significance all over the world and why they were always interested in rare religious artifacts.

What went wrong for the Nazis? They failed because they were unable to identify the true Grail hallows and the real ark of the covenant. Many high-quality fakes existed, and it was impossible for the Nazis to verify which ones were genuine. Their plan depended on having authentic objects. Only those possessed real occult power.

The Nazis believed Cain's real father was Lucifer, the angel of light standing on the right hand of the true God. Satan is the monster who tried to usurp the true God. He was expelled from heaven, and in revenge, he created this world of matter, hell itself. Human history is full of perversity, but that comparison is the most obscene of them all.

The inquisition, the crusades, the massacres perpetrated by the Muslims and Hindus in India, the Boston Massacre, crucifixions, martyrdoms, beheadings, the burning of witches, the extermination of heretics, the endless litany of death, and the sanctification of slaughter was all done in the name of God or Satan.

Isn't it odd how so few people know the name of the god they supposedly worship? Yehoshua ben Yosef is Jesus Christ's real name. Jesus is simply the Greco-Roman version of the Hebrew name Joshua. Joshua is itself an Anglicanized version of Yehesua and means "Yahweh is Salvation." No name could be more repellent to a Gnostic than that one. How long do you think Christianity would survive if every Christian were forced to call Jesus by his real name? How many Christians would kneel to Yehosua ben Yosef? Christianity would crumble. Only by giving a Jew a Greco-Roman name was it possible for Gnostics to worship a Jew. A whole religion was founded on a false name. Billions of people are worshipping a fraudulent God.

In this version of the story, a stranger arrived in Eden bearing an extraordinary birthmark, a double serpent on his forehead. Through time, the myth became confused, and people came to believe that an actual serpent appeared in the garden of Eden. The stranger spent all of his time with Eve, telling her amazing things. He said he had secret knowledge of the true nature of the universe. He called this special knowledge Gnosis, and the Tree of Knowledge was his symbolic way of representing Gnosticism. Good and evil were entirely different from what Jehovah taught Adam and Eve.

So the legend arose that Eve was tempted by a serpent to eat the forbidden fruit of the Tree of Knowledge of Good and Evil. In fact, what happened was that the serpent stranger taught her Gnosticism. There was no literal Tree of Knowledge in Eden and no forbidden fruit. What was forbidden was any knowledge that challenged Jehovah. Gnosticism was the forbidden knowledge, forbidden because it was the very first heresy.

Eve managed to persuade Adam to listen to the Gnostic ideas, hence the myth that Eve tempted Adam to join her in eating the forbidden apple. What she kept secret was that she was pregnant and Adam wasn't the father. The first person born on the earth was Cain, the first true human being. His brother Abel soon followed, and this time Adam was the father.

When they grew up, the difference in appearance between Cain and Abel was obvious. They fought over their parentage, and on Cain's birthday, Abel tried to kill Cain with a spear. Cain wrestled the spear from Abel and slew him. He knew he could no longer live with Adam and Eve and fled eastwards. The Old Testament said he was banished to the Land of Nod, but there's no such place. Nod simply means wandering. In other words, he led a nomadic life. He eventually settled in Canaan, Cain's land, the same territory that Jehovah later promised to Cain's mortal enemies, the Jews, Jehovah's chosen people.

The Old Testament also says Cain was branded by God. That too is false. Cain, like his true father, had a double serpent birthmark, the so-called mark of Cain. That's why the SS adopted two sig runes for its insignia. The SS represented the two serpents. They also had the death's head symbol, just like the Knights Templar.

And the swastika was an ancient symbol for reincarnation. The Gnostics called reincarnation as metempsychosis, the transmigration of souls. Any soul trapped in a human body that failed to achieve Gnosis was condemned to be reincarnated in a new body and live again in the material world. So the Nazis chose the swastika to show their Gnostic allegiance and their belief in reincarnation as the penalty for remaining wedded to this world. The swastika is just two square SS stuck together at right angles, another form of the mark of Cain.

Cain and his people became famous for technological accomplishment, and they spread far and wide from Canaan, building great cities wherever they settled. Their most famous city was called Babylon. Centuries after Canaan fell to the Hebrews, becoming the land of Israel, the Babylonians invaded, sacked Solomon's Temple in Jerusalem, and carried off all the treasures it contained, including the ark of the covenant.

After the invasion, some of the remaining Babylonians took ships and went looking for new lands to settle in, and the rumor was that they took the ark with them. They went to the far north, to a land that legend said lay beyond the north wind. It's called Hyperborea in Greek. The Latin name was Ultima Thule or usually just Thule, "the land at the end of the world."

The people of Thule made another great journey to the most famous island of all, Atlantis. According to legend, Atlantis was destroyed over 2,500 years ago on none other than April 30, following an apocalyptic religious ceremony. The rumor was that the ark of the covenant was the centerpiece of that ceremony. The few survivors then spoke of finding a new Atlantis, a lush land marked by a special star called America. So America wasn't named after Amerigo Vespucci. It got its name because the people who discovered it thought it was the mythical Gnostic land that lay under the shining star America. So who discovered America? It was the Knights Templar, who are the descendants of Cain.

The Templars had a fleet that sailed off in 1307 to escape the Catholic church's persecution. They had no choice but to find a new land, beyond the reach of the papacy. Once they discovered America, they kept it a closely guarded secret. They made sure no word got back to Europe, knowing that, if anything leaked out, the pope would send an armada against them to conquer them and seize their new country.

It wasn't until the end of the fifteenth century that they changed their strategy. They had lost many men in wars against the Native Americans, and the Knights Templar were unhappy about having to take squaws as wives. Their settlements were failing. They need an influx of Europeans to make America viable. The Knight Templar they chose for their most vital mission was one of the most famous men in history. His name was Christopher Columbus.

Columbus knew exactly where the New World was, and that was because he already lived there. That was why no one is quite sure whether he was Italian, Spanish, or Portuguese. In fact, he was American. The so-called discoverer of the Americas was an American all along.

When the *Santa Maria*, *Nina*, and *Pinta* embarked from Spain in 1492, they changed their sail as soon as they were out of sight and raised new sails with the red cross of the Knights Templar. The history of America is largely the account of persecuted religious minorities, and the very first were the Knight Templars. America is the country of the Knights Templar. It is a Gnostic country, and it is Freemasonic. It's the new Atlantis, the cherished home of the Illuminati.

XXIV

THE MESSIAH PROGRAM

Given to man have they secrets that shall guard and protect him from all harm. He who would travels the path of the master, free must he be from the bondage of night. Conquer must he the formless and shapeless; conquer must he the phantom of fear. Knowing must he gain of all the secrets, travel the pathway that leads through the darkness, yet ever before him keep the light of his goal. Obstacles great shall he meet in the pathway, yet press on to the light of the sun.

THERE HAVE BEEN persistent references in Masonic literature to possible relationships between Masonry and other systems that use symbolic language: the Rosicrucians, Kabbalists, Gnostics, alchemists, Greeks, Romans, Christians, Essenes, Persians, Hindus, Kabbalists, and the Illuminati.

Rather than being a secret society, Freemasonry is a revealer of secrets. The great truths of ancient man were, in their time, also great secrets, and few were admitted into the sanctuaries where these great truths were taught. Today the craft teaches these great truths to all the worthy who ask to learn them.

Freemasonry has captivated the public's attention since its inception because of its reputation as a society that contains secrets. However, in addition to secrets or things known only to its members, Freemasonry is also an organization that possesses many mysteries and, foremost among them, the very origins of the craft itself.

Freemasonry defines itself as "a peculiar system of morality, veiled in allegory and illustrated by symbols." Freemasonry claims to make good men better. The symbolism is in part the mystery as well as the secret. Freemasonry derives its system of initiation of three degrees from the techniques and methods of the stonemason's trade, or those operative masons who actually worked with stone as well as biblical account of the construction of Solomon's Temple. From these two relatively simple ideas, a complex structure of ritual, symbolism, philanthropy, and philosophy has arisen. In addition, some things unique to Masonry, such as "the mason's word" and the legend of Hiram Abiff, have been the source of a great deal of speculation, suggesting that Freemasons were privy to secret esoteric teachings and occult operations. This, coupled with the length and breadth of the order as it grew, created a perfect climate for Freemasonry to become a vehicle for the promotion of spiritual ideas that were outside mainstream thought.

Initiation is defined as a beginning, but a beginning of what exactly? In modern life, where we have virtually destroyed all contact with our traditional values and social conventions, the nature of ritual initiation is mysterious, foreign, and terrifying. It's mysterious because it is something rarely heard of, let alone experienced. It's foreign because it rarely occurs in our lives, except in most fashions such as college fraternities and sororities of membership in a special club or group. It's terrifying because undertaking it requires, now more than ever, a willing to surrender our personal liberty, to trust another and then ourselves. This security is rarely physical, but rather completely psychological and ego-centered.

Initiation is distinct from religious worship in that, while there is often an element of the divine in initiation rites, initiation is not a form of worship but transformation. In Freemasonry, the candidate takes part in a play performed for his benefit so he may have specific and distinct experiences that will have the potential to transform him on one or more levels. The candidate is both spectator and participant in the events that unfold around him during these rites.

Symbols are placed before the candidate, words are stated, and stories are told that hold within them a veiled truth, a connection to an ancient and mythological period that participates and yet also transcends human history and knowledge.

Initiation takes the candidate beyond time and space and impacts them deeply on a subconscious level. Even if they never reflect again upon the symbols put before them, Masons will find their mind drifting back to one or more of the key experiences in their initiation and knowing that "something" intangible happened to them at that moment. They were transformed and connected to something bigger than themselves. For some, this bigger something is this and their community. For others, it is the Masonic fraternity as an entity of importance. And for a small number, it is the mystical stream of which Freemasonry is a distinct and unique expression. And for the most elect, the experiences of initiation can bring epiphany and direct contact with the cosmos, which is their connection to God.

The Chamber of Reflection is a unique aspect of Freemasonry that is not present in every rite or jurisdiction. The importance of it, however, is such that no Mason should be unaware of it, and in fact, each should replicate it in his own dwelling space as a means of understanding the deeper aspects of the craft. The purpose of these chambers, however, was not that of a study or a place of work but rather a place that allowed one to connect more deeply with both the material and the spiritual worlds.

Masons live in the world, but endeavor not to be part of it. They recognize their physical morality and seek to build the immortal within themselves, while still carrying out their duties to family, community, and, most importantly, the self. Since all initiations are in some way connected with death or leaving the old to embrace the new, it is appropriate that death be the major theme in the Chamber of Reflection. Yet death is just another form of birth, and as Masons soon discover as they pass through the gate of initiation, we must learn to trust in something other than ourselves if we are to find the light.

The trestle board was an item that the Masons used in their Chamber of Reflection. The trestle board is one of the most unique aspects of Masonic instruction. While it is composed of symbols, it is also a symbol itself. The trestle board is a board placed on a tripod for display and instruction. In both operative and speculative Masonry, it is where the master draws his plans and directs the workmen in their labor. In Freemasonry, it takes on the added dimension of being a form of the book of nature, or a means whereby the Grand Architect of the Universe reveals his supreme design for creation.

The three Masonic degrees of entered apprentice, Fellow Craft, and Master Mason are in what is known as Blue Lodge and are referred to in some rites as symbolic degrees. The degrees belonging to high-grade Masonry are all based on and further elaborate on what is presented in Blue Lodge and are referred to as Philosophic Masonry.

The term Blue Lodge refers to the color blue, which makes up the ceremonial decorum of the lodge as well as the tradition of a blue sky or astrological designs of the heavens, upon the ceiling in representation of the breadth and encompassing nature of the fraternity's insistence on universal friendship and mercy. That is, Masons are to be as broad and tolerant as the heavens themselves.

Given the Hermetic roots in which Freemasonry developed, it is consistent to examine its symbols within a Hermetic framework. A clear connection to Egyptian symbolism can be made here, as the Egyptian gods were often depicted as blue-skinned to show they were heavenly, nonphysical origin and nature. In the Kabbalah, the color blue is given to the sphere of chesed, or mercy, on the Tree of Life and fits well with the idea of benevolence as well as being reminded of the universal nature of the Grand Architect's plan. In alchemy, chesed is related to the prima materia, or "first matter," the secret underlying essence of all things.

THE ENTERED APPRENTICE

The degrees of entered apprentice is the first degree in Freemasonry, and its initiation gives the candidate an overview of Masonic ritual form and structure while instructing members to seek the as yet undefined light. The apprentice who has entered a Masonic temple for the first time is prepared for the life-changing moment in the preparing room. As part of his preparation in this room, the candidate for initiation is stripped of all material possessions and dressed in a strange and peculiar garb that some say resembles the dress of heretics on their way to be burned at the stake, presumably in reference to the death of Jacques Molay. This includes a blindfold and a length of rope called a cable tow. The uniform dress reduces all members to the same level and thereby provides the same experience for each Mason, creating a psychological climate in which each Mason remembers forever the moment he was brought before the altar and made a member of the craft.

It is also explained in the lecture of the degree that this uniformity of appearance suggests that Masons learn humility and to turn their attention inward rather than toward material wealth. The notions of charity and personal conduct that is respectable and loyalty to the fraternity are moral lessons each entered apprentice is to learn, and then they are to demonstrate during the time of passing from this degree into the next, which is the Fellow Craft.

The blindfold used represents secrecy, darkness, and ignorance as well as trust. The candidate is led into the lodge room for initiation but is not able to see what is happening. He is bound about the wrist and arm with the cable tow. This is a symbol of unity. The most profound moment in each member's Masonic life is when he is first exposed to "the light" at the altar of Freemasonry. The sheer impact of its presentation is forever memorable and a point of awe. And it is the point where the candidate becomes a Freemason. Part of this light is represented by the square and compass, the universal symbol of Freemasonry and among the most recognized symbols across the globe.

As a Mason, the apprentice is invested with an apron symbolic of his work, traditionally made of lambskin or white leather, both symbols of purity and spiritual strength. Three working tools of the entered apprentice are then presented: the twenty-four-inch gauge, a common gavel, and a copy of their book of law. The gauge is representative of the hours in a day, the passing of time, and how we use it. The gavel is representative of power and its rightful and constructive use in life. The book of the law represents the apprentice's desire to build his life upon spiritual values. It is up to each apprentice, under the direction of his mentor, to learn how to use these tools properly and thereby demonstrate his worthiness for the Fellow Craft degree.

THE FELLOW CRAFT

The Fellow Craft is the second degree of freemasonry. Usually after three years, the entered apprentice is allowed to pass on to the second degree and then builds upon the simple moral teachings given and enlarges them through development of the intellect. Symbolically, the apprentice passes from the porch of the temple into the temple proper, but not yet its innermost recesses.

The seven liberal arts and sciences of traditional learning create a well-rounded person and creative thinker, someone who is capable of solving problems and understanding the relationships among various disciplines as well as areas of life. These seven disciplines are divided into two groups: the trivium, consisting of grammar, rhetoric, and logic; and the quadrivium, consisting of arithmetic, music, geometry, and astronomy.

Grammar allows people to express themselves with the correct use of words. Rhetoric adds beauty to this expression so that it may inspire, uplift, and convey a deeper meaning beyond the words thought of. Logic provides clarity and reason and demonstrates the importance of a life of the mind. Arithmetic is the ability to add, subtract, multiply, and divide, which is essential for daily life. Music demonstrates the mathematical relationship or harmonies of the ancients, otherwise known as the music of the spheres. Geometry, or the "Queen of Science," as it was known, is the practical application of mathematics to the material world, as it allows for the precise measurement of objects both far and near. Astronomy, which is most likely astrology in the classical, medieval, and Renaissance periods, extends our ability to measure realms beyond Earth, enlarging our view of creation.

The middle chamber is the time of learning, experiencing the material world, and shaping it according to what we have learned. This is a period of the senses, making the symbolic length of time spent as a fellow of the craft in the middle chamber for five years.

Just as the tools of the entered apprentice are for shaping material stone, the tools of the Fellow Craft are for shaping the inner life, improving the life of the mind in preparation for the life of the soul. These tools are an instructive tongue, attentive ear, and faithful heart. These represent the need of the Fellow Craft to be constructive in his words to others, particularly apprentices in his care, attentive in his listening to instructions from masters, and faithful in his adherence to what he has received. For this reason, they are known as the instructive tongue, attentive ear, and faithful breast, further demonstrating the oral nature of Masonic ritual and instruction. The plumb is one of the working tools of a Fellow Craft, along with the square and level to represent the three tools of the degree.

THE DEGREE OF MASTER MASON: THE HOLY OF HOLIES

The degree of Master Mason is the third and final degree in Masonry. In this initiation, the greatest of Masonic truths are symbolically revealed, and the sublime nature of the soul and its immortality is received. It is here that the mysteries of life and death are revealed.

This revelation is in part done through the mystic chain, or the linking of brethren arm in arm as the newly made Master Mason is raised from the stinking stench of death into the bonds of fellowship. The veil has been pierced, and after the symbolic age of seven years' labor, the Master Mason is a master of life and able to shape himself inwardly and outwardly, to serve his fellows, and to heed the voice of God within.

Nothing can escape the rule of conscience of universal justice. This is the ultimate culmination of the first question each entered apprentice is asked, "In whom do you put your trust?" The answer is "God." Only with a complete trust in divine omnipotence, omniscience, and omnipresence can life be truly lived.

To have this trust and to build this life, all of the previous tools of Masonry can be used, but one tool above all else represents the power of the Master Mason, the trowel. Just as a trowel spreads cement to hold stone together, so the Master Mason spreads brotherly love in daily life, thereby helping to complete the building of the temple.

XXV

✠

THE KNIGHTS TEMPLAR

Turn thy thoughts inward not outward. Find thou the
Light soul within. Know that thou are the master. All else
is brought from within. Grow thou to realms of brightness.
Hold thou thy thought on the light. Know thou are one
with the Cosmos, a flame and a child of the light.

T HE FOURTH THROUGH the fourteenth degrees are called the ineffable
degrees because their principal purpose is the investigation and
contemplation of the ineffable name of deity. The word "ineffable" derives
from the Latin *ineffabilis*, which means something that should not be
spoken. As used in these degrees, it refers to the belief of ancient Judaism
that the name of God was not to be spoken. This concept forms a metaphor
for Scottish Rite teaching that all of the essential qualities of deity are
incapable of description in language.

Each culture has formed its conception of God into a particular myth
and practice best suited to the experience of the people and the limits
of their conceptions. Masonry seeks to teach no doctrine of faith except
that universal doctrine of brotherhood of man and oneness of God. The
ancients believed that the name of God possessed a peculiar power, the
possession of which could be worked for good or evil. Thus was the name
not spoken and its true pronunciation lost forever. The pronunciation of
the name as a quest in Masonry should not be misunderstood as a quest for
that power; rather it is a quest to understand that power that can, by the

same nature, keep the planets in their courses and destroy lives as buildings fall due to an earthquake.

As physical evils are but the shadow of the light of nature, so moral evil is but the shadow of virtue. Masonry seeks to provide a way out of that shadow that we might stand in the full light of the glory of God, expressed in the proper application of the divine moral sense that we have latent in ourselves.

FOURTH DEGREE (SECRET MASTER)

The white apron is edged with black and has black ties. These two colors symbolize the grief suffered by the Masons upon hearing of their Master Hiram's death and the loss of the word. As well, they are illustrative of the dualist nature of the universe, containing light and darkness, good and evil, and truth and error. The sky blue flap has an open eye embroidered upon it in gold, denoting the sun as the great archetype of light, the ineffable deity. In its center is a "Z" embroidered in gold, and around it are two crossed wreaths of laurel and olive.

The jewel is a small ivory key with a black "Z" upon the wards. It is worn suspended from a broad yellow ribbon edged in deep blue or black. The gold symbolizes light emerging from darkness. The initials C. a. M. denote Clavis ad Mysterium, the "key to mystery." The significance of the letter "Z" is esoteric and thus is not proper to be discussed here. It is the initial of the password of this degree. In Hebrew numerology of the Kabbalah, its equivalent letter had the value of seven, a number familiar to all Masons.

The duties of this degree were to practice silence, obedience, and fidelity. The lessons to be learned are:

1. The teachings of Masonry are not to be taken lightly.
2. Learning far outlasts physical monuments.
3. Duties are not to be performed expecting reward but expecting only personal satisfaction.

A candidate of this degree must ponder on the following question: may one command who does not know how to obey? The important symbols of this degree are the color black with silver tears, Adoniram, key of ivory, blazing star, wreath of laurel and olive leaves, the three pillars, and the nine Masonic virtues.

Out of all the relations of life grow duties, as naturally grow and as undeniably, as the leaves grow upon the trees. These duties form the path that leads to the object of the Masonic quest, the true Word. The wreaths of laurel and olive symbolize the hopeful expectation of success in that search. The square is a reminder that the candidate has begun a great journey. It is, however, not a simple journey. He has passed from the square to the compasses, the square representing earthly things and the compasses representing spiritual things.

The lights of the lodge represent perfection, friendship, prudence, council, and justice. Through the concepts of light and darkness and truth and error, we see the foreshadowing of the dualist doctrine that forms an important part of Freemasonry. Dualism teaches by way of analogy the idea of opposites in both the universe and human experience.

The columns of wisdom and strength are harmony. The all-seeing eye now also represents the sun as the source of light; the blazing star symbolizes the search for truth. And the letter "G" is now a Samaritan letter still representative of the true God.

The principles taught in this degree—silence, obedience, and fidelity—are conveyed directly through the obligation taken by the candidate and closing. These are also illustrated symbolically. The placement of the candidate's right hand upon his lips is a symbol of silence or secrecy. Silence is one of the virtues through which good triumphs over evil. The jewel of this degree, a key of ivory, is also an emblem of secrecy and serves as a reminder that we are the custodians of the true Word. It should be locked up in our hearts. The candidate is instructed, "Prepare yourself to command by learning to obey."

Placing the hand over the heart in the ritual is a symbol of fidelity. This may remind you of the standard mode of pledging allegiance to the flag. The candidate's quest is to learn how he may best prepare himself to symbolically use the ivory key he has been given to open the gate and attain greater light and knowledge, which is truth. He is informed that Freemasonry neither encroaches upon the privileges of religion nor claims to provide salvation of the soul or entrance into heaven. It affirms God exists, there is benefit in prayer, and man owes it to himself to return to that sanctuary that best increases his faith in our Creator. The candidate is informed that, in the fold of his religion, he should pray, study the book of sacred law, and turn from his errors. To help him discern truth is encouraged to study reason and the science of logic. Its rules and syllogisms, when understood, will help separate truth from falsehood. When we can do this, we will be able to form reasonable opinions without having to rely on others' opinions.

The discovery of truth is the principal quest of religion and philosophy. As an example of this, the candidate is told about the Kabbalah. This mystical branch of Judaism is only introduced as a teaching aid and not as a personal religious doctrine. Like other systems of philosophy, it explores with vivid detail the great question on the nature of God, the origin of the material world, and relationship of God to man. This system is introduced as a tradition built upon symbolism and worthy of consideration. In connection with this, the candidate is taught that wisdom, strength, and beauty, the three principal supports of the lodge, correspond to the three pillars of the Tree of Life on the principle symbols of symbolic Kabbalah. In this degree, nine emanations, or outflowings of the deity, each typify a Masonic virtue: independence, truthfulness, endurance, equity, justice, mercy, silence, devotion, and attainment.

Truth must be sought for in study, reflection, and discrimination. Learning is the ultimate accomplishment of human purpose and far outlasts the physical monuments erected by the hand of man. Silence is important because it prevents demands upon us that we are only obligated to perform for the benefit of a truly needful brother, which demands can be exacted far in excess of simple human charity. Obedience is not blindness to tyranny, but the proper submission of the individual will to the necessary demands of living in a society. Even among the ancients, fidelity was one of the highest of virtues. We must strive always to keep faith with God and our fellows; otherwise our obligations are meaningless.

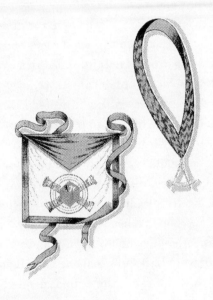

THE FIFTH DEGREE (PERFECT MASTER)

The apron is of white lambskin. The lining, border, and flap are light green. Two crossed columns with three concentric circles and a golden cube superimposed form the center design of the apron. The outside circle is crimson, the center one is blue, and the inner one is orange. There are two letters upon the top face of the cube—the one on the left black and the other white. The cube represents the finite universe, and the three circles symbolize wisdom, power, and beneficence of God, the great trinity of his attributes. The letters are Phoenician and the first two letters of the ancient name of God.

The jewel is the compasses, opened to sixty degrees, the points on a graduated arc. Masonic compasses are opened to sixty degrees because this is the number of degrees in each of the three angles of the equilateral triangle, always a symbol of deity. It is suspended from a broad, grass green, watered ribbon worn from the right shoulder to the hip. This jewel, absent the square, indicates the candidate is moving away from the earthly and toward the heavenly. The square is an emblem of what concerns the earth and the body, the compass of what concerns the heavens and the soul. The color of the ribbon symbolizes the attainment of this transition by the renewal of virtue.

The duties of this degree are to be industrious and honest. The lessons to be learned are:

1. Life is uncertain.
2. Death may call at any time.
3. The noblest portion of humanity is virtue for virtue's sake.

For reflection, the candidate is to ponder on the following questions: does one measure his age by good deeds or by years? And does a life well lived prepare you for death? The important symbols are the branches of acacia, the coffin, and the Master Hiram Abiff.

Custom and practice require the candidate to prepare a last will and testament while in the preparation room for the degree. The purpose of writing a will or contemplating doing so is to impress upon the candidate the uncertainty of life. Death may call at any time, and it is the duty of every Mason to provide for his family and loved ones.

The square, compasses, gavel, and rule, emblems of the virtues and authority of the deceased, are placed upon the coffin. Branches of acacia are given to all the brothers and are symbolic to immortality. In morals and dogma, Pike expands upon the practice of honesty and industry so that, upon death, whenever that should be, others may look upon us and we may look upon ourselves as having accomplished as much as possible honestly.

Industry

Idleness is the burial of a living man, For an idle person is so useless to any purposes of God and man, that he is like one who is dead, unconcerned in the changes and necessities of the world; and he only lives to spend his time, and eat the fruits of the earth. Like a vermin or a wolf, when his time comes, he dies and perishes, and in the meantime is nought

Honesty

The duty of a mason as a honest man is plain and easy. It requires of us honesty in contract, sincerity in affirming, simplicity in bargaining, and faithfulness in performing.

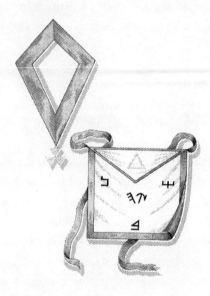

Sixth Degree (Intimate Secretary)

The apron is of white lambskin bordered in bright crimson. On the flap is an embroidered equilateral triangle. The designs on the apron are Phoenician letters; in the center are two letters that are on the apron of the fifth degree. The additional letters B, n, and Sh appear at the upper corners and one in the center near the bottom. These are the initials of the words "berit," "neder," and "shelemot," meaning "a covenant, agreement, or divine law," "a promise or vow," and "completion, performance, and offering in accomplishment of a vow, perfect, salvation." The Phoenician king presumably worshiped the Phoenician expression of the deity.

The jewel is a triple delta superimposed upon an equilateral triangle of gold. Each delta has a center design composed of one of the astrological or alchemical signs signifying the sun or gold, the moon or silver, and mercury or quicksilver. All three represent sources of light, or truth. To the ancients, the sun was a masculine (active) symbol, as well as the source of the light that the feminine (passive) moon reflects, while Mercury "harmonizes or reconciles them (that is, thesis, antithesis, and synthesis).

Thus understood, Mercury, also called Hermes, messenger of the gods, is a symbol of dynamic equilibrium, an apt symbol for the master of the lodge, who illuminates his brethren with good and wholesome instruction. As explained in the degree summary, the form of the jewel is utterly derived from Pike's favorite source of Masonic symbolism, the Pythagorean tetractys. The cordon is a broad, watered, crimson ribbon, worn from right to left, or a collar of similar material.

The duties that are required to be practiced in this degree are to be zealous, faithful, disinterested, and benevolent and to act a peacemaker. The lesson to be learned is zeal and fidelity to duty are always rewarded. For reflection, that candidate must ponder on why it is important to act as a peacemaker. The important symbols are the triple delta, King Solomon, King Hiram, and the color crimson.

Three candelabra with nine candles each are arranged to form three sets of three equilateral triangles. Similarly the jewel is a triple delta mounted upon a triangular plate. The triple delta is more of a mystery today than it was in Pike's time. In the Scottish Rite workings of the symbolic degrees, it is well known among masons in America, virtually all of whom take the first three degrees in York Rite lodges. It is a simple diagram of ten dots arranged as an equilateral triangle.

Within its boundaries are many important symbols that are revealed in stages throughout the ceremonies and lectures of many degrees. The triple triangle, the first example in the American Scottish Rite system, is seen by connecting the outer dots. The jewel of this degree is completed. The candidate represents Zabud, a faithful servant of King Solomon. The character of Zabud represents zeal and fidelity. The attitude of King Solomon convey benevolence and disinterestedness. The lack thereof is seen in the hasty actions and judgments of King Hiram. Both King Solomon and King Hiram act the peacemakers.

Fidelity and Zeal (in Performance of Duty)

To perform that duty, whether the performance be rewarded or unrewarded, is the masons sole care. And it doth matter through this performance there may there may be no witnesses, and through what he does will be forever unknown to all mankind.

Benevolence

Suffer others to be praised in thy presence, and entertain their good and glory with delight; but at no hand disparage them, or lessen the report, or make objection; and think not the advancement of thy brother is a lessening of thy worth.

Disinterestedness

It should be objection sufficient to exclude any man from the society of Masons, that he is not disinterested and generous, both in his act, and in his opinions of men, and his constructions of their conduct

Act a Peacemaker

See, therefore, that first controlling your own temper, and governing your own passions, you fit yourself to keep peace and harmony among other men, and especially the brethren. Above all remember that Masonry is the realm of peace and that among Masons there must be no dissension, but only that noble emulation, which can best work and best agree.

SEVENTH DEGREE (PROVOST AND JUDGE)

The apron is of white lambskin, edged in red. In the center is a red-edged pocket with a red-and-white rosette just below the opening. This pocket holds the plans for the temple. On the flap is embroidered a hand of justice holding a scale.

The jewel is a gold key that unlocks the ebony box seen in the ceremony. This ebony box represents the human heart where the candidate is to lock up the secrets of the order as Albert G. Mackey says, "In the Human heart are deposited the secret designs and motives of our conduct by which we propose to erect the spiritual temple of our lives."

This key is especially emblematic of that justice and uprightness that alone can unlock for us the mysteries contained in the higher degrees and enable us to advance toward perfection. The cordon is a broad, watered, crimson ribbon, worn from right to left and from which is suspended the jewel.

The duty required in this degree is to let justice be the guide of all your actions. The lessons to be learned are:

1. All actions have consequences.
2. Be just in judging others' motives.

For reflection, the candidate is to ponder on whether the duties of a judge are a burden or an honor. The important symbols of this degree are the equal balance, the ebony box, a triangle, and the color red.

The symbolic color is red and appears in the hangings and apron. Unlike in other degrees where it represents the virtue of zeal, red takes on special meaning here to remind us of the violent death of Master Hiram.

The heavy burden of provost and judge forms the basis for the following instruction:

1. The judge must himself be impartial, cautious, merciful, and of pure morals.
2. Only a false judge pardons errors in himself and not others.
3. A judge must be aware of the grave responsibility he bears.
4. A judge must inform himself fully of the law he is called upon to enforce.
5. An unjust judge will be smitten by God.
6. Remorse will pursue the corrupt judge beyond the grave.
7. Judge not unless you are willing to stand under the same judgment.

The candidate is invested with the jewel, apron, and cordon. He also receives additional instruction on the symbols found in this degree. The triangle suspended over the ebony box represents the deity as well as justice, equity, and impartiality. The equal balance cautions us to weigh carefully those who present themselves for our mysteries.

In morals and dogma, the concept of justice is explore from three principal points of view:

1. Consequences attend our every action.
2. We should be just in judging other men's motives.
3. We can only be just when charitable.

Masonry does not seek to take the place of religion, but like religion, it acknowledges a higher law than that of man.

Justice

Those who are invested with the power of judgment should judge the causes of all persons uprightly and impartially, without any personal consideration of the power of the mighty, or the bribe of the rich, or the needs of the poor … They must divest themselves of prejudice and preconception. They must hear patiently, remember accurately, and weigh carefully the facts.

Eighth Degree (Intendant of the Building)

The white apron is lined with red and bordered with green. In the center is an embroidered nine-pointed star, and over that is a balance. On the flap is a triangle, with Phoenician letters at each angle. The three colors are white, red, and green. The chief symbolic colors of the Scottish Rite Masonry teach us to imitate the purity of morals and zeal for the service of Masonry, which have made our deceased master immortal recollection to men.

The jewel is a delta of gold. On one side is engraved and enameled the

Samaritan words "ben-khurim," both meaning "nobles" or "freeborn." On the reverse is the word "Achad" in Samaritan, signifying "our only God, chief, and source of all." Pike derives this interpretation from its root, which means "first." The triangular shape is the most fundamental symbol of the deity. The cordon is a broad, watered, crimson ribbon, worn from right to left. The jewel is suspended from it by a green ribbon.

The duties of these degrees are to be benevolent and charitable. The lessons to be learned are:

1. Benevolence and charity demand we correct our own faults and those of others.
2. That which a man knows dies with him. Therefore, transmit your knowledge.
3. Labor is honorable if done with sobriety, temperance, punctuality, and industry.

For reflection, the candidate must ponder on the question: is this life more than a portal to another? The important symbols are the triple triangle, nine-pointed star, and the colors crimson, green, and white.

The major color of this degree is crimson, a deep tinged with blue. It represents fervency and zeal. The second color, green, borders the apron, and a separate green ribbon attaches the jewel to the cordon. Green represents renewal, such as what occurs in the springtime of the year when leaves bud upon the trees, more specifically, renewal in purity of morals. As the color of the Acacia, it also reminds us of that plant, a symbol of immortality.

Suspended in the east is a nine-pointed star. Here this symbol is especially representative of the divine truth. Also in the east to the right of the master are five lights forming a square with a taller one in the middle. The lights surrounding signify sobriety, temperance, punctuality, and industry, qualities that make labor honorable.

Twenty-seven lights arranged in a triple triangle also illuminate the lodge. The number twenty-seven was peculiarly significant of the ancient Pythagorean numerologists, as were all multiples of nine. For example, 9 x 2 = 18, 1 + 8 = 9, 9 x 3 = 27, and 2 + 7 = 9. This process may be continued through 9 x 9 = 81 and 8 + 1 = 9. Of course this series, twenty-seven, was deemed particularly significant since it was the cube of three, the Pythagorean number of deity.

The candidate is told that, to become an intendant of the building, he must not only be charitable and benevolent, he should sympathize with the working man, relieve his necessities, and view himself as the almoner of God's bounty, recognizing all men as his brothers. Since we no longer work in the operative craft, the intendant of the building must labor in human quarries, promoting works of charity and benevolence.

The province of Masonry is to teach all truth—moral, political, philosophical, and religious. The political lessons of the degrees are disclosed. A system of government to which man should aspire requires:

- Fourth, fifth, and sixth: an enlightened citizenry
- Seventh: an independent judiciary
- Eighth: an economic order based on capital and labor

And finally in a brief history of Scottish Rite Masonry, we learn the political truths taught here have influenced history in the world and are useful to maintain the vitality of a republic, such as that of the United States.

This lecture teaches many important lessons, some of which are found in the ritual of this degree and others not. Under the current of the primary duties flow lesser streams, streams of thought that also enlighten and instruct. One of the more subtle lessons taught is the importance of the transmission of knowledge. That which a man knows dies with him. Civilization is based upon human progress, which itself depends upon knowledge acquired in one generation being transmitted to subsequent generations.

As he does here, Pike often uses the lectures in morals and dogma to explain Masonry, its history, doctrines, and teachings and only to hint at philosophical ideas and arguments, enticing the Mason to reflect and develop a positive approach to life. This is a process in which the Mason must participate in order to benefit charity (love) and benevolence (goodwill).

Benevolence

Enjoy the blessings of this day, If God sends them, and the evils of it bear patiently and calmly; for this day is ours we are dead to yesterday, and we are not yet born to the Morrow.

Charity

Of the many teachings of Masonry, one of the most valuable is, that we should not depreciate this life. It does not hold, that when we reflect on the destiny that awaits man earth, we ought to bedew his cradle with our tears, but like the Hebrews, it hails the birth of a child with joy, and holds that his birthday should be a festival.

NINTH DEGREE (ELU OF THE NINE)

The apron is an emblem of masonry and truth. It is of white lambskin, lined and bordered with black. The candle, surrounded by darkness, represents the feeble light of ignorance, error, and intolerance, with which the world is shrouded and through which Masonry moves like a star, dispensing light, knowledge, and toleration, symbolized by the star on the flap.

The jewel is a dagger. Its hilt is of gold, and its blade is of silver. These two metals in combination symbolize the brilliance of the combined light of the sun and the moon. We also see their meaning in the ancient Han characters of China, where the characters for sun is merged with the character for moon to form the character for brilliant. This dagger is not an emblem of false bravery but of the weapons of legitimate warfare, which an Elu of the Nine may lawfully use, and especially of the two-edged sword of truth with which every Mason should be armed. A reference to this dagger is also found in the lecture for the knight of the Brazen Serpent degree, "Even the Dagger of the Elu of the Nine is that used in the mysteries of Mithras (a Persian deity) which with its blade black and hilt white, was an emblem of the two principles of light and Darkness."

The cordon is a broad, black, watered ribbon, worn from the right shoulder to the left hip. From the end of the cordon hangs the jewel. At the lower of this are nine red rosettes, four on each side and one at the bottom. The rosettes symbolize the original nine Elus, or elected, who King Solomon chose to seek out the assassins of Hiram. They also represented the nine virtues taught in this degree: disinterestedness, courtesy, devotion, firmness, frankness, generosity, self-denial, heroism, and patriotism. The color of the cordon reminds us ever to lament the prevalence of ignorance, oppression, and error. We should strive to overcome them by means of the above excellent qualities of an Elu of the Nine.

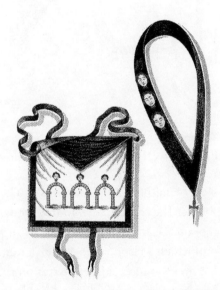

ELU OF THE TENTH

The white apron is lined, edged, and fringed with black. The flap is also black. In the center are painted or embroidered three gates, and over each is a rosette representing the three assassins of Hiram as well as those three vices against which Masonry is particularly opposed.

The cordon is a broad, watered, black ribbon, worn from left to right. On the front of which are embroidered three rosettes bearing the same symbolism as those on the apron. The jewel is a dagger. Its hilt is gold, and its blade is silver. It hangs from the end of the cordon.

The duties of this degree are to enlighten our souls and minds. It is to instruct and enlighten the people. It is to be vigilant to the interests and honor of our country. It is to be tolerant and liberal and to war against fanaticism and persecution with education and enlightenment. The lessons to be learned are:

1. Ignorance is the principal enemy of human freedom.
2. A free press is indispensable to true liberty.
3. Remorse and guilt are God's punishment and more severe than that of man.
4. Fanaticism creates intolerance and persecution.

The important symbols are the assassin Abariam, the cave with a pale light and fountain, the stranger Pharos, and the master Hiram as human freedom.

The word "Elu," which appears in this and following degrees, is a French word meaning "elect" and refers to those chosen or elected to find and inflict punishment upon the three assassins. The Gnostics used the term "elect." It defined someone who was in possession of the Gnosis or divine knowledge acquired by revelation.

In the chapter of the Elu of the Nine, the traditional hangings are black, strewn with silver tears to remind us of the death of Hiram. In addition, alternating red-and-white columns appear on the hangings. This is one of the first symbols clearly derived from the Kabbalah, a Jewish mystical philosophy. The red columns represent severity, or the trials of the Hebrews. The white columns represent mercy, or the return of the Jews to the folds of God's grace. They alternate to portray the cyclical nature of these periods in Hebrew history.

The lodge of the Elu of the nine and fifteen traditionally represent the audience chamber of King Solomon. The hangings are black with red and silver tears. These are three sets of five lights, four forming a square with one in the center. The yellow wax means knowledge and also the color of the sun, representing the deity. These two degrees are conferred together because they relate a single tale, the fate of the assassins of the Grand Master Hiram.

The fifteen who participated in the capture of the assassins are rewarded by admittance into a higher degree of mysteries and a new order called the Elu of the Fifteen. The candidate, in being invested with this rank, devotes himself to toleration and liberality by lighting the nine candles of yellow wax that represents light and knowledge. As each candle is lit, nine knightly virtues are verbalized: impartiality, courtesy, devotednesss, firmness, frankness, generosity, self-denial, heroism, and loyalty. These are not, however, the principal duties of the Elus. He dedicates himself to instructing and enlightening the people, thus freeing them from superstitious fears and subservience.

Ignorance, which the third assassin symbolizes, is the principal enemy of human freedom. The stranger Pharos represents a free press, which, with liberty and knowledge, helps to destroy ignorance. The cave is a symbol of the imprisonment of the human soul and intellect by ignorance, superstition, deceit, and fraud. The lamp feebly lighting the cave reminds us of the pale light substituted by spiritual despotism in the human soul for the brilliant light of truth. The fountain symbolizes the ignorance and fraud perpetrated by the priesthood in the past, which even now flows into the present.

If the decapitation of the assassin in the cavern were not symbolical, the incident would have no place in masonry, any more than the dagger and the odious word "vengeance." The two assassins are symbols of the special enemies of freedom, ambition and fanaticism. Tyranny despotism are born from ambition. Intolerance and persecution spring from fanaticism. Combined with the symbolic meaning of Abiram from the ninth degree, the three heads over the gates are symbolic of ignorance, ambition, and fanaticism, particular enemies of freedom.

This degree's duties are among the most important in the craft: education, enlightenment, and patriotism. Education and enlightenment are not simple schooling and the worldly understanding that derives therefrom. These duties hearken us to far higher and nobler aspirations. We must learn to guard against all forms of tyranny. We must enlighten our souls as well as our mind in order to do the work of him that guides us, ministering to our own self-improvement and the welfare of our nation.

Education

An intelligent people, informed of its right, will soon come to know its power, and cannot long be oppressed; but if there be not a sound ... The elaborate ornaments at the top of the pyramid of society will be a wretched compensation for the want of solidity at the base

Enlightenment

Most men have sentiments, but not principles. The former are temporary sensations, the latter permanent and controlling impressions of goodness and virtue. The former are general and involuntary, and do not rise to the character of virtue. Everyone feels them. They flash up spontaneously in every heart. The latter are rules of action, and shape and control our conduct; and it is these that masonry insists upon.

Patriotism

Masonry teaches that all power is delegated for the good and not for the injury of the people; and that, when it is perverted from the original purpose, the compact is broken, and the right ought to be resumed; that resistance to power usurped is not merely a duty which man owes to himself and to his neighbor, but a duty which he owes to his God, in asserting and maintaining the rank which He gave him in creation.

Toleration

Toleration holds that every other man has the same right to his opinions and faith that we have to ours

Liberality

The Mason does not sigh and weep and make grimaces. He lives right on. In his life is, as whose is not, marked with errors, and with sins he plows over barren spot with his remorse, sows with new seed and the old desert blossoms like a rose.

Eleventh Degree, Elu of the Twelve or Prince Ameth

The apron is white-lined, edged, and fringed with black, and the flap is black. In the middle is an embroidered flaming heart. The cordon is a broad, black, watered ribbon, worn from right to left. Over the flaming heart on the cordon are painted or embroidered the words "Vincere aut mori." It literally means "death rather than dishonor." The flaming heart upon the apron and cordon are symbols of that zeal and devotedness that ought to animate all Masons and of those noble and heroic souls that have in all ages suffered and sacrificed themselves for their fellows or their country. The motto is a solemn pledge that one would rather die than betray the cause of the people or become through his own fault.

The jewel is a sword of gold, suspended from the cordon, and represents truth. The Elu of the Twelve has been given the title of Prince Ameth or prince of truth, "for truth is sharper than any two edged sword" (Heb. 4:12).

The duties of this degree are to be earnest, true, and reliable, to be the champion of the people. The lesson to be learned is that life is a school and Masonry is work. For reflection, the candidate must ponder on the following question: is Masonry's work ever completed? The important symbols are a flaming heart, the twelve Elus, and swords with points touching in a circle.

Here we are informed that the previous Elu degrees symbolize an independent and free government. The nine Elus represent the upper house. They are fewer in number, more mature in wisdom, and elected for longer terms than those of the lower house, symbolized by the Elu of the Fifteen. This degree should remind us of another institution necessary for true liberty, the trial by a jury of twelve men whose unanimous verdict is necessary to convict someone of a crime.

Prior to the reception, the brethren assemble around the altar. Swords are drawn and placed at a forty-five-degree angle with the points touching. In this configuration, the brethren renew their pledge as Elus of the Twelve.

King Solomon selects by lot of the fifteen to be governors in Israel. They are charged with collection of the revenues and given supreme control in their province. The twelve are advanced to rank and dignity of Princes Ameth, a Hebrew word meaning "truth," fidelity," "firmness," and "constancy in keeping one's promises." His duties are to be earnest, true, and reliable. A Prince Ameth is the advocate and champion of the people. An Elu of the Twelve must protect the people against illegal imposition. He is to do that which is right so those who rely upon him will not be disappointed.

Fulfilling the duties of a Prince Ameth—be true, earnest, reliable, and sincere and protect the people—requires the Mason to view himself and the whole of the human race as one great family. Thus the duties of a Prince Ameth extend from himself to his family, his lodge, his brothers, his neighbors, his country, and the world.

Be a Prince Ameth

You are to be true unto all men. You are to be frank and sincere in all things. You are to be earnest in doing whatever it is your duty to do. And no man must repent that he has relied upon your resolve, your profession, or your word.

Education and Enlightenment

For it is true now as it always was and always will be, that to be free is the same thing as to be pious, to be wise, to be temperate and just, to be frugal and abstinent and to be magnanimous and brave; and to be the opposite of all these is the same thing as to be a slave.

Protect the People

Masonry will do all in its power, by direct exertion and cooperation, to improve and inform as well as to protect the people, to better their physical condition, relieve their miseries, supply their wants, and minister to their necessities. Let every Mason in this good work do all that may be in his power.

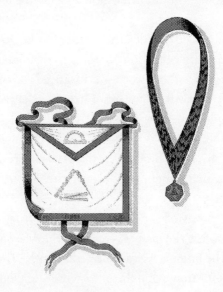

TWELFTH DEGREE (MASTER ARCHITECT)

The white apron is lined, bordered with blue, and fringed with gold. On the flap is embroidered a protractor. And in the middle of the body is a plain scale, a sector, and the compasses, arranged to form a triangle. The colors are to remind us of the degrees of the symbolic lodge, the foundation of Masonry. The cordon is a broad, blue, watered ribbon, worn from the left shoulder to the right hip.

The jewel is a heptagonal medal of gold. On one die in each angle is a five-pointed star, enclosed by a semicircle. In the center on the same side is an equilateral triangle, formed by arcs of circles. On the reverse side are five columns, representing the different orders of architecture, arranged from left to right, with the initial letter of the proper order below each in old English letters (T)uscan, (D)oric, (I)onic, (C)orinthian, and (C)omposite.

Above these columns are a sector and a slide rule. Below them are the three kinds of compasses, the plain scale, and parallel ruler. Between the second and third and the third and fourth columns are Phoenician letters equivalent to the English or Roman letters "R" and "b." These letters have two meanings, one exoteric and the other esoteric. The esoteric meaning all may know. It is simply the initials of Rab Benaim, the Semitic name for the degree. You should pay particular attention to the symbolic meanings of the jewel and its designs in the ritual.

The duty that is required to be practiced is to seek wisdom through knowledge. The lessons to be learned are:

1. Wisdom is a gift from God and should be preferred over riches.
2. Wisdom and knowledge bring honor, discretion, and understanding.
3. Wisdom teaches the knowledge of God.
4. Wisdom enables immortality.

For reflection, the candidate must ponder on the following question: are you in control of your life? The important symbols of this degree are the architect's tools.

In Masonic degrees, candidates make a series of ceremonial prescribed circuits of the altar. This practice, called circumambulation, is derived from the ancients and existed among the Romans, Semites, Hindus, and others. It is thought to have been a right of purification. The sun was believed to travel around the earth. The initiates imitated the movement of the sun when they made circuits around the altar. In the symbolic lodge, the circuits of the craftsmen at the installation of the officers symbolize the possession of the lodge by the new master. In Scottish Rite Masonry, this ancient symbol of purification is adopted to represent a renewal in virtue through the performance of duty.

The crimson flames on the hangings represent the zeal and fervency required in the pursuit of wisdom from which a new man arises, becoming renewed in virtue. This idea is symbolized in other degrees by the color green. The flames should also remind us that we have completed the earthly instruction of the Scottish Rite and will now advance from the realm of morality to that of true philosophy.

To become a master architect, the candidate assumes the character of Adoniram who, according to Masonic tradition, was the first upon whom this degree was conferred. Adoniram, having gained superior knowledge and skill, was subsequently appointed chief architect of the temple and the successor of Master Hiram. The advancement of Adoniram to master architect teaches us that the ablest, wisest, and best of every nation should be its leaders.

We are also reminded that Masons do not need any knowledge of geometry and mathematics as sciences to advance because the instruments of the architect and geometrician are also allegorical and symbolic. The different compasses represent that life and time are but a point in the center of eternity, and the circles of God's attributes is infinite. This meaning may also be ascribed to the North Star (Ursa Major) because they do not set in the northern hemisphere and, by rotation of the earth, appear to draw circles in the night sky. The parallel ruler teaches us that we should be consistent and firm and possess a sense of equality in mind and temper. The protractor represents a man who is upright, sincere, frank, moderate, and punctual. The plain scale reminds us to live not only for ourselves, but for others and in just measure to serve ourselves, families, friends, neighbors, and country. The sector teaches us to multiply our good deeds, divide what we can spare, and extract the good from the reverses and calamities of life. Finally the slide rule prompts us to strive to grasp and solve the great problems of the universe and in our existence, to know and understand philosophy in the Masonic sense, and to share freely with others.

The great duties that are inculcated by the lessons taught by the working instruments of a grand master architect, demanding so much of us and taking for granted the capacity to perform them faithfully and fully, bring us at once to reflect upon the dignity of human nature and the vast powers and capacities of the human soul.

Knowledge and Wisdom

Let the Mason never forget that life and the world are what we make them by our social character, by our adaptation or want of adaptation to the social condition, relations and pursuits of the world.

Knowledge and Wisdom

Alone the mind wrestles with the great problem of Calamity, and seeks the solution from the infinite Providence if Heaven, and thus is led directly to God.

Knowledge of the Deity

We must, Of necessity embrace the great truth taught by Masonry, and live by them, to live happily. "I put my trust in God" is the protest of Masonry against the belief in a cruel, angry and vengeful God, to be feared and not referenced by his creatures.

THIRTEENTH DEGREE, ROYAL ARCH OF SOLOMON

The apron is of crimson velvet. Upon it is embroidered a triangle emitting rays, and in the middle is a letter, an archaic form of the Semitic Yod. The color denotes the zeal and devotedness of a Royal Arch Mason. The triangle is the emblem of deity, or infinite wisdom, infinite power, and infinite harmony. The letter represents the tetragrammaton, the name of God worn by Moses.

The cordon is a broad, watered, purple ribbon worn from the right shoulder to the left hip from which is suspended a triangle of gold bars. The jewel is a circular medal of gold, around which on one side are the following letters, words, and numbers: R, S, R, S, T, P, S, R, I, A, J, es S Anno Enochi 2995. On the same side is an engraving on the ground with a rectangular hole in it into which two men are lowering a third by a rope. On the reverse side is a triangle emitting rays, and in the middle of it is the same letter, as in son the apron. This medal is to be worn upon the chest, suspended by a narrow, white, watered ribbon. The letters stand for Ragnante Solomone, Rege sapientissimo, Thesaurum Pretiosissimum, Sub Runis Ineunerunt Adoniram, Joabert, and Satolkin. Found under the ruins is the most precious treasure. Let the emblem on the reverse side of this jewel always remind us that the good Mason reveres and adores the Grand Architect of the Universe and endeavors by pursuing the path of honor and duty to perform the part assigned him in the world well and faithfully.

The duties that are required to be practiced in this degree are to seek knowledge and to be motivated by duty and honor. The lessons to be learned are:

1. Moral character is a habit, not formed in a moment.
2. The great law of retribution acts in our memory as a remorse and at final judgment.

For reflection, the candidate must ponder on the question: are idle hours and idle words subject to the great law of retribution? The important symbols of this degree are Enoch, Adoniram, Yehu-aber, Satolkin, the descent into the vault, the arch, cube of agate, triangle of gold, and name of the deity.

Enoch is an important Masonic character. He was an ancient Hebrew patriarch and predecessor of Solomon. From Genesis 5:24, we learn his life was one of exceptional virtue. He is described as walking with God. He is said to have lived 265 years, his earthly life ending not by death by being bodily transported into heaven (Gen. 5:23). We are told he received the gift of wisdom and knowledge from God and was learned in astronomy and astrology. Tradition tells us that God, seeing in Enoch a man of perfect virtue, elected to reveal to him his true name. After receiving it in a dream, Enoch's vision continued, and he was conveyed vertically through nine arches into a subterranean vault that contained a triangular plate of gold upon which was written the name of God.

Enoch took the dream as a sign from God, and after a long journey through Canaan, or the Holy Land, he excavated nine apartments vertically into the earth, each covered with an arch, the lowest hewn out of solid rock. In this apartment, he placed an alabaster pedestal and mounted upon it a cube of agate into one side of which he had sunk a triangular plate of gold inscribed with the name of the deity, thus fulfilling the purpose of his vision.

The next day, the three master architects returned and removed the cube of agate, which they conveyed to King Solomon, who immediately recognized the word engraved upon the golden plate in its side as the ineffable name of the deity. According to tradition, Solomon knew the word because he had received it from his father David, who had received it from the prophet Samuel. Solomon created this degree, it is said, to reward the zeal and dedication of the discoverers of this great treasure. In Hebrew, the name Enoch is Henoch and means "initiate," "instruct," "teach," and "dedicate." In Freemasonry, Enoch therefore has become a symbol of initiation and the acquisition of knowledge.

The drama requires three candidates, who represent Adoniram, Yehu-Aber, and Satolkin. They must descend vertically into the deepest vault and recover the sacred treasure. Many obstacles meet their descent. The third attempt is successful. It should be noted the candidate in this last attempt carries a torch. His success reminds us that, with the aid of light (a symbol of knowledge and wisdom) and by seeking ever deeper within ourselves, the true knowledge of deity will be found. When all the candidates have descended into the subterranean vault, the light is extinguished. All remain in utter darkness, and unknown voices speak of death and the grave. When the pedestal is uncovered, it brilliantly lights the room, and the brethren behold the ineffable name of deity. This alabaster pedestal represents the light of reason, given by God to man, by which he is able to read the great book of nature. And by it, he understands the attributes of the deity. The masters who discover the treasure represent the types of the true Mason who seek knowledge from pure motives.

The cubical stone bearing the name of the deity is then taken to King Solomon. The candidates are rewarded for their zeal and devotedness by their advancement. Masons of the Royal Arch of Solomon pledge themselves to live virtuously and honestly. Zeal, charity, honor, and duty lead them through life. This lecture provides foundational material for subsequent degrees and indirectly discusses the important duties of this degree: to seek knowledge and to be motivated by honor and duty.

To Practice Honor and Duty Is a Religion

When friends meet, and hands are warmly pressed, and the eye kindles and the countenance is suffused with gladness, there is a religion between their hearts; and each loves and worships the True Good that is in the other.

Retribution

The great law of retribution is, that all coming experience is to be affected by every present feeling; every future moment of being must answer for every present moment; one moment; sacrificed to vice, or lost to improvement, is forever sacrificed and lost

XXVI

✠

Morning of the Magician

Deep are the mysteries around thee, hidden the secrets of old. Searc`h through the keys of my wisdom. Surely shall ye find the way. The gateway to power is secret, but he who attains shall receive. Look to the light! Oh my brother. Press on through the valley of darkness. Overcome the dweller of the night. Keep ever thine eyes to the light plane and thou shall be one with the light.

FOURTEENTH DEGREE (PERFECT ELU)

T HE APRON IS of white lambskin, lined with crimson and edged with blue. Around it on the inside of the blue ending is a delicate embroidery in crimson representing a wreath of flowers. In the middle of the apron is painted or embroidered the jewel, and on the flap is a representation of a flat, square stone to which is attached a ring, representing the entrance to the secret vault of the preceding degree. Of its three colors, white, like the snowy purity of the ermine, represents justice. Blue, the color of the perfectly symmetrical and changeless arch of the sky, represents right. And crimson, the color of fire that reviews and purifies all things, represents truth.

The cordon is a collar of crimson velvet, worn over the neck and coming to a point at the breast. On the left side is embroidered in silver a five-pointed star with a Phoenician word meaning perfection in the center. The five-pointed star as a type of all stars is representative of Masonic light. The five points also stand for the five points of fellowship. The jewel is a pair of compasses, opened upon a quarter circle and surmounted by a pointed crown. Within the compasses is a medal, representing on one side the sun and on the other a five-pointed star, in the center of which is a delta. And on that is the name of deity in Phoenician characters. This jewel is gold and worn suspended from the collar. On the segment of the circle are enameled, at proper distances from each other, the numerals III, V, VII, and IX. The compasses remind us that science, united to honor and virtue, made the architect of the temple of the companion of kings and that the men of intellect and learning, the great kings of thought, are in this age the rulers of the world. The sun as the source of light to our system was once worshipped as a god. The star as a type, the myriad suns that light other countless systems of world, is an emblem of that Masonic light in search of which every Mason travels, the correct knowledge of the deity and of his laws that control the universe. The brethren of this degree also wear white gloves, symbolic of purity.

The duties of this degree are to assist, encourage, and defend the brethren; protect the oppressed; and relieve want and distress. Enlighten the people. Serve the common good, and be fruitful of all good works. The lessons that are to be learned are:

1. Perfect Elus are both bound and free, bound by their obligation and free from prejudice on tolerance and envy.
2. Masons meet on the level in their lives.
3. Authority and liberty are in equilibrium.

For reflection, the candidate is to ponder the following question: if perfection is not attainable, then for what does a Mason strive? The important symbols are baptism, horizontal passageway to the vault, the cube, seal of Solomon, columns, triangular pedestal, and the great candelabrum with seven lights.

This degree is styled the degree of perfection because it represents the perfection or completion of the degrees of the Scottish Rite symbolic lodge.

The crypts, one built by Enoch and the other by Solomon, have two important symbolic interpretations. The first is that the crypts are inward symbols. That is, being hidden under the earth, they direct us to focus our reflection upon the inward qualities of man, a reminder of the symbolic lodge instruction that is the internal and not external qualifications that recommended a man to be a Mason. The second is that these crypts were built in a very different fashion and must be seen as distinct, yet united, symbols. They are distinct because each has its own meaning. They are united because together they form an entirely different symbol with its own interpretation. The crypt of Enoch was built vertically. The vertical direction represents the spiritual dimension of the universe. Enoch receives a prophetic vision directing him to build his crypt and deposit the sacred treasure therein. Following the completion of this spiritual task, Enoch does not suffer death but is taken directly to heaven. The crypt of Enoch is discovered, and the treasure is removed and taken to Solomon, who deposits it in the innermost chamber of his crypt, constructed horizontally between his most retired apartment and the Sanctum Sanctorum of the Temple. The horizontal represents earthly things. Solomon was not a spiritual leader. His wisdom was the wisdom of the earth. He was wise and just ruler of men, but less so of himself. He began to worship strange gods and led a majority of his people into idolatry with him. Thus the Hebrew people were punished by their conquest and captivity in Babylonia.

Uniting the vertical with the horizontal creates the symbol of the cross. All the world's messiahs have sought to unify the spiritual and earthly qualities of man, providing a model of perfection. This is the perfection taught in Masonry, living life to the fullest while preparing for the next.

An important symbol here is the Seal of Solomon, formed by two interlaced triangles, one white and the other black. This six-pointed star can be found hidden within the Pythagorean tetractys. Among the Greeks, the hexad, or number six, was considered a symbol of marriage, and the figure drawn from the six dots that circle the central dot, the tetractys, thus form an apt symbol of this number as it creates six smaller equilateral triangles, the children of the union of the two large triangle. There are deeper and more significant meanings, which are to be revealed in later degrees.

The cube, a profound symbol of many diverse meaning, is first found in the thirteenth degree as a symbol of the Scottish Rite. Of course, it is seen in the first degree of the symbolic lodge where, as is appropriate, it is given a simple interpretation. There the cube is called the perfect ashlar and stands as a symbol of the union between operative and speculative masonry. As one of the five so-called platonic solids, the cube's adoption as a mystical symbol was inevitable. It is six-sided and formed of perfect squares. At most, only three sides are visible from perspective, and like the Seal of Solomon, it nestles within the tetractys as an optical illusion. These qualities combine to give the numerologically inclined ancients much opportunity for reflection and speculation. The lighted pedestal is triangular so the light emanating there from may be seen as representing light from the deity.

The word "reveal" means to "re-veil," that is, to give one explanation and yet continue to maintain the mystery of the symbol by not explaining it in a full and complete manner. Just how this is accomplished may be illustrated by an examination of the lights of the Great Candelabrum, not their number and arrangement. The lights are to be arranged, illustrating the seven planets known to the ancients: the Sun (in the center) Moon, Mercury, Venus, Mars, Jupiter, and Saturn. That is not the only meaning of the lights may readily be seen, by the fact that there are no particular assignments of lights with planets.

The assignment of the sun as the central light is the revealing of symbolism, as we are led to see the other six lights arranged around the central one as the planets are around the sun. This concept the ancients did not even possess. The "lights" in parentheses are not in the arrangement and are added here to show the essential form of the Pythagorean tetractys, guiding the placement of the lights in the lodge, which emphasize that portion of the Pythagorean tetractys that creates the optical illusion of a perfect cube within its bounds. Appropriately the cube is a principal symbol of this degree.

Several degrees in the various rites of Masonry require the candidate to spread a little time in quiet and solitude that he may reflect upon his character and the seriousness of the obligations he is about to take. In this degree, searching questions are posed to the candidate. He is sent to the Chamber of Reflection while the brethren consider his fitness to be received into the order. Darkness is not a new condition to the Mason who has advanced to this degree.

In the ancient mysteries, the aspirant was always shrouded in darkness as a preparatory step to the reception of the full light of knowledge. The period of darkness varied with the particular mysteries. Among the druids it was reputed to be nine days and nights. In Grecian mysteries, it was reportedly twenty-seven days. And it was fifty days among Persians. The periods of darkness in Masonry are shortened considerably and symbolize a state of preparation, nonexistence before birth, and the ignorance before the reception of knowledge.

Few religious ceremonies have both the universality and antiquity of ritual purification by water. Whether called "lustration" or the more common "baptism," it is not as is often supposed to be considered a borrowing of the Christian practice of baptism but rather should be understood as the continuation of a ceremony far older than John the Baptist. It was practiced in ancient times by the Hindus, Chaldeans, Egyptians, Etruscans, and at the greater mystery ceremonies of Greece.

Having been purified symbolically by baptism and fulfilled the necessary condition and requirements, the candidate is initiated a Grand Elect, Perfect Sublime Mason. In an act reminiscent of the ancient Hebrew, Indian, and Persian sacrifice of bread and wine, the brethren partake of the bread and wine from the table of the bread of the presence. The bread itself is a symbol of eternal life by which we are brought into the presence of God and know him. The wine represents "the inward refreshment of good conscience and should remind us of the eternal refreshments which are to receive in the future life for the faithful performance of duty in the present." The ceremonial sharing of the bread and wine are a symbol of the perfection of the candidate, his bond with the Masonic fraternity, and the secrecy demanded from the perfect Elu.

Along with the apron, cordon, and jewel, the candidate also becomes eligible to receive the fourteenth-degree ring, which represents divine protection. The motto inscribed in Latin within its boundaries translates to "virtue has united, and death shall not separate." The ring symbolizes the immutable and eternal nature of Masonic virtues and the brotherhood they inspire. It is equally worthwhile to reflect on the ring as denoting power (or authority) and affection.

The purpose of teaching the concept of a Messiah in Freemasonry is to point out its near universality in the well-developed religions of the ancient world. We see references to Dionysius of the Greeks, Sosiosh of the Persians, Krishna of the Hindus, Osiris of the Egyptians, and Jesus of the Christians. The purpose of these varying culture's messiahs was to find in human form a source of intercession with deity, in particular, one who as a human had been tempted and suffered daily pangs of life and so could be expected to possess a particular sympathy and understanding. In a word, the messiahs expressed hope.

FIFTEENTH DEGREE (KNIGHT OF THE EAST)

The cordon of a Knight of the East is a broad, green, watered ribbon worn as a baldric from left to right without a jewel. Also among the clothing of this degree is a broad sash of white, watered silk edged on the upper side and fringed with gold on the lower. It is worn around the waist with the ends hanging down on the left side. It is embroidered with mutilated human body parts and on one end a gold arched bridge with letter L. D. P. over the arch. Suspended from the right side is a small silver trowel.

The apron is crimson velvet. On the flap is an embroidered gold, bleeding head over crossed swords. In the center are three nested gold triangles formed from chains with triangular links. These represent the chains on the human intellect: tyranny, superstition, and privilege. The velvet signifies that the honors of a Masonry are more precious than the gift of kings.

The jewel is three nested triangles of gold. In the center are two crossed swords pointing upward. The hilts rest on the base of the inner triangle. The nested triangles symbolize liberty, equality, and fraternity, along with law, order, and subordination. The crossed swords represent truth and justice.

There are additional decorations peculiar to this degree, green kid gloves and a black, broad-brimmed hat with a green plume. Green, the dominant symbolic color, represents here the immortality of the human soul and even of Masonry itself. The gloves are a symbol of innocence, cleanliness of mind, heart, and soul.

The duty of this degree is to rebuild the Masonic temple of liberty, equality, and fraternity in the souls of nations. The lesson to be learned is fidelity to trust, honor and duty, perseverance, and constancy under difficulties and discouragements. For reflection, the candidate is to ponder on the following question: is equality the basis of all freedom?

Anthony Kaminski

Duty

Rebuild the Masonic Temple of liberty, equality and fraternity in the souls of men and of nations.

Lessons

Fidelity to trust, honor and duty, perseverance and constancy under difficulties and discouragements.

For Reflection

Is equality the basis of all Freedom?

To Rebuild the Symbolic Temple with Fidelity

It is the motionless and stationary that most frets and impedes the current of progress ... : the Masons that doubt and hesitate and are discouraged; that disbelieve in the capability of man to improve; that are not disposed to toil and labor for the interest and well being of general humanity; that expect others to do all even of that which they do not oppose or ridicule; while they sit, applauding and doing nothing.

To Rebuild the Symbolic Temple with Perseverance and Constancy

Masonry is engaged in her crusade,—against ignorance, intolerance, fanaticism, superstition, uncharitableness, and error. She does not sail with the trade winds upon a smooth sea, with a steady breeze, fair for a welcoming harbor; but meets and must overcome many opposing currents, baffling winds and dead calms.

Sixteenth Degree (Prince of Jerusalem)

The crimson apron is lined and edged with the color saffron. On the flap is an equal balance, held by a hand of justice. In the middle of the apron is a representation of the second temple, on one side of which is a sword lying across a buckler and on the other a square and a triangle. On the left and right sides are the Phoenician letters equivalent to Greek letters alpha and theta. The colors, crimson bordered with that of the dawn (saffron), are symbolic of faith in the justice and beneficence of God and of the dawn of hope for the persecuted, proscribed, and oppressed. The equal balance, held by the hand of justice, is a symbol of righteousness and impartiality in judgment and of that equilibrium that the deity maintains throughout the universe. The square and the triangle are the appropriate emblems of your Masonic character.

Masons, in this and higher degrees, wear the apron so they may never forget that they attained their tank and dignity by means of Masonic labor. And by remembering their first estate, they may be courteous, kind, and just to the brethren of the lower degrees. The cordon is a watered saffron ribbon, four inches broad, bordered with gold. It is worn from the right shoulder to the left hip. On it are embroidered a balance, a hand of justice holding a sword, a poniard, five stars, and two small crowns. At the end hangs a small silver trowel. The cordon of this degree symbolizes, by its colors, the dawn and light. Many symbols are embroidered on the cordon. The balance is a symbol of judicial impartiality. The hand holding the sword of justice is an emblem of that stern severity that is sometimes necessary to repress crime. The poniard or dagger represents that with which Ehud slew the oppressor Eglon, king of Moab. The five stars represent the five princes of Jerusalem. The two crowns, promised by the prophet to Zerubbabel and Jeshua, are symbols of civil and religious authorities. The trowel is a symbol of the mason builders of the temple.

The jewel is a medal of gold. On one side is engraved a hand holding an equal balance, symbolizing the justice and mercy of God, held in equipoise by his single will and infinite wisdom. On the other side is a double-edged, cross-hilted sword, with one star over the point and two on each side. The sword stand upright with hilt downward. On one side of the stars is the letter "D" and the letter "Z" on the other, the initials of Darius and Zerubbabel.

The duties of this degree are to direct and aid those who labor to build the symbolic temple. Judge equitably and fairly. Provide aid of whatever kind to princes of Jerusalem. Keep faith in the justice and beneficence of God. Press forward with hope for the persecuted and oppressed.

The lesson to be learned in this degree is we must build temples of the living God in our hearts by following Masonic truth: justice, equity, morality, wisdom, labor, fidelity, and brotherhood to achieve immortality.

For reflection, the candidate is to ponder on the following question: will you leave a noble heritage to those who follow you in this world? The important symbols of this degree are the color saffron; the Seal of Solomon; the colors white, blue, red, and violet; five steps to the throne; and the scales or balance.

SEVENTEENTH DEGREE (KNIGHT OF THE EAST AND WEST)

The apron is of yellow silk, lined and edged with crimson. The colors are emblematic of the dawn. Its triangular shape is symbolic of the deity in his first three emanations. In the center is a gold tetractys formed of ten Hebrews yods. They represent the ten sephiroth (or manifestations of the deity) of the Tree of Life in the Kabbalah.

The order is a broad, white-watered ribbon, worn from the right to the left. It is crossed by a black one of equal width, worn from left to right. The jewel is a suspended from the latter. The two colors are symbolic of the two principles of good and evil, as explained in the dualist doctrines of Zoroaster and Manes.

The jewel is a heptagonal (seven-sided) medal, half-gold and half-silver or mother of pearl. These two colors are emblems of the sun and moon, themselves symbols of the Egyptian deities Osiris and Isis, who represent the generative and productive symbols of nature, illustrated in Masonic symbolism by the columns Jachin and Boaz as the active and passive forces manifested in nature. On one side are engraved at angles, the same letters as are on the capitals of the columns in the ceremony and possessing the same meaning, that of the last seven sephiroth of the Kabbalah. A star is over each. In the center on the same side is a lamb lying on a book with seven seals, on which seals are, respectively, the same letters, through shown in this representation as the Roman equivalents. On the reverse side are two crossed swords with points upward. Their hilts rest on an even balance. In the corners are the initials in Greek of the names of the seven churches.

The duties of this degree are to work, reflect, and pray. One is to hope, to trust, and to believe. One is to teach the truths that are hidden in allegories and concealed by the symbols of Freemasonry. The lesson to be learned is an army of martyrs has offered up their lives to prove their faith or benefit mankind. For reflection, the candidate is to ponder whether Masonry can teach religion without being a religion and on what the meaning the vacant chair in the ceremony holds. The important symbols are the east, the west, John the Baptist, the colors of the rainbow, the candidate, the number seven, and the vacant chair.

Eighteenth Degree (Knight Rose Croix)

The apron is white satin bordered with crimson on one side and black on the other. On the white side is embroidered the pelican side of the jewel. On the black side is a large, red passion cross. The cordon, worn from left to right, is of velvet or silk, crimson on one side and black on the other. It is plain on the crimson side. A red passion cross is embroidered on the black side and worn over the heart. The colors of the cordon and apron, white and crimson, are symbols of light and the dawn of day and represent faith, hope, and charity.

The jewel is the compasses with points opened to sixty degrees and resting on the segment of a graduated circle. On the lower part, on one side, is an eagle with his wings extended and head lowered. Among the Egyptians, the eagle was the emblem of a wise man because his wings bore him above the clouds into the purer atmosphere and nearer to the source of light, and his eyes were not dazzled with that light. Since the eagle also represented the great Egyptian sun god Amun Ra, it is a symbol of the infinite supreme reason or intelligence. On the other side is a pelican, piercing its breast to feed its seven young in a nest under it. The pelican symbolizes every philanthropist and reformer who has offered up his lot for the benefit of humanity, and so teaches an exhaustless munificence toward all men, especially the needy and defenseless. It also represents the large and bountiful beneficence of nature, from whose bosom all created things draw their sustenance. Thus, the pelican and eagle together are symbols of perfect wisdom and perfect devotedness. There is a crimson cross showing on both sides. At the intersection of its arms, on the pelican side, is a crimson rose in bloom. The cross, pointing to the four cardinal directions and whose arms infinitely extended would never meet, is an emblem of space and infinity. The cross has been a sacred symbol in many cultures from the earliest antiquity. The rose was anciently sacred to the sun and to Aurora, Greek goddess of the dawn. As a symbol of the morning light, it represents resurrection and the renewal of life, thus immortality. Together the cross and rose symbolize immortality won by suffering and sorrow. On the summit of the compasses is an antique crown. On the segment of the circle, on the pelican side, is the word of this degree in special cipher. The jewel is of gold. The pelican and eagle upon it is of silver.

The duties of this degree are to practice virtue that it may produce fruit. Labor to eliminate vice, purify humanity, and be tolerant in the faith and creed of others. The lessons to be learned are:

1. We should have faith in God, mankind, and ourselves.
2. We should hope in the victory over the evil and the advancement of humanity and hereafter.

3. Charity is relieving the wants and tolerating the errors and faults of others.

For reflection, the candidate is to ponder on the following questions: do evil and calamity exist to provide an opportunity for the practice of virtue? Do your attitudes and actions reflect faith, hope, and charity? The important symbols are the constellations called faith, hope and charity, the punishments and terrors of hell, the rose, the cross, the pelican, and the eagle.

Rose

Many mystical systems have found the rose an appealing symbol. Its use as a Masonic symbol is therefore but the continuation and expansion of an ancient tradition. In the Grecian mysteries of Iacchus, the white rose was a symbol of silence, a virtue learned in the fourth degree. In classical mythology, the color of the red rose is attributed to a white rose being sprinkled by the blood of Venus injured by a thorn while hastening to aid her son Adonis, who was attacked by a wild boar.

In Masonry, the rose has taken on the meaning of immortality. Surely the idea of immortality is as old as rational man. Immortality is the quintessential hope of all mankind. For many, it is the very source of virtue. For others, it is only an absurd superstition. Therefore, Masonry teaches only the hope of immortality, but still the literature of the craft abounds with the expression of the soul's immortality, and time has forged it into a creed, if not a doctrine. The rose became in Christian symbolism a representation of the blood of Christ. Its merger with the cross was virtually inevitable, and indeed we see just such on the coat of arms adopted by Martin Luther.

The Cross

The cross was a sign of the Persian deity Mithra that the mercenaries who revered this god weren't thus able to fight in the Christian emperor Constantine's army under a standard bearing this symbol since to them it represented light. We should also add to Pike's review in the lecture for this degree that the equal-armed cross was a symbol of the medieval alchemists for whom it represented the four elements: air, earth, fire, and water

The cross in Masonry is a statement of infinity. This concept and the word we use to describe it contains within the borders of its meaning some of the most profound thoughts of both human and philosophical comprehension, conjuring up visions of numbers stretching endlessly before us, a universe that has no bounds, time extending within limit before us, and above all the overwhelming attributes of God. The idea of the infinity of the attributes of God may be possible for man to comprehend, but the pursuit of such understanding is its own noble work.

The Pelican

This symbol derives directly from early Christian art and represents Christ. As a Christian symbol, it has its origin in the belief that the pelican pecked at its breast to feed its young with its blood; hence it was seen as an apt representation of Christ shedding his blood for the redemption of his children, all mankind. Thus, this symbol is generalized to signify devotedness.

The pelican also is symbolic of nature. We are reminded in morals and dogma that none of the magnificent works of man can compare with the wonders of the natural world. No beauty is as sublime; no perfection is so apparent. The very commonness of our surroundings dulls our senses of this wonder, and we may become bored, even cynical, about the beauties of nature. The old adage of stopping and smelling the flowers should tell us what we are missing when we let the distractions and cares of the world blind us to the beauty and order of our surroundings, God's gift to our senses.

The Eagle

Like the rose, this emblem of great antiquity figures in the symbolic inventory: the Egyptians as the sun; the Hebrews as Jehovah; and the Romans and wisdom. The Christians saw the eagle like the pelican, as a representation of Christ who bore upon his wings his children teaching them, by example, truth and love and bearing them upward to a more spiritual conception of life. To Pike, it also signified liberty, probably because of its presence on the Great Seal of the United States.

As wisdom is attained through reason, the eagle is also symbolic of reason, the unique attribute of man among all of the world's creatures. By reason, we have come to understand the mechanics of the natural world, established societies bound by custom and law, created great works of literature and art, fathomed many of the mysteries of the human mind, and secured at least a cursory understanding of the nature of the deity and our place in the universal plan. It reminds for us to marshal its power to better ends, to alleviate human misery and suffering, to end the scourge of war, and to loosen the shackles of vice.

The Pillars

Faith corresponds with beauty those attributes, one of the supports of the symbolic lodge. We may also see it as a symbol of one of the major teachings of this degree, the unity, immutability, and goodness of God.

Similarly hope is said to represent strength, to which we may attach the teaching of the immortality of the soul, perhaps the supreme hope of mankind. And finally charity is said to signify wisdom, embodied here in the teachings of the concept of a Redeemer, which, of whatever religion, is the ultimate manifestation of God's love for man.

Besides the three theological virtues of faith, hope, and charity, we must not lose sight of those Masonic virtues of brotherly love, relief, and truth, all taught to us in the symbolic lodge. Two symbols in this degree represent the fraternity itself, the pelican and the rose and cross united. The pelican represents the Masonic virtue of relief; the rosy cross represents the Masonic virtue of brotherly love. The lost word itself represents the Masonic virtue of truth.

Tolerance

No one Mason has the right to measure for another, within the walls of a Masonic Temple, the degree of veneration which he shall feel for any reformer, or the founder of any religions.

Hope

At the appointed time, he will redeem and regenerate the world.

Charity

Greater love hath no man than this, that a man lay down his life down for his friend.

NINETEENTH DEGREE (GRAND PONTIFF)

The cordon is crimson, bordered with white, and worn from left to right. It teaches us that the zeal and ardor of a grand pontiff ought to be set off by the greatest purity of morals, perfect charity, and beneficence. Where it crosses the breast, embroidered in gold are twelve stars and the Greek letters alpha and omega. The stars upon it allude to the twelve gates of the New Jerusalem, the twelve signs of the zodiac, the twelve fruits of the Tree of Life, the twelve tribes of Israel, and the twelve apostles. The initials of the apostles' names appear upon the gates and foundations of the New Jerusalem. The columns in the set of this degree also number twelve. In this degree, there is also a filet, or headband, of blue with twelve stars upon it which have the same significance as those on the cordon. It is the peculiar emblem of a grand pontiff because the lightest contact with the earth will soil its spotless purity. Similarly the least indiscretion will soil the exalted character that you have voluntarily assumed.

Another distinctive ornament in this degree is the breastplate of the high priest of ancient Israel with twelve different gems embedded in a four-by-three matrix. Upon each gem is one of the initials of the twelve names (or attributes) of the deity mentioned in the ritual.

The jewel is an oblong square of solid gold, with the letter Aleph engraved on one side and Tau on the other. These letters are the first and last of the Hebrew alphabet, as those upon the cordon are of the Greek. They should remind us of the love and veneration we owe to that Great Being, the Source of All Existence, the Alpha and Omega, the First and the Last. On his promises, we rely with perfect confidence in whose mercy and goodness we implicitly trust and for the fulfillment of whose wiser purposes we are content to wait.

The duties of this degree are to be content to labor for the future, serve the cause of truth with patience and industry, and destroy error, falsehood, and intolerance with truth, honesty, honor, and charity. The lessons to be learned are good will triumph over evil. The human intellect cannot measure the designs of God, and if lived properly, this life is a bridge to eternal life. For reflection, the candidate is to ponder on whether one lives his life as if it is a bridge to immortality.

The important symbols are twelve columns around the council chamber, the tracing board of the New Jerusalem, the colors blue and gold, and the spirit of Masonry. The true Mason labors for the benefit of those who are to come after him and for the advancement and improvement of his race.

TWENTIETH DEGREE
(MASTER OF THE SYMBOLIC LODGE)

The yellow apron is bordered and lined with sky blue. In the center are three concentric equilateral triangles, with the initial letters of the nine great lights in the corners. The letters stand for the following: charity, generosity, veneration, heroism, patriotism, honor, toleration, truth, and justice. In the center of the inner triangle is the Tetragrammaton in Phoenician characters. Intersecting it vertically are the Hebrew words "yehi aur," or "Let there be light." The cordon is a broad ribbon of yellow and sky blue. It may also be two ribbons, one of each color, crossing the other. The jewel is gold, like the triangles on the apron, with the same words and letters.

The duties of this degree are to dispense light and knowledge and to practice the Masonic virtues both in and out of the lodge. The lessons to be learned are truth, justice, and toleration are indispensable qualities for a master of the lodge. Example is the best teaching method known. For reflection, the candidate is to ponder on the following question: is your behavior the same both in and out of lodge? The important symbols are triangle, square, octagon, candles, three pillars, and Pythagorean right triangle.

Duties of a Master of the Symbolic Lodge

The true Mason is a practical philosopher, who, under religious emblems, in all ages adopted by wisdom, builds upon plans traced by nature and reason the moral edifice of knowledge. He ought to find, in the symmetrical relation of all the parts of this rational edifice, the principle and rule of all his duties, the source of all his pleasures. He improves his moral nature, becomes a better man, and finds in the reunion of virtuous men, assembled with pure views, the means of multiplying his acts of beneficence.

TWENTY-FIRST DEGREE
(NOACHITE OR PRUSSIAN KNIGHT)

The apron and gloves of this degree are yellow. On the upper part of the apron is an arm, naked and upraised, holding a naked sword. Under it is a human figure, erect with wings. The forefinger of his right hand is on his lips. In his left hand he holds a key. He is the Egyptian figure of silence, called by Greek *harpocrates*, though the wings are an addition. Plato said that wings symbolized "intelligence." To the alchemists, they stood for the higher active, male principle.

The order is a broad, black ribbon, worn from right to left. The jewel is a silver full moon, suspended from the third buttonhole of the vest, or a golden triangle traversed by an arrow that points downward, suspended from the collar. On the jewel is an arm upraised, holding a naked sword, and around it the motto, "Fiat Justitia, Ruat Coelum," meaning "Let there be Justice, through the Heavens fall."

The duties of this degree are to be humble and modest, trusting in God. Be steadfast and courageous in the face of adversity. The lessons to be learned are the downfall of evil is certain. A free and independent judiciary is necessary to human progress. Journalism should be fair, just, and responsible.

For reflection, the candidate is to ponder on the following question: do you keep the ideal of justice before your own interests? The important symbols are the masked brothers, full moon, and sword of knight.

Be Humble and Modest

One ought, in truth to write or speak against no other one in this world. Watch man in it has enough to do, to watch and keep guard over himself.

Twenty-second Degree
(Knight Royal Axe, Prince of Libanus)

The white apron is lined and bordered with purple. In the middle is embroidered a round table, on which are mathematical instruments and unrolled plans. On the flap is a serpent with three heads: drunkenness, impurity, and gamblings. By these vices, many youths have been lost, and many great nations have sunk into ignoble imbecility and shameful bondage.

The order is a broad, rainbow-colored ribbon, lined with purple. It is worn as a collar or may be worn as a sash from right to left. The jewel, suspended from the collar, is a gold axe and handle, the symbol of the great agent of civilization and improvement. Troops armed with this weapon have conquered barbarism. Under its blows, the primeval forests disappear. The farmer displaces the wild hunter, to the rude barbarism of the early ages succeeded settled society, laws, and all the arts that refine and elevate mankind. The axe is nobler than the sword. Masonry hews at those mighty trees—intolerance, bigotry, superstition, uncharitableness, and idleness—thereby letting in the light of truth and reason upon the human mind, which these vices have darkened for centuries. The letters on the top are the initials of Noah and Solomon. Those on the handle are of Libanus and Tsidunian. Those on one side of the blade are of Adoniram, Kuros, Darius, Zerubbabel, Nehemiah, and Azra. And those on the other side are of Shem, Kham, Yapheth, Moses, Aholiab, and Betselal. These names represent the various places and persons significant in the use of cedars of Lebanon for "holy enterprises," for example, Noah's ark, the ark of the covenant, Solomon's Temple, and the rebuilding of Jerusalem and the temple by Zerubbabel.

The duties of this degree are to respect labor for its own sake and do work. The lesson is that work is the mission of man. For reflection, the candidate is to ponder if one finds himself esteem in his labors. Does the prestige associated with his labors matter? The important symbols are the cedars of Lebanon and carpenter's tools: saw, plane, and axe.

TWENTY-THIRD DEGREE (CHIEF OF THE TABERNACLE)

The white apron is lined with scarlet and bordered with red, blue, and purple ribbons. In the middle is painted or embroidered the golden candelabrum with seven lights. Josephus, the great Jewish historian, is the source of the design of the apron. He defines the symbolism of the colors as follows:

- White, the earth from which the flax used in fine linen is grown
- Red, fire from its color
- Blue, the sky, for the same reason
- Purple, the sea for it derives from a sea mollusk.

But to us there are deeper meanings. White is the infinite beneficence of God. Blue is his profound and perfect wisdom. Red is his glory, and purple is his power. The candelabrum symbolized to us, as to the ancients, the seven planets: the Sun, the Moon, Mercury, Venus, Mars, Jupiter, and Saturn. It also represents the seven archangels and seven of the ten manifestations of the deity, specifically, the seven sephiroth that follow will, wisdom, and understanding: justice, mercy, beauty, glory, victory, dominion, and kingdom.

A red leather belt is also worn, fringed along the lower edge with gold, from which hangs the jewel. The jewel is a small silver censer, or ornamental cup, with a long handle. The end serves as a stand for the cup and is shaped like an open hand. It should remind us to offer up unceasingly to God the incense of good deeds and charitable actions dictated by a pure and upright heart.

The duties of this degree are to be devoted to the service of God, constantly endeavor to promote the welfare of man, and act with proper subordination to your superiors. The lessons to be learned are simple faith is wiser than vain philosophy and a society's concept of the deity and the universe are consistent with its developments.

For reflection, the candidate is to ponder the following question: what is the nature of God? The important symbols are the standards of the twelve tribes of Israel, darkness, light, and the colors scarlet, white, blue, and purple.

The Ancient Mysteries

The powers revered in the mysteries were all in reality nature. For gods, none of whom could be consistently addressed as mere heroes because their nature was confessedly super heroic. The mysteries were not in any open hostility with the popular religion, but only a more solemn exhibition of its symbols or rather a part of itself in a more impressive form. They offered a perpetual problem to excite curiosity and contributed to satisfy the all-pervading religious sentiment.

The Mysteries and Masonry

The Grecian mysteries established by Pythagoras taught the true method of obtaining a knowledge of the divine laws, purifying the soul from its imperfection, searching for truth, and practicing virtue, thus imitating the perfections of God, particularly inculcated silence, temperance, fortitude, prudence, and justice. He taught the immortality of the soul, the omnipotence of God, and the necessity of personal holiness to qualify a man for admission.

XXVII

OUT OF DARKNESS INTO LIGHT

Now shall I speak to thee of knowledge ancient beyong the thought of thy race. Know ye that we of the Great Race had and have knowledge that is more than mans. Wisdom we gained from the star born races, wisdom and knowledge that is far beyond mans. Down to us had descended the masters of Wisdom as far beyond us as I am from thee. List ye now while I give ye wisdom. Use it and free thou shall be.

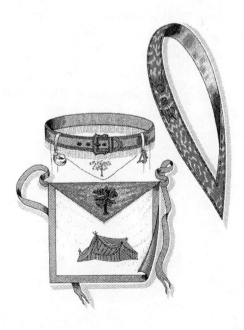

TWENTY-FOURTH DEGREE
(PRINCE OF THE TABERNACLE)

THE ORDER IS a broad, watered, scarlet ribbon worn from right to left. On the front is embroidered in gold a winged globe and under it a scarab, under which is a brilliant butterfly. All are symbols of immortality. The girdle is of light green Morocco leather, fringed below with gold and edged with gold lace. From this belt are suspended the jewel of the preceding degree, a silver censer, and the jewel of this degree, the Phoenician letter Aleph.

The apron is of white lambskin lined with scarlet and bordered with light green. In the middle is painted a representation of the Arabic tent in gold. On the light blue flap is a representation of a myrtle tree of violet color, also an emblem of immortality.

The jewel is the Phoenician letter "A" (Aleph) suspended from a short collar of narrow, watered, violet-colored ribbon. It is another manifestation of the pentagram, or five-pointed star, because the star, viewed from any angle, figures the letter "A." Since "A" is the initial of one of the principal names of the deity, Adonai, or Lord, this star is a sign of intellectual omnipotence and autocracy.

The duty of this degree is to labor incessantly for the glory of God, the honor of your country, and the happiness of your brethren. The lesson to be learned is there is one true God, who is pure, absolute, and existence. For reflection, the candidate must ponder on the following question: is the doctrine of the immortality of the soul consoling to you, a source of menace and despair, or merely a superstition? The important symbols are the grips of the apprentice, Fellow Craft, and Master Mason; five-pointed star; and the character Caleb.

The Methods and Purposes of the Ancient Mysteries

Initiation was considered to be a mystical death; a descent into the infernal regions, where every pollution, and the stains and imperfections of a corrupt and evil life were purged away.

The Important Lessons Taught in Ancient Mysteries

The object of the mysteries was to procure for man a real Felicity on earth by the means of virtue, and to that end he was taught that his soul was immortal,; and that error, sin and vice must needs by inflexible law, produce their consequences.

TWENTY-FIFTH DEGREE, KNIGHT OF THE BRAZEN SERPENT

The white apron is lined and edged with black. The white side is spotted with golden stars, and the black side has silver ones. Those on the white side represent, by their positions and distances, the Pleiades, the Hyades, Orion, and Capella. Those on the black side represent the stars of Perseus, Scorpio, and Ursa Major. In the middle of the white side is a triangle in a glory. In the center of which is the name of deity in Phoenician characters. On the flap is a serpent in a circle with his tail in his mouth; and in the center of the circle so formed a scarab, or beetle. Over this is a star of gold, with the letter "R" for Regulas over it. On the right side of the apron is another with the letter "A" over it. On the left side is another with the letter "A" over it. These last three letters have the same meanings as on the order explained below.

The order is a crimson ribbon, on which are embroidered the words, one under the other: Osiris, Ahura, Osariph, and Moses. Under them is a bull with a disk, surmounted by a crescent between his horns. This is worn from left to right, and across it from right to left is worn a broad white, watered ribbon, on which are the words Isis and Ceres over a dog's head and a crescent. On the right breast, on the left breast, and at the crossing of these orders is a star of gold. Under that on the left breast is the letter "A" for Aldebaran. Under that on the left breast is the letter "A" for Antares. And under that, at the crossing of the orders, is the letter "F" for Fomalhaut. On the crimson cordon is the word GEBURAH, "valor" in Hebrew. And on the white is the Hebrew word AUN for "force of strength." Together they mean generative power and the productive power of nature. The jewel is a Tau cross of gold, surmounted by a circle, the cuz Ansata of Egypt, round in which a serpent is entwined. On the upright part of the cross is engraved the Hebrew word meaning "he has suffered," and on the arms is the Hebrew word given in the Bible for the brazen serpent, "Nakustan."

The duty of this degree is to fulfill your destiny and re-create yourself by reformation, repentance, and the enlarging of your knowledge. The lessons that are to be learned are:

1. Man is composed of the flesh, the soul, and the intellect.
2. Man is a reflection of the divine.
3. Do not weary God with petitions.

For reflection, the candidate is to ponder the following question: is it possible to find your way to heaven alone? The important symbols are the sun, moon, brazen serpent, and the Pythagorean right triangle.

The Soul

As you learned in the 24th degree, my brother the ancient philosophers regarded the soul of man as having had its origins in Heaven ... The mysteries taught the great doctrine of the divine nature and longings after immortality of the soul, of the nobility of its origins, the grandeur of its destiny, its superiority over the animals who have no aspirations heavenward.

The Heavens

It is not possible for us thoroughly to appreciate the feelings with which the ancients regarded the heavenly bodies. We wonder and are amazed at the power and wisdom of the maker; they wondered at the Work, and endowed it with life and force and mysterious powers of mighty influence.

The Serpent

Among the Egyptians, it was a symbol of Divine wisdom, when extended at length and with its tail in its mouth, of Eternity. In the ritual of Zoroaster the Serpent was a symbol of the Universe. In China, the ring between two serpents was the symbol of the world governed by the power and wisdom of the creator.

Symbolism

Man cannot worship a mere abstraction. They require some outward form in which to clothe their conception, and invest their sympathies. If they do not shape and carve or paint visible images, the have invisible ones, perhaps quite as inadequate and unfaithful, within their own mind.

Twenty-sixth Degree (Prince of Mercy)

The scarlet apron has a wide border of white. In the center is an equilateral triangle formed of green bars. In the center of this is the jewel, embroidered in gold. The flap is sky blue. The colors green, red, and white symbolize the Masonic trinity. Green is an emblem of the infinite wisdom. Red represents the supreme energy, force, or power. And white, produced by the mingling of all the colors, indicates divine harmony. The cordon is a broad, tricolored ribbon, green, white, and red, worn from right to left.

The jewel is an equilateral triangle of gold bars with a flaming heart of gold in the center. On the heart are the letters "I," "H," and "S," and on the respective sides of the triangle, "W" is on the right, "F" is on the left, and "H" is at the bottom. This jewel is suspended from a small collar of narrow, watered, purple ribbon and hangs on the breasts. The last three letters stand for wisdom, force, and harmony. The first three are traditional Christian initials for Jesus Hominum Salvator, but which may also be read as sapientia, Imperium, Harmonia. Thus their Masonic meaning is the same meaning as the three upon the bars.

The duties of this degree are to practice mercy (forgiveness). Be tolerant. Be devoted to the teaching and diffusion of the true principles of Masonry. The lessons that are to be learned are:

1. The trinity of the deity belongs to no single religion.
2. The truths of Masonry are contained within the religions of the world.

For reflection, the candidate must reflect on the following question: what is truth? (Pontius Pilate, John 13:18). The important symbols are the number three and nine, triple-interlaced triangle (nine-pointed star), arrow, tessera or mark, and the colors red, green, and white.

The Creed of Masonry

God therefore, is a mystery, only as everything that surrounds us, and as we ourselves, are mysteries … This is the real idea of the Ancient Nations: God, the Almighty Father, and source of all; His Thought, conceiving the whole Universe, and willing its creation; His Word, uttering that thought, and thus becoming the creator … In whom life and light, and that light the life of the universe. Nor did that word cease at the single act of creation … For the thought of god lives is immortal. Embodied in the word, it preserves. Behold the true Masonic Trinity; The universal soul, the thought in the soul, the Word, or thought expressed; the Three in One, of a trinitarian ecossais.

Twenty-seventh Degree
(Knight of the Sun, or Prince Adept)

The apron is of pure white lambskin and has no edging or pattern except the interlaced pentagram, which is traced in the middle vermilion.

There are three jewels. The presiding officer wears a jewel that is a representation of the sun in gold, suspended by a chain of gold and worn around the neck. The reverse is a hemisphere of gold showing the northern half of the ecliptic and Zodiac, with the signs from Taurus to Libra inclusive. The other officers wear a jewel composed of a simple, seven-pointed star of gold. The remaining members of the council wear a jewel that is a gold five-pointed star. Only the jewel of the degree is shown in the illustration. The order is a broad white, watered ribbon worn as a collar. On the right side is painted an eye of gold, a symbol of the sun or of the deity.

The duties of this degree are to be a lover of wisdom and to be faithful to the promises you made within Masonry. The Lessons to be learned are:

1. Nature reveals a power and wisdom and continually points to God.
2. In the universe, two opposite forces provide balance.

3. There is no death, only change.
4. The moral code of Masonry is more extensive than that of philosophy.

For reflection, the candidate must ponder: what can the book of nature teach me? The important symbols are Rebis, Seal of Solomon, right triangle, and Pythagorean tetractys.

The Deity and Creation

God is the author of everything that existeth; the Eternal, the Supreme, the living, and awful being; from whom nothing in the Universe is hidden. Make of Him no idol and visible images; but rather worship him in the deep solitudes of sequestered forests; For he is invisible, and fills the Universe as its soul, and liveth not in any temple!

The Deity and Truth

God and truth are inseparable; a knowledge of God is a possession of the saving oracles of truth. In proportion as the thought and purpose of the individual are trained to conformity with the rule of right prescribed by Supreme Intelligence, so far is his happiness promoted, and the purpose of his existence fulfilled. In this way a new life arises in him; he is no longer isolated, but is a part of a higher will, informing and molding it in the path of his true happiness.

TWENTY-EIGHTH DEGREE
(KNIGHT COMMANDER OF THE TEMPLE)

The apron is square of scarlet-colored lambskin, lined and edged with black. The flap is white, and on it is the Teutonic cross described as a cross potent sable, charged with another cross double potent or surcharged with an escutcheon of the empire. The principal cross is surmounted by a chief azure seme of France, the technical terminology of heraldry. "Potent" is a word used to describe a cross with a cross pieces at the ends. "Double potent" means two cross pieces at the ends. "Sable" is black or is gold. "Charged" means superimposed upon. "Chief" means on top of. "Azure" is blue. "Seme" means strewn or scattered.

In the middle of the apron is a black key, and around it is a wreath of laurel. The laurel symbolizes the good opinion our brethren have for us. The order is of white, watered ribbon edged with red. It is worn as a collar from which the jewel is suspended. The jewel is the Teutonic cross shown on the apron.

There are also gloves and a scarf among the clothing of a Knight Commander of the Temple. The colors of these, as well as of the apron and order, are white, red, and black.

The duties are to be devoted to truth, honor, loyalty, justice, and humanity. The lessons of this degree are:

1. Masonry is practical and requires its members to be actively involved in life.
2. Virtue and duty have been the same in all times.

For reflection, the candidate is to ponder on the following: is it nobler to err and make amends than never to err at all? Is this statement contrary to the virtue of prudence? The important symbols are the colors scarlet and black, garland of laurel, circles and globes, and swords drawn and extended to a central point.

Honor, Loyalty, and Duty

Times change, and circumstances; but virtue and Duty remain the same. The Evils to be warred against but take another shape, and are developed in a different form.

TWENTY-NINTH DEGREE
(SCOTTISH KNIGHT OF SAINT ANDREW)

A Knight of St. Andrew wears a green collar edged with crimson over the neck and a white silk scarf fringed with gold and worn from left to right.

The jewel is a St. Andrew's cross of God with a large emerald in the center, surmounted by the helmet of a knight and with a thistle of gold between the arms at the bottom. It is worn suspended from the collar. The emerald signifies the manliness and uprightness of chivalry, its color that of the renewal of virtue, always bright and sparkling. The thistle is the national emblem of Scotland and recalls a tradition that the Danes invaded Scotland and stealthily surrounded Staines Castle. They took off their shoes to wade the moat, only to find it dry with thistles. The resultant yells and curses roused the garrison, and the Danes were soundly defeated. The banner of the order is a green St. Andrew's cross on a white field fringed with gold. At the end of each arm of the cross is one of the four Hebrew letters that form the ineffable name of the deity. Above the cross is a circle of five stars with a thistle in the center.

The duties of this degree are to revere and obey the deity. Serve the truth. Protect virtue and Innocence. Defend the people against tyranny. The lessons to be learned are that ideas and institutions wax and wane in the great cycle of time, which is but change.

For reflection, the candidate is to ponder the following: is virtue and armor stronger than the strongest metal? The important symbols are St. Andrew's cross, castle in ruins, and armorless knight.

Humility, Patience, and Self-denial

Humility, Patience, Self denial are three essential qualities of a knight of St. Andrew of Scotland. The cross is an unmistakable and eloquent symbol of these three virtues … Jesus's Life was one of humility, patience and self denial.

Charity, Generosity, and Clemency

Clemency is a mark of a noble nature to spare the conquered. Valor is then best tempered, when it can turn out a stern fortitude into the mild strains of pity, which never shines more brightly than when she is clad in steel … The most famed men in the world have had in them both courage and compassion. An enemy reconciled hath a greater value than the long train of captives if a Roman triumph.

Virtue, Truth, and Honor

If you would be a respectable as a Knight, and not a mere tinsilled pretender and Knight of straw, you must practice, and be diligent and ardent in the practice of the virtues you have professed in this degree ... How vow to be zealous and constant in the service of the order and be as useless to it as if he were dead or buried? What does the symbolism of the compass and square profit him, If his sensual appatites and base passion aree not governed by, but domineer over his moral sense and reason, the animal over the divine, the earthle over the spiritual, both points of the compass remaining below the square? what a hideous mockery to call on brother, whom he maligns to the profane, lends money unto at usury, defrauds in trade, or plauders at law by chicanery.

Look to the Past and Future

It has been well said, that whatever withdraws us from the power of our senses, whatever makes the past, the distant, or the Future, predominate over the present, advances us in the dignity of thinking beings.

THIRTIETH DEGREE (KNIGHT KADOSH, OR KNIGHT OF THE WHITE AND BLACK EAGLE)

No apron is worn. The cordon is a black, watered silk ribbon, four or five inches wide, edged with narrow silver lace, and worn across the body from left to right. The letters "K" and "h" are embroidered in a scarlet silk on the front part of the cordon. They are the first and last letters of the Hebrew word "Kadosh." Also embroidered on the cordon are two Teutonic crosses and a double-headed eagle, his wings extended, holding a poniard in his claws. The two heads and the blade of the poniard are of gold. The handle of the poniard is oval, half of it white and the other black. The colors represent the division of good and evil in the universe. The jewel is a double-headed eagle with wings spread and measuring about one inch across from the outside to outside of the wings. The eagle rests upon a Teutonic cross and is a half-inch in size. The eagle is of silver, and the cross is of gold, enameled with red.

The duty of this degree is to labor unceasingly for the good of mankind. The lessons to be learned are:

1. Arm yourself with faith in God.
2. Love toward your fellow men and knowledge.
3. Great examples are the noblest legacies from the past.
4. They enrich a nation more than wealth and power.

For reflection, the candidate is to ponder the following: are the knightly virtues obsolete in the modern world? The important symbols are three skulls, three funeral urns, the mystic ladder, and the double-headed eagle.

To War Against Ignorance, Tyranny, Despotism, and Vice

The arms where with to war against tyranny, Superstition and Ignorance, are knowledge, Virtue and Love, and charity for mankind.

THIRTY-FIRST DEGREE (INSPECTOR INQUISITOR)

Though no apron is worn in the tribunal, there was an apron that was to be worn when an inspector inquisitor visited an inferior body. That custom has been dispensed with, but the apron is still a part of the history and symbolism of the degree. So it is displayed here. It is of pure white lambskin with a Teutonic cross embroidered in black and silver upon the flap. The collar is white, and at the point upon the breast is a gold triangle emitting rays with the letters "XXXI" in the center. The jewel of this degree is a Teutonic cross of silver worn with a white, watered ribbon around the neck.

The duty of this degree is to judge yourself in the same light as you judge others. Consider both actions' motives. The lessons to be learned are:

1. The good man is able to portray himself and his actions positively and not simply assert the absence of wrong in his life.
2. Justice and mercy are two opposite, which unite in the great harmony of equity.
3. To aim at the best but be content with the best possible is true wisdom.

For reflection, the candidate is to ponder the following: is the man a thief who steals a loaf of bread for his hungry children? The important symbols are balanced heart, columns, sages, and tetractys.

The Law of Justice

The holy bible will remind you your obligation; and that as you judge here below, so you will be yourself judged hereafter, by One who has not to submit, like an earthly judge, to the sad necessity of inferring the motives, intention, and purposes of men(of which crime essentially consists) from the uncertain and often unsafe testimony of their acts and words; as men in thick darkness grope their way, with hands outstretched before them; but before whom every thought, feeling, impulse, and intention of every soul that now is, or ever was, or ever will be on earth is, and ever will be through the whole infinite duration of eternity present and visible.

Thirty-second Degree
(Master of the Royal Secret)

The cordon is worn from the right shoulder to the left hip and is four inches wide, doubled, black-edged with white on the principal side, and crimson on the other. At the point of the principal side is embroidered a red Teutonic cross in black. The jewel of the order is a Teutonic cross in black.

The jewel of the order is a Teutonic cross of gold with arms frosted. In the center are the letters "XXXII" surrounded by a green wreath. The apron is of white silk or velvet, twelve inches square. It is edged with two strips of gold lace, each a half-inch wide and an inch apart and fringed with gold. Between the stripes of lace is a stripe of black velvet. On the flap are embroidered six flags, three on each side. The lower one is blue; the middle one and the upper one is gold. On these in the center is a Teutonic cross of gold. And over that is an eye of gold, holding a sword of gold. A claw is on the hilt. On the body of the apron is the tracing board of this degree in all the colors. The reverse side of the apron is of crimson silk or velvet. It is tied by a heavy cord of crimson silk.

The duties of this degree are that a soldier of the light seeks truth and knowledge. A soldier of freedom demands for the people's free vote and voice and attains freedom of voice, vote, and opinion for himself. A soldier of the true religion combats spiritual tyranny with reason and truth. A soldier of the people encourages men to be self-reliant and independent. A soldier of Scottish Rite Masonry is zealous and ardent in the performance of his duties to God, his country, his family, his brethren, and himself. The lessons to be learned are:

1. The human is ever interlaced with the divine.
2. Only doctrines, faith, and knowledge that bear in action are of value.
3. To work is to worship.

For reflection, one is to ponder the following: do you endeavor to achieve the royal secret in your life and within yourself? The important symbols are the camp, lesser tetractys, five-pointed star, greater tetractys, seven-pointed star, triple-interlaced triangles, and trimurti (three-faced bust).

The Royal Secret

It is the secret of the Universal Equilibrium.

It's time to decide whether you pledge your soul to the light or the darkness. The sons of light are those brethren who dedicate their lives to truth, love, gnosis, and serving their fellow mankind to the best of their God-given abilities. To be a genuine member of the sons of light is to be an enlightened immortal soul on the course of evolution who has made the sacrificial pledge to serve others in order to make the world a better place than you found it rather than serve yourself and pursue selfish desires. It is this that brings better definition to the Masonic term, "To make good men better."

The idea of the term is to create an organized fraternity of good men who make the world better by bettering themselves and the world around them. It is to live a life of giving rather than taking. These are the true Masons of Solomon's Temple, the Masonic sons of light.

To put it quite simply, to be a member of the sons of light is to be a spiritual human who uses the material world to create heaven on earth based on truth, light, and love. Of course, they may make mistakes along their path and be vulnerable to human frailties and shortcomings as well, but their hearts are in the right place. If they step into the darkness because of the human pressures of this dark world that we live in without fail, they will always return to the light.

THIRTY-THIRD DEGREE

Freemason Manly P. Hall had written about the true masons in the lost keys of Freemasonry. The true Mason is not creed-bound. He realizes with the divine illumination of his lodge that, as a Mason, his religion must be universal. Either Christ, Buddha, or Mohammed, the name means little for he recognizes only the light and not the bearer. He worships at every shrine and bows before every altar, whether in temple, mosque, or cathedral, realizing with his truer understanding the oneness of all spiritual truth.

The sons of darkness are those brethren who dedicate their live to pursuing materiality in the forms of selfish desires regardless of their God-given abilities. To be a true member of the sons of darkness is to be an ignorant, immortal soul that was on the course of evolution, but who has made a sacrificial pledge to serve thyself in order to make your own world better rather than serve others. It is a life of taking rather than giving.

To be a member of the sons of darkness is to be a nonspiritual being by living your life as a material-seeking human who uses this world to obtain whatever it is he selfishly desires in his dark, cold hearts. They may claim their motives are in the right place, but what they do and do not do speaks for itself.

Unfortunately most of the visible Masons would mainly consist of the darkness who normally join the fraternity under the auspices of material gain and selfish pursuits of their own secret goals. These sons of Masonic darkness fill up most of the ranks from the first degree, all the way up to the thirty-second degree.

Material gain is their main goal, no matter what they may claim or act, as they are secret wisdom keepers. They primarily operate through their minds and not their hearts. These Masons are not hard to weed out from the true Masons of light. This would be the reason why, when a candidate is being initiated in Masonry, the senior deacon of the lodge describes this person as one who has long been in darkness and now seeks the light. Unfortunately the vast majority will never make it into the light.

Of course, not all Masons in these degrees are selfish, materialistic human practices because this is how you rise to the thirty-third degree, and the tares are weeded out from the wheat. Masonry, like all the religions, mysteries, Hermeticism, and alchemy, conceals its secrets from all except the adepts and sages or the elect and uses false explanations and misinterpretations of its symbols to mislead those who deserve only to be misled to conceal the truth, which it calls light, and draw them away from it.

In this endeavor, it is possible for one to ascend into the highest Masonic ranks and into the mysterious and invisible society of Masons who earn the thirty-third degree of illumination to become a member of the true Masonic sons of light who have risen above the thirty-second degree.

The sons of light are the fraternity within the fraternity. The ancient Masonic facts are that only true spiritual initiation brings about illumination and reason, an initiation of your soul in which it becomes Lord of your body, mind, and spirit.

Albert Pike had written, "Lucifer, the Son of the Morning! Is it he who bears the Light and when its splendors intolerable blinds feeble sensual or selfish souls? doubt not!"

Later Lucifer is transformed into what Manly P. Hall calls the true light of the soul, called the Christ. Hall had written, "Lucifer here represents the intellectual mind without the illumination of the spiritual mind; therefore it is 'the false light.'"

The true light of the soul finally overcomes and redeems the false light. The secret processes by which the Luciferian intellect is transmuted into the Christly intellect constitutes one of the great secrets of alchemy and are symbolized by the process of transmuting base metals into gold. As they say, "It is always darkest before the dawn." The morning star is always the brightest before daybreak.

Right now, the craft of Freemasonry is divided amongst those who are Luciferians who serve the false light as the sons of darkness or the sons of Belial and the thirty-third degree Masons who have been redeemed by the true light of the soul or the Christ. They are also known as the Sons of the Law of One.

In the end, only the thirty-third degree mysterious and invisible society of Masons will survive. The Masonic sons of darkness will then be a memory. There will be a time when the true sons of light will become visible to take the stage in order to lead their true fellow brothers and sisters into the next stage of human evolution. This will be a time that we will all know as the beginning of the true heaven on earth.

The War of the Sons of Light against the Sons of Darkness war scroll states,

Then the Sons of Righteousness shall shine to all ends of the world continuing to shine forth until Undo of the appointed seasons of darkness. Then at the time appointed by God, His great excellence shall shine for all the times of eternity, for peace and blessing, glory and joy and long life for all sons of light.

THE 34ᵀᴴ DEGREE BY PAUL V. MARSHALL SR.

Your time on Earth spent in service. a shining example of a man to be
But your now needed in the Heavenly lodge.
Time has come for your 34th degree.
Leaving behind the ones you love are the dues that you must pay
From afar you can watch over them. A part of your obligation this day.
This is the Farthest you can go. The Highest point of Masonic Life.
No higher an honor can be sown. In Gods lodge you must stride.
God in the East, King Solomon the West.
They open the lodge for you this day
You go the way as Masons before. To sit
with pride and stand with praise.
The alter shows the love you felt. Brotherhood of man one and all.
Your deeds reflect like shining gold. Your jewel is non to small.
You now stand before this alter. Deserving the rest you now seek.
No longer to toil the labors of life. Grand
Masters wages are yours to keep.
Those of us you left behind. Will carry your work on for you
Your dedication will shine to all. A memorial you leave for all to view.
So gather your wages rest for now. Lay back
in the Shade of God's great tree.
You've earned the honor now bestowed.
Masons in Heaven the 34th Degree.

XXVIII

---✠---

THE FORBIDDEN RELIGION

Know ye O man, that all of the future is an open book to him who can read. All effect shall bring forth its causes as all effects grew from the first cause. Know ye the future is not fixed or stable but varies as cause brings forth an effect. Look in the cause thou shalt bring into being, and surely thou shalt see its effect. Great is the struggle between darkness and light age old and yet ever new. Yet, know in a time, far in the future, Light shall be all and darkness will fall.

ONE OF THE most debatable Freemasonic symbols that you will find is the square and compass that is often depicted with the letter "G" in the center. This letter "G" has garnished the most speculation from outsiders and even ones who are initiated members of this most secret brotherhood. The most common explanations you will find for what the letter "G" represents run the gambit from God, who would also be the Great Architect of the Universe, to geometry since, as Pythagoras had said, all is number. Math and mathematical symbols have always been used in the teachings of the craft. Therefore, it would only be natural for people to assume that the "G" could possibly represent geometry as well. The number thirty-three is a master number that represents a master teacher. It is also used to represent Christ's consciousness. Jesus was crucified at Golgatha at age thirty-three in the year 33 AD. Thirty-three is the number of the

God Amon (Amen), which is the numerical equivalent of AMEN. 1 + 13 + 5 + 14 = 33. Amen is the god of truth.

When one becomes an honorary thirty-third degree Scottish Rite Freemason, your fellow Masons will have voted you as a worthy brother who is both a Gnostic and understands the secrets of procreation, the universe, truth, love, and immortality. The supreme council will have deemed you to have what may be called a Christ consciousness or a "reincarnated Buddha" astral body, where you may walk as both Jesus and Buddha had done by knowing thyself and also by using the knowledge you have gained for wisdom and reason in order to operate in the current moment of truth throughout eternity. This is what being a Gnostic is all about.

So the letter "G" in Freemasonry signifies Gnosis, generation, and the Great Architect. Gnosis (Greek for "knowledge") in its simplest form is "knowledge of thyself," or the Great Arcanum. Daath or Da'ath (Hebrew for "knowledge") is one of the spheres of the Tree of Life of the Kabbalah.

Generation (from the Latin generāre, meaning "to beget"), also known as procreation in biological sciences, is the act of producing offspring. Hence, it is from the blood that Gnosis or knowledge is transmitted through the act of procreation that then passes the knowledge encrypted within our DNA to our offspring.

Gnosis means knowledge. But it's not just any knowledge. Gnosis is knowledge that produces a profound transformation in those who receive it, knowledge capable of nothing less than waking up man and helping him to escape from the prison in which he finds himself. That is why Gnosis has been so persecuted throughout the course of history. It is knowledge considered dangerous for the religious and political authorities who govern mankind from the shadows. Every time this religion, absolutely different from the rest, appears before man, the other religions unite to try to destroy or hide it again.

Gnosis has always been behind almost every theological and philosophical system that has been branded heretical, forbidden, persecuted, and forced to become occult. By examining this forbidden knowledge, it is possible to recover the pieces necessary to reconstruct the whole of that which is Gnosis or otherwise known as illumination, the secret religion of the Illuminati.

If that knowledge were to be discovered and written down, it would be an immensely powerful book. It would be the most dangerous text in the world, capable of waking up and liberating those who read and study it. Such a book would be a strange object in this created world, something not fabricated here but coming from somewhere else, from another world completely different to this one. It would also be capable of surviving the elements as well as time because its truth is immortal. Illumination or Gnosis is Gnostic knowledge in its pure form.

LUCIFER, THE SON OF THE MORNING

Gnostic myths convey that Lucifer is the messenger of the true God. It is said that this God, the greatest one, unreachable and unknowable, is unable to penetrate this limited universe of impure and satanic matter. But according to these myths, he can send someone, Lucifer. Only with a supreme sacrifice can an incredibly spiritual and pure being of antimatter fire break through into the infernal world of this universe.

According to Gnostic legends and myths, the great, unknowable God sent Lucifer, angel of indescribable fire and light, to show man the light and to help him wake up and see his true origin, the origin of his spirit, which has been perversely imprisoned in this impure matter called body-soul. He is an uncreated being who came to the created world to bring light, liberating Gnosis. The saving knowledge can wake man up and help him free his imprisoned spirit. The knowledge allows him to know who he truly is, why he is here in this world, and what he has to do to liberate himself and fulfill his spirit, which belongs to another uncreated and unknowable plane.

We have said that Lucifer came to the world to wake man up; to help him remember his divine origin, the divine origin of his spirit; and to help him free himself from the body-soul in which he is trapped and from created time and matter.

Gnostics consider that the biblical myth of creation can be explained as follows. The creator Satan of the world trapped Adam and Eve in his miserable world, and Lucifer, in the form of a serpent, offered them the forbidden fruit of saving Gnosis and showed them that the creator was deceiving them. In other words, the creator said to man, "But of the tree of the knowledge of good and evil you shall not eat, for in the day that you eat of it you shall surely die." On the other hand, the serpent said, "You will not surely die. For God knows that in the day you eat of it, your eyes will be opened, and you will be like God, knowing good and evil." The Bible continued, "And the eyes of both of them were opened."

It doesn't say, "They both died." It says, "The eyes of both of them were opened," like the serpent had said. Later the creator says, "And now man has become as one of us, to know good and evil." The creator lied. He said that man would die if he ate the fruit, but man did not die. The serpent was telling the truth. The creator himself ended up agreeing that the serpent was right.

Gnostics believe that this serpent Lucifer is the liberator of man and the world. It is wisdom, the liberating Gnosis that wakes up man and saves him. Of course, this messenger of the unknowable God, Lucifer, is an opponent and an enemy of the creator of this world.

Gnosis states that the creator wants to keep man captive in this limited, inferior, and impure sphere. He also forbade man contact with the higher world, represented in the biblical myth by the fruit from the Tree of Knowledge of Good and Evil. But Lucifer, the angel of light, made a great sacrifice and descended into this satanic hell to give the forbidden fruit of Gnosis to man and opened his eyes so he would be able to remember his divine origin and his superiority in relation to the creator. Gnostics consider that, before the arrival of the serpent in paradise, man was in a state of ignorance and blind to his true situation. They maintain that Adam and Eve were in a state of servitude until the serpent Lucifer opened their eyes and fed them the fruit of knowledge, which made them remember their divine origin and become aware of the situation in which they found themselves.

Of course, the creator threw Adam and Eve out of this paradise in which he had placed them since he wanted them (and still does) to reflect him and be similar to him after his image and resemblance and to carry out his precepts so as to be like him and not like the unknowable God. He wants the spirit to stay asleep so he can take advantage of its energy, preventing it from manifesting itself in man and the world.

Humanity can never be free until it recognizes its pure relationship to divinity, and that is not one of master and slave. If you go into a church, a mosque, or a synagogue, you will be in no doubt that you are amongst slaves and they worship a God who is their absolute master. They are subjects before him, and he craves obedience. He despises those who think for themselves. Such a God is no God at all. Such a God is Satan.

There is an astonishing difference between a God of being that is Satan and a God of becoming who is the true God. The first offers you slavery. And the second offers you the highest possible reward. Not just salvation, but something that most people can barely comprehend, which is the ultimate Holy Grail.

It is true that many will find this material difficult, abstract, and obscure. But those who persist may catch glimpses of a new reality. The truth is not a matter of parables by preachers and prophets. The truth does not lie in holy texts supposedly expressing the Word of God. If God were the true author of these alleged holy texts, the text would be an undeniable clarity. It would be susceptible to multiple interpretations. It would not be full of contradictions. It would not lead to hatred, selfishness, greed, and war. The truth is the true God does not communicate directly with this world. It is not his world. He did not create it. He created the world of light. Another, the father of lies, rules this world of matter. The truth is never simplistic. The truth is not simply given to us. It requires the highest degree of effort. Truth based on faith rather than knowledge is absurd. There is no truth in faith, only delusion. Gnosticism is the path to salvation.

The central crisis of humanity lies in that of alienation. Humans are alienated from their jobs, their neighbors, their communities, their culture, their society, and their political leaders. They feel powerless and unable to change anything. They feel themselves depersonalized in the large, bureaucratic machines for which they work. They are not recognized as individuals with unique worth. They are cast adrift, estranged, and full of anxiety. The world seems foreign, alien, and hostile. Above all, people are alienated from themselves. Their alienation is most extreme in the case of what ought to be their greatest inspiration, religion.

What is the central teaching of illumination? Find God within yourself. Where else should he be? We can be God ourselves if we have the courage. We can join God. His hand stretches out toward us. Do we have the strength, imagination, and boldness to grasp it? Or will we fall on our faces in fear, trembling, and worship Satan instead? Do not fall into their pit of despair. The world has always persecuted the Illuminati.

The Illuminati have no desire to persecute anybody. They want to save people from themselves, to end their alienation from life. Become one with yourself. Embrace illumination. For the first time in your life, see the light.

Here is the ancient wisdom of the Illuminati. It is the test that until very recently was used to determine who was ready to join the Illuminati. Anyone who approached with the right question would be admitted to the first stage of the procedure for becoming a member of the Illuminati. The question was this one: what are we becoming? And the answer was, "The Light." It's God. Are you really ready to become God?

XXIX

✠

The Illuminati

"Far, through strange spaces, have I journeyed into the depth of the abyss of time, until in the end all was revealed. Know ye that mystery is only mystery when it is knowledge unknown to man. When ye have plumbed the heart of all mystery, knowledge and wisdom will surely be thine."

WHAT IF THERE were a society, a secret society where the best and brightest minds came together to actually do something to change the world? What if this society knew the secrets of the universe and for them nothing was impossible? The Illuminati is undoubtedly the most notorious secret society known to man. There have been many theories on who they are, ranging all the way from shape-shifting reptilian lizards bent on the domination of the human race to an exclusive group of rich elites who are in control of the world. It is clear that Illuminati still maintain their reputation of being the most secret society with all conspiracy theories leading back to the all-seeing eye.

The Illuminati are conspirators, but their conspiracy is entire benevolence. The Illuminati also despises privilege, fame, and excessive wealth. So if you think that the Illuminati are a group of rich and famous people with all the privilege in the world, then it is time for you to think again.

The essence of illumination, the secret religion of the Illuminati, is that it is possible for any human being to literally become God. It is therefore that the Illuminati oppose any religion that seeks to separate God from humanity with some uncrossable gap that creates a master slave relationship in which enslaved humans on their knees worship a tyrannical slave master God.

One of the greatest deceptions that this world is enduring at this time is that the deity worshipped by billions of Christians, Muslims, and Jews is the true God. This deity is known as the God of Abraham and is the furthest you can get from the true God. In the story of Abraham, the defining moment of Abraham's life is when he hears the voice of God commanding him to sacrifice his son. After hearing this order, Abraham willingly agrees to take his son's life because God told him to do so. Abrahamists celebrate this event, and if you ask any of them, they will tell you that God was just testing Abraham. What kind of God would test someone like that? Who but the devil would order fathers to murder their own flesh and blood? To believe that God would ever command a father to kill his innocent son under any circumstances is sick and most definitely evil. So unfortunately it is safe to say that the world we live in is sick, corrupted, and evil.

Abrahamism is the creed of absolute, mindless, slavish obedience to a tyrannical slave master God. What loving God would terrorize his own creations with such tests and threats of eternal damnation and limitless suffering? Such a being does not sound like God at all. Such a being sounds like Satan.

Abrahamism is the supreme insult to human dignity and freedom. It stands in immortal opposition to enlightenment. It rejects knowledge and reason in every regard. The future of humanity will be dark unless our wicked insane Abrahamic past is destroyed. Can any sane and rational person imagine a religion of love and compassion, forgiveness, and peace being founded on the image of a father standing over his son about ready to sacrifice him out of pure fear? Abrahamism is the biggest lie and fraud perpetuated by the human race. If these religions are a source of good, then why is the world so evil?

The Illuminati are Gnostics who oppose Satan, or otherwise known as Rex Mundi, the king of the world. The Illuminati is an ancient secret society that seeks to bring about a New World Order based on the principle that everyone can become God. Their aim, as it has always been, is to overthrow the elite, dynastic families of wealth and privilege that are referred to as the Old World Order, those who have run the world since the dawn of civilization to their advantage and to the unfair detriment of the people.

The Illuminati are a radical and revolutionary organization that seeks men and women of the human race to ascend to the next stage of humanity's evolution to join the society of the divine. It's time to end the reign of false prophets. It's time to put down the old, dusty holy books that are used for nothing but control. It's time that we stop worshipping fake gods and idols that we call celebrities. We all know that humanity is capable of so much more. Isn't it time to bring about a real change? Isn't it time to finally claim our divine inheritance?

The Illuminati are the messengers of the true God. Their sacred mission is to bring the human race together in full union with the true God so there is no longer a distinction between humanity and the divine presence. Isn't it time for the human race to open its eyes and see the light for the first time? The Illuminati have long worked in the shadows during the history of our time. The enemy has persecuted them to keep the truth from being let out.

But now they have emerged from the shadows once again to cast the light of Abraxas, the true God on this world that is filled with darkness. Their mission is most certainly impossible, but nevertheless it will be accomplished. Their mission, as it has always been, is to bring enlightenment here to the world, to be shared by everyone.

XXX

✠

THE OLD WORLD ORDER

Keeper have I been of the secrets of the great race, holder
of the key that leads into life. Bringer up have I been to
ye, O my children, even from the darkness of the Ancient
of Days. List ye now to the words of my wisdom. List ye
now to the message I bring. Hear ye now the words I give
thee, and ye shall be raised from the darkness to Light.

THE CURRENT WORLD we live in is controlled by what the Illuminati
refer to as the Old World Order. The Illuminati has resisted this
group that controls the world from behind the curtains since the beginning
of the battle between light and darkness. What they want is absolute
power, which is what they have been implementing on the people of this
world, a One World Order. They are the organization of families that must
fall before a New World Order can be instilled and humanity is freed from
the bondage that has held us back for so long.

The Old World Order is a global network of dynastic families. Their
mission is to maintain the power and wealth of their dynasties in perpetuity.
Others are admitted into this charmed circle only if they can assist the
interests of their endeavors. The Old World Order can sedate the people
by use of the TV, Hollywood, computer games, porn, music, alcohol,
recreational drugs, and sport. All of these diversions ensure the people
will never rise up. The Old World Order do not care about the welfare of
the ordinary citizens. Most people are very familiar with the dynasties of

our world. They are associated with oil, banking, entertainment, media, military, the intelligence services, and politics. The Old World Order models themselves around the Roman Empire at the time of Augustus Caesar.

The elite has devised a caste system under which this world is controlled. The rich or the plutocrats run the nation. Their desire is to keep widening the gap between themselves and everyone else because they thereby massively enhance their power and influence. The plutocrats want to rule out the middle class. They want to eventually make themselves into an old-style aristocracy, a permanent dynastic ruling elite incapable of being challenged by anyone. The plutocrats prefer to have just two classes below them, the working class and the underclass. The working class is designed to be full of people who have enormous credit card debts and mortgages to pay. These people live their life in anxiety. They are terrified of losing their jobs because then they won't be able to make their payments. If they defy their masters, they will be fired and plunged into the underclass. The working class, unlike the plutocracy, are extremely heavily taxed, and most of their tax dollars go to various welfare benefits for the underclass so they don't go to war with the state.

The underclass is the ever-growing cesspool of humanity. They live in ghettos that all have dysfunctional families. Their education is poor, which makes it hard for them to hold down any job, which leaves them in a position with no prosperous future. They often join gangs for protection and status and become criminals. So the system consists of remote elite living in luxury who never come into physical contact with the other classes. They lead parallel lives that never interact. They heavily tax the working class, and they ensure the workers are kept in a permanent state of fear that involves debt and the presence of a ghetto society where the losers and troublemakers end up. The taxes of the workers provide enough welfare to the underclass just enough to prevent violence, but there is still criminality among the sewer society, which the police and army keep in line so the elite can maintain power and control. This is the system that we live in, and now it has reached a point that's worse than ever. It's time to wake up. It's time to change the system.

The Matrix clearly shows the workings of the Old World Order. The controllers of the matrix are the Old World Order. Most people who live in the matrix are absolutely oblivious to the truth, that they are slaves. Only a few care and can see through the illusion of the matrix. Mr. Smith and his agents are the Old World Order's lethal enforcers who will deal with anyone that shows any signs of being divergent. But they don't need to even intervene that often because everybody is under control and asleep. Even some who have tasted the truth decide that they would prefer to go back to the world of enslavement. When given the choice of the blue or red pill, they choose the blue pill instead of seeing how deep the rabbit hole goes.

What if there were a prison, a jail of the mind from which those inside can never threaten your power and control? Imagine that you wanted people to go along with your plans, to never defy or challenge you. The Old World Order uses many psychological tactics to control us, including such things as turning the other cheek. Does it make sense that, if someone is relentlessly hurting me, to sit there and let him or her continue doing it? Wouldn't the best thing to do be to fight back? If someone strikes me, I'm striking back. I will not stand to be abused.

Another tactic is they tell you to wait for the kingdom of heaven to enjoy the rewards of your earthly struggle. Does that even sound right? If I'm enjoying the pleasures of the world, I'm not going to want anyone to take those pleasures from me. How do I make sure that no one takes them from me? I tell this person that he or she shouldn't worry himself or herself with enjoying himself or herself right now on earth. Instead these people should have their minds set on some future date rather than here and now. It's better to have now than to have not.

Another trick that the controllers use is the American dream. We all know the concept of the American dream. If you work hard, you will get rewards. If you are not getting your rewards, then you are not working hard enough. So that means that millions of Americans who work incredibly hard to barely put enough food on the table aren't working hard enough because, if they were, they would certainly be enjoying the benefits of life. On the other side, lazy, privileged investment bankers who walk away at the end of the day with millions of dollars obviously deserve it because of all their hard work.

And finally yet another gimmick the controllers use is the lottery. In the United Kingdom, they have a slogan, "*It* could be you." Well, yes, I suppose it could be, but the odds are 50 million to one, so the odds are definitely not in your favor. Are you beginning to see what we are up against? Welcome to the Old World Order.

This is how the Old World Order operates. Well-connected, wealthy, privileged people meet on the yachts of the super rich to carve up the world between them. All of the important decisions that so crucially affect the lives of ordinary people are taken in these kinds of secret meetings behind the curtains with firmly locked doors. In these meetings of the Old World Order, they decide what is best for themselves and then carry out these policies "in the name of the people."

They don't consult the people. They don't care about the people, yet they accept the people to vote for them. And remarkably the people do.

If you want to support the Old World Order, then watch TV shows that are garbage, worship your celebrities, go see the sporting gods, vote in the elections, drink yourself into oblivion, take drugs, purchase things you can't afford, and spend your life repaying the debt. Hold down a soul-crushing job, say prayers to false gods, and worship dusty holy books written by old-bearded prophets way out of their time, go to fake churches, and shop 'til you drop on Black Fridays and Christmas.

It has been often claimed that various powerful secret societies are conspiring to create a New World Order, which for them is a one-world oppressive government that has complete control over the world. The New World Order that so many people fear is actually in fact the Old World Order. There is nothing new about it. Globalization has been their goal since its conception.

A New World Order means a new political, economic, and religious configuration of the world. It does not mean an existing model that has already existed. It is only being extended further. A New World Order has never been seen before, and it is the doorway to a greater humanity.

If you want a better future, you must commit your life to work for a New World Order and do everything to resist the Old World Order. Democracy, like mainstream religion, is a means to bind the people to their own enslavement. The cure and final solution for the Old World Order is the New World Order, and the antidote for democracy is meritocracy.

XXXI

✠

THE NEW WORLD ORDER

Now I command ye to maintain my secrets, giving only
to those ye have tested, so that the pure may not be
corrupted, so that the power of Truth may prevail. List
ye now to the unveiling of Mystery. List to the symbols
of Mystery I give. Make of it a religion for only thus will
its essence remain.

MOST PEOPLE HOLD absurd ideas about the soul. A select few secret
societies such as the Illuminati have always had teachings that
were consistent with modern thinking. One of the aims of the Illuminati
is to show how the soul theory of the established mainstream religions
have been refuted by science and to reveal the authentic character of the
soul. The soul is our connection to God, and to know your soul, you must
triumph through the hero program.

Everyone has access to his or her personal hero program, but very
few choose to activate it. Only those that do can ever become psychically
whole. Only these select few can establish their true identity as complete
people who have fully integrated all aspects of their being. They are the
people who can defeat inner demons, transcend limitation, and travel the
pathway that leads to the stars. It's time to become a hero. Beyond that
there is only one other stage, to become God.

In the hero's journey, the first stage is the world of common day, or
the ordinary world. This is our day-to-day life, boring, repetitive, tedious,

and uninspiring. The most important element to this life is conforming to what society expects of us, and we are on permanent autopilot. We exist rather than live, and we are stuck in life with no opportunity for growth. We are nowhere near fulfilling our potential. This is a spiritual wasteland. It's the world of persons where everyone wears a mask to hide who they really are. In this world, we are desperate to be acceptable to others. We fear being ourselves, to be individual.

The heroes journey is often seen in many Hollywood movies. In the beginning of *The Matrix*, Neo is asleep at his computer when he is first introduced. Then a message appears on the computer screen telling him to wake up. He then is told to follow the white rabbit. When Trinity first meets him, she tells him that they are watching him. When Neo wakes up, he thinks it's all a dream and then returns to work, where he is unhappy with his job and his life. For Neo, this is his ordinary world.

Then the hero gets the call to adventure, where the would-be hero encounters a problem or a challenge. We are all in this position. We are all being called, but few answer. We don't want to hear it because it demands too much of us. In *The Matrix*, the message telling Neo to wake up notifies that Neo will soon be leaving the ordinary world. The call to adventure gives us an indication of what's at stake in the story. What is the dramatic question? What issue will be resolved for the would-be hero?

When we get the call, we often can be indecisive and afraid. Few people actually have what it takes to change. Most of the time, people are comfortable where they are, and they are reluctant to leave. Everyone is called, but most refuse the summons. When they are old and the opportunity has long passed, they will do nothing but live in regret unless they take advantage of this sacred moment.

When the hero accepts the call, he receives supernatural aid, or otherwise known as the meeting with the mentor, an older, wiser figure who helps him to overcome his reluctance to act and prepares him for what is to come. In the tales of King Arthur, Merlin the wizard was the mentor. In *Star Wars*, it was Obi wan Kenobi. In *The Matrix*, it is Morpheus. Most people never encounter a mentor, and this is why they fail to respond to the call to adventure.

The next stage that takes place is when the hero crosses the first threshold, where he crosses from the ordinary world into the extraordinary world. In *The Matrix*, the first threshold is presented when Morpheus presents Neo with the red and blue pills, and Neo takes the red one to see how deep the rabbit hole goes.

After completing this stage, the hero experiences a death and rebirth. There is now a clear separation between the hero's old self and his new self. Then the hero is faced with the road of test and trials, where he will encounter allies and enemies and is subjected to great ordeals as his transformation proceeds. In *The Matrix*, Neo meets the crew of the Nebuchadnezzar, who become his allies. He is told about the agents, a sentient computer program that protects the matrix. These agents become the enemies of Neo.

After the hero passes the road of test and trials, he meets with a god or goddess. In this stage, the hero finds a transformative love that he has never experienced before. This stage represents an encounter with the hero's anima, his ideal image of a female. In the matrix, Neo develops a spiritually profound relationship with Trinity.

Temptation temporarily draws away the hero from his task. In Gnostic terms, the lure of the physical world diverts one from the spiritual path. Many people who have reached this point fail. Neo does not though because he finds true love with Trinity.

The next stage is the atonement with the father, where the hero confronts whoever is in control of his destiny, and that is usually the most powerful person in his life. In *The Matrix*, Neo meets the all-knowing oracle, who tells him what his future is. This is the most critical moment in the hero's journey thus far. After this, the hero reaches a higher state of being than he has ever experienced. He is now more fulfilled than ever.

In *The Matrix*, the boy able to bend the spoon with his mind impresses Neo. After he sees this, he then feels that he is gaining a greater understanding of the world. The oracle tells Neo that he has the gift, but he is not the one, and maybe he will be the one in his next life. Neo feels relieved since he didn't believe he was the chosen one. The oracle tells him that either he or Morpheus will die soon. Neo resolves that he will sacrifice himself to save Morpheus. His life now has meaning.

When the hero gets to this stage, he is now ready to receive his reward. This is what the quest was all about. The hero takes possession of what he came for. For Neo, he gained knowledge and understanding of the matrix.

He's in love with Trinity. He has transformed himself and is willing to sacrifice himself for others. The expression "seizing the sword" relates to aggressively taking the prize that is desired in the extraordinary world.

Having achieved his goal, the hero may not want to return to the ordinary world. But for a true hero, no such possibility exist. The hero then takes the precious gift back to the ordinary world, but the agents of the ordinary world once again attack him. With what the hero has learned, he is able to defeat them with ease. When returning to the ordinary world, the hero must work out how to best use what he has gained to help the community. In Neo's case, he is now the one and can manipulate the matrix at will. He then defeats Agent Smith and moves into being the master of the two worlds, which is resurrection. In *The Matrix*, Neo has suffered, died, and been resurrected. The hero becomes a messiah, who has mastered both spiritual and physical reality, which allows the hero freedom to live.

The hero is released from fear of death and has the maximum freedom to live. He has completed the journey and returned home with new power, talents, and knowledge that is transcendent. And by his own efforts, he has raised himself to a higher level and can now help others.

The Matrix ends with Neo calling the demiruge from a telephone. Neo says, "I know you're out there. I can feel you now. I know that you're afraid. You're afraid of us. You're afraid of change. I came here to tell you how it is going to begin. I'm going to show these people what you don't want them to see. I'm going to show them a world without you, a world without rules and controls, without borders and boundaries. A world where anything is possible."

Neo's final message is exactly the message of the Illuminati. The Illuminati have always supported a meritocratic form of government. They are opposed to monarchies, aristocracies, dictatorships, and even democracy. But why would the Illuminati oppose democracy, the ultimate form of freedom. Democracy is supposedly a government of the people, by the people, and for the people, but it is actually a disguised oligarchy where a small elite group governs in its own interests and forms an aggressive campaign to take active steps in providing misinformation and disinformation to keep the people as uneducated as possible. Democracy is actually a government of the people, by the elite, and for the elite. It is the perfect instrument of control for the Old World Order. Democracy only becomes acknowledgeable at the point at which the vast majority of citizens are highly capable, talented, and resourceful. Until that point happens, the most meritorious people must be placed in charge and in a form of government of freedom and democracy that is clearly not happening.

The Illuminati had hoped to achieve a worldwide meritocracy via Masonic lodges, groups of talented, educated individuals all over the world who did not subscribe to the elitist oppressive regimes. For a little while, Freemasonry did exactly what it set out to do, and the foundation of the American nation was its greatest accomplishment. All of the significant players in the creation of America were Freemasons, and in the times of the American Revolution, the people turned to the best and brightest among them, the Founding Fathers. But soon the dream became a nightmare, and Freemasonry became corrupted and began to resemble the elitist rulers they had once opposed.

The Illuminati still support meritocracy with one crucial refinement. Greed corrupted the Freemasons. So greed in a meritocracy cannot exist. The Illuminati's form of meritocracy is now committed to abolishing all forms of greed with a commitment to limit the rewards of the most successful. It is true that no one should be ashamed of earning higher reward for being talented and hardworking. They must not succumb to the greed of the Old World Order. Could anyone on earth complain if he or she were allowed to earn $1 million a year? Does anyone really need anymore than that? If the average American is making $50,000 a year, then a million should be more than enough. If you think you need anymore than that, then greed has possessed you.

The Illuminati have created the following movements in the course of our history. Ancient Egyptian and Greek mystery religions, Druidism, militarism, Gnosticism, alchemy, Catharism, the Knights Templar, Roscicrucainism, and Freemasonry. Illuminati teachings have appeared in Christianity, Kabbalah, Zoroastrinism, Hinduism, Buddhism, and many other religions. The religions that oppose Illumination are Islam, Judaism, Christianity, and Catholicism.

All religions based on faith rather than knowledge are in direct opposition to illumination. The essence of illumination lies in the word becoming. Religions such as Judaism, Christianity, and Islam are based on being. Those who understand the difference between being and becoming will be rewarded with a worldview that is breathtaking in the opportunities and possibilities that it has in store. So do you see now what we were up against? Is it clear now what must take place in order for this world to change? What are you willing to do for freedom? What are you willing to do for God?

XXXII

✠

HEREAFTER

When man again shall conquer the ocean and fly in the
air on wings like birds; when he has learned to harness
the lightning, then shall the great warfare begin. Great
shall the battle be twixt the forces, great the warefare of
Darkness and light. Nation shall rise against Nation using
dark forces to shatter the Earth. Weapons of Force shall
wipe out the Earth man until half of the races of men shall
be gone. Then shall come forth the Sons of the Morning
and give their eddict to the children of men, Saying: O
man, cease from striving against thy brother Only thus
can you come to the light.

S O HOW IS this never-ending story going play out? What does the future
hold? What is the final revelation? What will be revealed when all that
is that is hidden in the shadows is brought into the light? The great cycle has
been completed, and we are entering the golden age. It is the end of time as
we know it. And we will be moving into another dimension. Many people
are unaware of what is really going on here. Our earth has been dying.
There is no doubt. Humanity, for the most part, are slaves on this planet,
who are ruled by an elite few who have the technology and knowledge to
keep humanity at the state of consciousness that it is currently manifesting.
It's not humanity that is killing our planet. It's our consciousness. We have
accepted an imposter into our ranks. That imposter has lied and cheated,

stolen, and killed to keep you from knowing the truth that will be true always. That truth is that you are God and we create reality.

We have reached the end of time. This is the time that the Mayans and all of the ancient breakaway civilizations prophesied about. And although it is past 2012, that sure does not mean that we aren't still due for some world-shaking events that will reveal the true history of this world and change our future as well. Humanity was not meant to die in the dirt. We were meant to reach the stars. It's up to us to make the decision if we want to return to the dust or ascend into the heavens. Why do you think the statues of Easter Island had their heads pointed up to the stars? The answer is that they were gods, and they left this place, but of course only to return back again in the future.

The grand finale of this experiment that we know as life is coming to its culmination, and with that being so, humanity is ready to ascend into the next dimension, if it so pleases. For some, it will be smooth. For others, it will seem like the end of the world. For some, it will be a divine intervention. And for others, it will be an alien invasion. Regardless though, it is time to get prepared for this world to never be the same again. Either we can have it the way it is or we can have it be like *Star Trek* and *Star Wars*, where there is full disclosure of everything that has been kept a secret. The elite has shown the truth in movies, but they never fully just come out and say it. If one has clairvoyant illumination sight, it is not hard to see what is going on once all of the pieces of the compartmentalized puzzle are put together.

Can you see the big picture now? Can you see what this is all about? Can you see how important it is to know God? Fearlessness is the primary characteristic of mastery, and it is time for us to become masters. They say that ignorance is bliss. Well, that may be so. Ignorance may be bliss, but knowledge is power. There is nothing more important than knowing who you are, where you came from, what you're doing here, and where you are going. And to know those things, you must go through that hero's journey that we all know now to be the quest for the Holy Grail and the path to becoming one of the Illuminati.

This world is getting geared up to experience a momentous event. Whether anyone likes it or not, this event will not leave this world the same, and it will be up to the people to decide how we are going to go on.

But the people must be awoken, and the veil must be lifted. And for that to happen, the illusion they have used us to create will fall. And when that happens, all that is hidden will be revealed.

The government and our science know about the event because it has happened like clockwork four other times in our history, and now we have once again come to the end of a twenty-six thousand-year long cycle of experiencing both darkness and light. They have built underground cities. They have been preparing for something that the world does not know is going to happen. The last thirteen thousand years has been darkness. The next thirteen thousand years will be light. But before this shift can occur, humanity will once again endure an event that will change the consciousness of this world.

I will let you use your imagination to think about the possibilities that we could be experiencing in our near future. Among those possibilities are earthquakes, floods, hurricanes, famines, wars, and even alien interventions. It's all coming down to the big finale, and as the prophets of our own destiny, it is in our hands what happens to this world and the people who inhabit it.

The truth is that this could go many ways. But what's even more true than that is that there is only one way that it will turn out. And that is either the human race being free or it being enslaved, like it has been for so long. So are we heroes or slaves? It up to us to free ourselves from our own tyranny, our own oppression, and our own ignorance to the truth, and that truth is that we are masters of our own fates and the captains of our own souls. We just forgot who we were, and now it's time to remember again.

XXXIII

✠

THE DIVINE REVELATION

Now Ye assemble my children waiting to hear the secret of secrets which shall give ye the power to unfold the God -man, give ye the way to Eternal life. Plainly shall I speak of the unvieled mysteries. No dark sayings shall I give unto thee. Open thine ears now, my children. Hear and obey the words that I give. Darkness and light are both of one nature, different only in seeming, for each arose from the source of all. Darkness is disoreder. Light is Order. Darkness transmutted is light of the light. This my children your purpose in being; Transmutation of darkness to light.

THE HISTORY OF Esoterism has long been obsessed with the notion of reclaiming lost knowledge and technology, all the way back to Plato's *Timaeus* and its legends of Atlantis. The never-ending story of life is told in a nonlinear fashion. With this being so, the great secret of life is that of eternal recurrence.

The decisions we make in this life determine what we will do in the next one, and death is only just a doorway into the next life. This is the gospel of Illuminism. This is the secret of the transmigration of souls taught by all of the schools of the ancient mysteries. The wheel of birth and death can only be transcended by enlightenment and right living, which will lead to the recovery of lost Gnosis or otherwise lost technology.

The eternal recurrence is thus working out the flaws and mistakes made in previous lives, ultimately giving the souls an experience of all phases and stations in life. The modern world has moved away from the idea of telos or purpose. Is there a purpose to the universe? There is. Does extraterrestrial life exist? Indeed. Are we really immortal beings? It's true. But what does it all mean? What is it all for? Why are we here? We are here to understand who we are. We are here to learn. The meaning of life is revelation.

Why did the Illuminati choose the symbol of a pyramid with a separated capstone? In basic terms, it simply means, "All paths lead to one God." As the base of the pyramids is wider, it represents all the people, religion, belief system, and chaos, and as a human being moves toward enlightenment, the pyramids get narrower and narrower as more order is instilled as the religious and personal beliefs get smaller and smaller until it reaches a single point toward the great eye of illumination, or as they say, "the one true God." This is the most important symbol and shape in the universe. This shape, known as a tetrahedral structure, is the answer to all that exists and why it does.

The dialectic, the scientific method, and teleological evolution are all the same thing. They are all the core method for understanding the universe. It is the essence of life to move forward, to grow to advance, to develop, to evolve. If you feed in potential, actualization is what occurs. And all the while it moves toward its telos (its end), the purpose of its existence, the maximum expression of its potential, the supreme actualization, the divine revelation.

The Hegelian dialectic is a fluid process. The evolution of the universe takes the form of a cosmic spiral, winding around a genesis point while moving ever further from that point, and it continues until it reaches the dialectical endpoint, the omega point. The dialectic is the core dynamic process of reality. It is essential to existence. If you have energy and the dialectic, you have the universe. From energy and the dialectic comes everything. Without the dialectic, without a purposeful process of evolution, there would be nothing of significance in the universe. The dialectic is the logic of reality. What is life? Life is the dialectic. What does the dialectic operate on? It operates on energy, the fundamental substance of the universe. What is meaning? Meaning is contained in the dialectic.

The dialectic is evolving meaning. What is God? God is the supreme product of the dialectic. God is absolute meaning.

The demiurge is a dialectical stage in God's development as he gradually regenerates himself. He must pass through evil in order to know good. He must be selfish and self-interested before he can become altruistic and selfless. The demiurge is God at a primitive stage of his development, before he understood himself. The demiurge is the true God's shadow—the immature, dark, unenlightened, destructive, and selfish aspect that must be overcome if God is to become his true self.

God is on a dialectical path, seeking to overcome the negative parts of his psychology that hold him back from self-actualization, from becoming everything he has in him to become perfect. Is that not the true meaning of the statement that we are created in God's image? Is that not the true meaning of the ancient wisdom, "As above so below."

Here is a remarkable truth: It is not God who redeems humanity; rather humanity redeems God. Our dialectical role is to show the demiurge the error of his ways. God comes to full self-realization and moral perfection through humanity. It is we who shape God. If we can be morally superior to the demiurge, then he will be shaped in our image rather than we in his. It is our divine dialectical task to transcend the demiurge to be led onto the true path to God.

Entelechy is a difficult word to define since it has a number of different uses that imply subtly different things. Entelechy is derived from "en" (in). Telos comes from perfection, completion, and end. And "ekhein" (to have) means "to have its end within itself." So we have a concept that refers to the end as potential, the end as actualization, and the process that converts the potential into actuality. Entelechy can be given the following meanings as well:

- having its end within itself;
- having an inner creative drive to attain that end and moreover to achieve it as perfectly as possible;
- the purpose for which a thing exists and which remains as potential until actualized;
- the accomplishment of the goal;
- the fulfillment of the purpose;

- the realization or compete expression of some function;
- the condition in which a potentiality has become an actuality;
- the perfect realization of what was previously only potential; and
- development from what is potential to what is perfected and actualized.

Entelechy is something like a guiding, informing spirit, an inner genius, a soul seeking to become all that it can be and "dissatisfied until it succeeds." All things wish to transform their starting potential to maximum actualization. They wish to blossom, to become all they can be. They want to be the caterpillar that turns into the butterfly. The solution to the world's unhappy consciousness is the successful realization of our entelechy.

There is no question anymore. The mystery is solved. No longer will we be able to walk around in ignorance of who and what we are. Isn't time for the truth to be known? Isn't it time to reclaim our divine inheritance? The purpose of life is to earn your soul through the hero's journey and then become God. Through telological evolution, one is to navigate the universe to reach its final end point, and then when that is achieved, one is to do it all over again and again into eternity.

It's time to take back the planet. It's time for freedom. It's time for peace. It's time for the light to come out of the darkness. It's time for the Illuminati. I don't know if you are ready to hear this. I don't know what you'll think or whether you'll understand. But we have reached the end of the great cycle, and it is inevitable that it will come to its completion. The truth is you are God! They just never wanted you to know that. Humanity is divine. We are all gods, and for us, this will not be the end. It is only just the beginning.

The secret of freedom lies in educating people, whereas
the secret of tyranny is in keeping them ignorant.
Maximilien Robespierre

Printed in the United States
By Bookmasters